Focusing on IELTS

Reading and writing skills

Second edition

Jeremy Lindeck
Jannette Greenwood
Kerry O'Sullivan

MACMILLAN

First edition published 2000 by the National Centre for English Language Teaching and Research, Macquarie University
Second edition published 2011 by
MACMILLAN EDUCATION AUSTRALIA PTY LTD
15–19 Claremont Street, South Yarra 3141

Associated companies and representatives
throughout the world.

National Library of Australia
cataloguing in publication data

Author:	Lindeck, Jeremy, 1961–
Title:	Focusing on IELTS: reading and writing skills / Jeremy Lindeck, Jannette Greenwood, Kerry O'Sullivan.
Edition:	2nd ed.
ISBN:	978 1 4202 3020 8 (pbk.)
Notes:	Subjects: International English Language Testing System. English language—Study and teaching—Foreign speakers. English language—Examinations, questions, etc.
Other authors/contributors:	Greenwood, Jannette O'Sullivan, Kerry, 1952–
Dewey number:	428.0076

Publisher: Vivienne Winter
Project editors: Claire Lavin and Kirstie Innes-Will
Editor: Kirstie Innes-Will
Illustrators: Andy Craig and Nives Porcellato
Cover and text designer: Anne Stanhope
Photo research and permissions clearance: Jes Senbergs
Typeset in 11.5 pt Sabon by Marg Jackson, Emtype Desktop Publishing
Cover image: Jenny Hall

Printed in China

Internet addresses
At the time of printing, the internet addresses appearing in this book were correct. Owing to the dynamic nature of the internet, however, we cannot guarantee that all these addresses will remain correct.

Contents

Unit 2: Writing 113

How to use this book

You can use this book independently as you prepare for the IELTS test or as a coursebook in an IELTS preparation course with a teacher.

Throughout this book there are **examples** to follow and **exercises** for you to complete. This book covers the Reading and Writing modules for both General Training and Academic candidates. You can easily select the particular sections to study based on your specific needs. To get the most out of this book and achieve your best possible result on the IELTS test make sure you do all the exercises related to your test: either General Training or Academic.

A full Answer key is provided at the back of the book.

Both Unit 1: Reading and Unit 2: Writing contain the following six sections.

1 What is in the test?

The first section describes the specific IELTS test, with information about its length, how it is conducted and structured, what kinds of questions there are, and how it is assessed. You should read this section in conjunction with the *IELTS Handbook* that you receive when you register for the IELTS test.

2 Test-taking tips

This section gives you advice about how to manage the test as successfully as possible. These tips will help you complete the test within the time allowed and get the best mark possible.

3 Getting to know the test

This section tells you what is included in each part or section of the test and how to approach these sections. For the Reading Test, this section introduces you to the various question types, and it includes exercises and examples for familiarising yourself with the requirements and nature of each question type. For the Writing Test, this section introduces you to the criteria used to assess each of the Tasks.

4 The strategies and skills you need

This is the main section of each unit because it explains the strategies and/or skills that you need to do well in the Reading and Writing modules and gives you opportunities to practise them. **Strategies** are the practical techniques you can use to meet the specific demands of the test – such as skimming and scanning the text quickly in the Reading Test. **Skills** are the abilities and language needed to perform well in the test – for example, the ability to organise your ideas logically in the Writing Test. Exercises are included throughout these sections to help you develop both strategies and skills. You should do these exercises without assistance and try to follow any time limits suggested.

5 Developing an independent study program

This section helps you develop a self-study program. This involves identifying your needs, finding appropriate practice materials and maintaining a regular study schedule. This section includes advice on improving your general reading and writing, as well as practising specifically for the IELTS test.

6 Practice IELTS tests

These practice tests simulate the real IELTS tests. You can do them before you start studying the other sections of the book to give you an idea of your current abilities, or you can do them after working through the units to consolidate your learning. You should do them without any assistance and follow any time limits given.

Acknowledgments

Author acknowledgments

I would like to especially express my gratitude to Mary Jane Hogan for her invaluable expert advice and Kate Chandler for her helpful feedback on the Reading section. I would also like to acknowledge and thank Vivienne Winter and Kirstie Innes-Will at Macmillan for their professionalism, ongoing support and suggestions. Lastly, thanks to my colleagues for their warm support and encouragement, especially Mark Henderson and Walter Slamer.

Jannette Greenwood

Publisher acknowledgments

The author and publisher are grateful to the following for permission to reproduce copyright material:

Photographs

Getty Images/Jetta Productions, 129, /Wire Images, 46; iStockPhoto/Adrian Baras,104, /Woraput Chawalitphon,167, /Robert Churchill,159, /Robert Hardholt, 82, /Johnnyscriv, 69, /Paul Morton,125, /RelaxFoto.de, 54, /Willi Schmitz, 72, /Devon Stephens,14, /Fekete Tibor, 45, /Juli-anne Whittle,183, /John Woodworth, 39 (middle), /Catherine Yeulet 195; NASA 177; Shutterstock/CandyBoxPhoto, 119, /EpicStock, 35, /Eric Isselée, 132, /Philip Lange, 135, /Laura Litman, 39 (bottom), /Sandy Maya Matzen, 23, /Dale Mitchell, 66, /Dusan Po, 18, /Vitaly Titov & Maria Sidelnikova, 39 (top), /David Sprott, 146.

Other material

Australian Bureau of Statistics for graph 'Annual Mean Temperatures for Australia', 147 (top), graph, 'Trends in Selected Working Arrangements and Types of Jobs for People Working as Full-Time Employees', 147 (bottom), graph, 'Risk factors by Index of Relative Socio Economic Disadvantage ranking', 154, graph, 'Overweight and obesity by sex and age 2007–2008', 155, graph 'Prisoners released in 1994–1997, reimprisonment rate by time to first reimprisonment', 213 (top), graph 'Prisoners released in 1994–1997, reimprisonment rate by age at release and time to first reimprisonment', 213 (bottom), adapted and used with permission; Extract, 'Eco-tourism and the tropics', from Eco-Resorts Planning and Design for the Tropics, by Zbigniew Bromberek, Copyright Elsevier (2009), 14–15; Extract, 'This winter, heat your home – not the Earth', from EnergyAustralia, <www.energysave.energyaustralia.com.au>, 75; Extract, 'Grameen Bank at a Glance', <www.grameen-info.org>, used with permission of Grameen Bank, 109–10; Extract, 'The World the Box Made', from The Box by Marc Levinson, © 2006, by Princeton University Press, Reprinted by permission of Princeton University Press, 10–11; Article, 'Seven ways to fast track success', by Jim Bright, *Sydney Morning Herald*, 31 January 2009, 7; Article, 'You'll never be happier but keep working', by Ross Gittins, *Sydney Morning Herald*, 3 October 2009, 12–13; Article 'Can't save them? Move 'em', by Suzanne Goldenberg, Sydney Morning Herald, 11 March 2010, 82; Extract, 'Types of Mobile Phone Systems', adapted from <www.topbits.com/types-of-mobile-telephone-systems.html>, 69–70; Extract, 'Guidance on Workplace Emergency Systems', from <www.ors.act.gov.au>, used with permission of WorkSafe ACT, 107.

While every care has been taken to trace and acknowledge copyright, the publishers tender their apologies for any accidental infringement where copyright has proved untraceable. They would be pleased to come to a suitable arrangement with the rightful owner in each case.

Reading skills and strategies summary

This table indicates which exercises provide practice at different question types, skills and strategies for the IELTS ReadingTest.

		1	2	3	4	5	6	7	8	9	10	11	12	13	14	15	16	17	18	19	20	21	22	23	24	25	26	27	28	29	30	31	32	33	34	35	36
Question type	Multiple-choice questions	✓																✓																✓	✓	✓	
	Identifying information		✓																										✓					✓	✓	✓	
	Identifying writer's views/claims			✓																												✓					✓
	Matching information				✓													✓																			
	Matching headings					✓													✓																		
	Matching features						✓																									✓	✓				
	Matching sentence endings							✓																													✓
	Sentence completion								✓								✓																		✓		
	Summary/note/table/flow-chart completion									✓	✓																		✓								✓
	Diagram label completion											✓																									
	Short-answer questions												✓						✓																		
Section of Test	General Training Section 1																															✓			✓		
	General Training Section 2																															✓			✓		
	General Training Section 3																																✓	✓			
	Academic Reading Passage 1																															✓		✓			
	Academic Reading Passage 2																																✓			✓	
	Academic Reading Passage 3																																✓				✓
Strategies	Skimming													✓			✓	✓	✓													✓	✓	✓	✓	✓	✓
	Scanning														✓		✓	✓	✓													✓	✓	✓	✓	✓	✓
	Reading intensively															✓	✓	✓	✓													✓	✓	✓	✓	✓	✓
Skills	Identifying question types																✓	✓	✓																		
	Dealing with vocabulary																			✓	✓	✓	✓	✓	✓	✓	✓	✓									
	Recognising text organisation and features																													✓	✓				✓		
	Recognising text types																															✓	✓	✓		✓	✓

Writing skills and strategies summary

This table indicates which exercises provide practice at the different parts of, and skills and strategies required for the IELTS Writing Test.

Exercise number

Aspect / Skill	Category	1	2	3	4	5	6	7	8	9	10	11	12	13	14	15	16	17	18	19	20	21	22	23	24	25	26
Aspects of the Test	General Training Task 1	✓	✓	✓	✓	✓	✓	✓	✓	✓	✓	✓	✓	✓	✓												
	Academic Task 1															✓	✓	✓	✓	✓	✓	✓	✓	✓	✓	✓	✓
	General Training and Academic Task 2																										
General writing skills	Editing your work			✓	✓																						
	Using a consistent tone																										
	Building up your vocabulary													✓													
	Linking your ideas										✓		✓									✓	✓		✓		
	Writing complex sentences											✓															
	Structuring your writing in paragraphs									✓																	
Specific writing skills for Test	Responding to the task	✓	✓	✓		✓	✓	✓	✓	✓	✓	✓				✓	✓	✓	✓	✓				✓			
	Organising your ideas logically								✓												✓	✓	✓		✓		
	Using appropriate vocabulary													✓												✓	✓
	Using a wide range of grammar features correctly														✓												

Exercise number

Aspect / Skill	Category	27	28	29	30	31	32	33	34	35	36	37	38	39	40	41	42	43	44	45	46	47	48	49	50	51
Aspects of the Test	General Training Task 1	✓	✓	✓	✓																					
	Academic Task 1	✓	✓	✓	✓																					
	General Training and Academic Task 2					✓	✓	✓	✓	✓	✓	✓	✓	✓	✓	✓	✓	✓	✓	✓	✓	✓	✓	✓	✓	✓
General writing skills	Editing your work																	✓						✓	✓	✓
	Using a consistent tone																									
	Building up your vocabulary																	✓	✓	✓	✓					
	Linking your ideas			✓																✓	✓	✓				
	Writing complex sentences																✓		✓							
	Structuring your writing in paragraphs	✓	✓		✓										✓	✓						✓				
Specific writing skills for Test	Responding to the task					✓	✓	✓	✓	✓	✓	✓	✓	✓		✓	✓	✓	✓	✓	✓	✓				
	Organising your ideas logically						✓	✓	✓	✓	✓	✓		✓		✓	✓									
	Using appropriate vocabulary													✓	✓	✓	✓	✓	✓	✓	✓					
	Using a wide range of grammar features correctly	✓	✓	✓	✓																	✓	✓		✓	✓

Unit 1
Reading

1.1 What is in the Reading Test?

The IELTS Reading Test has two formats: Academic and General Training.

Time allowed	60 minutes
Procedure	The Reading Test is the second section of the IELTS test. It is held in an examination room. You are given a question booklet and an answer sheet. As you complete each section, you write your answers directly onto the answer sheet.
Number of questions	40 questions, 1 mark per question Each section contains 12 to 14 questions.
Types of questions	Multiple-choice Identifying writer's views/claims Matching headings Matching sentence endings Labelling a diagram Summary/note/table/flow-chart completion Identifying information Matching information Matching features Sentence completion Short-answer questions
Structure	In both Academic and General Training there are three sections of increasing difficulty.
Reading passages	**Academic** Three passages from magazines, books, journals or newspapers on topics of general interest and of increasing difficulty. Each text may provide information and include description as well as analysis and evaluation. At least one text presents a detailed logical argument. **General Training** The texts for the three sections are taken from: **1** notices, timetables, advertisements **2** two short work-related texts – these are mainly information texts **3** one longer text, which may be a description or instruction text
Skills focus	**Academic** There will be a range of question types tested over each of the three texts. **General Training** **Section 1:** Extracting as well as matching general factual information from the texts **Section 2:** Identifying and extracting specific information on work-related topics **Section 3:** Locating information in longer texts and answering different question types
Scoring	You will receive a band score between 0 and 9 depending on how many questions you answer correctly. Scores can be reported in whole or half band scores, e.g. 8.0 or 7.5.

1.2 Test-taking tips

What should you do when you take the IELTS Reading Test? Here are some suggestions about how to manage the test as successfully as possible.

Be prepared

Make sure you arrive at the examination centre early so that you are relaxed and calm. Dress comfortably. Bring pencils, as answers to the Reading Test must be written in pencil.

Manage your time

The Reading Test requires careful time management and self-discipline. It is a good idea to look quickly through the whole test first before you start. There may be recommendations for how long you spend on each passage or section. If there are, you should plan out your time so you can stick to them. If there aren't, decide yourself how much time you need for each section. Remember that the sections increase in difficulty. For example, if more than about 15 minutes is spent on Section 1, then you will have less time for later and more difficult sections.

Read actively and quickly, using the skills introduced in this book, and try to predict answers.

Make sure you read the questions carefully – each needs a different approach so use the different skills you will learn in this book. When answering the questions you should spend no more than about a minute on any one question. If you cannot answer a question within this time, you should move on to tackle the next question. See the tips below for further advice.

Guess

Try to answer all the questions. If necessary, *guess* the answer. There are no penalties for wrong answers. Finalise all your answers as you complete each section – don't wait until the end of the test, as it will be difficult to go back to earlier sections and guess answers then.

Write accurately

Although this is a reading test, your ability to write accurate answers is also relevant. Incorrect grammar or spelling in your answers will be penalised. Remember to write your answers directly onto the answer sheet. As you write them, check whether you are using correct grammar and spelling. Make sure you write your answer next to the correct number. Also, do not write 'true', 'false' or 'not given' if 'yes', 'no' or 'not given' are required. You can cross out and change your answers – untidiness is not penalised, as long as your writing can be clearly understood.

Know what to expect

It is important to know what to expect in the Reading Test. Make sure that you are thoroughly familiar with both the content and the structure of the test. For both tests, you should prepare by reading widely, practising the reading strategies and skills introduced in this book, expanding your vocabulary and learning more about synonyms, paraphrasing and summarising. You will have practice in these areas in this book. Each test uses different types of texts; however, the reading strategies and skills required are the same, so you should complete all of the exercises in this book to give yourself the best advantage in the test.

Academic

In the Academic test, the reading passages are based on general topics. They become progressively longer (usually approximately 750–950 words for each) in each section of the text. Each passage is different in type. The first may be a more general description, the second may contain more analysis of a topic and the third is usually a longer argument that needs to be followed. This book will help you to identify the different features of each text type. It will also give you practice at reading longer texts.

General Training

There are three sections to the General Training test. The first section may have two or three short texts or several quite brief texts, such as advertisements or notices. The second section has two texts related to workplace issues. The third section will consist of a longer developed description or instruction text. This book will give you practice at reading these different types of texts.

1.3 Getting to know the test

The IELTS Reading Test assesses your general and specific reading ability, using eleven types of question. Each of these question types requires a different approach or strategy.

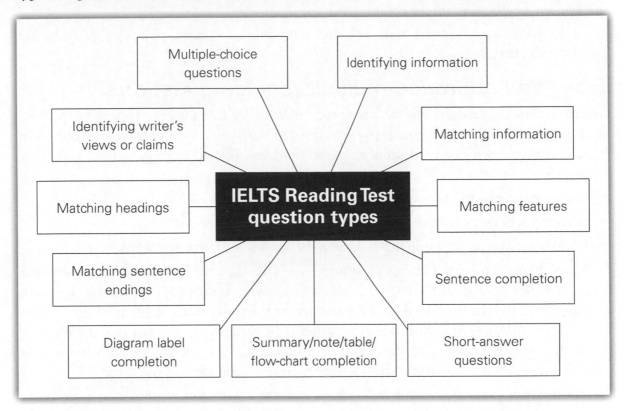

Knowing how best to handle these different kinds of questions is essential to performing well in the test. To familiarise yourself with these question types, work through exercises 1 to 12 in this section.

In some question types (for example, identifying information) the questions follow the same order in which the information occurs in the passage; in other question types (for example, matching information), the answers might be located anywhere in the text or texts.

Remember for all questions to write your answer directly onto the answer sheet. Always attempt all questions, even if you have to guess, because wrong answers are not penalised.

Multiple-choice questions

What do I have to do?

With multiple-choice questions, you need to select the best answer from a list of options. You may have to choose one answer from four options, or choose two or three answers from a longer list of options.

In some multiple-choice questions, you are given the start of a sentence (known as a sentence 'stem') and you have to choose the best **sentence ending** from three choices.

Multiple-choice questions may be either about specific information from the text or about the author's purpose overall. Multiple-choice questions that refer to the text overall are known as **global multiple-choice questions**.

Multiple-choice questions test your understanding of specific points or of the main points of the text.

How do I approach multiple-choice questions?

Multiple-choice questions will be presented in the order the answers appear in the text, so, to save time, make sure you answer the questions in order. Don't answer the questions based on your own personal opinions or knowledge. For all multiple-choice questions begin by:

▼ skimming the whole passage quickly for an overview

▼ checking whether you have to select one option only or several

▼ identifying and underlining key words in the question or sentence stem.

From there, you have a choice of approaches. One is to read the question or sentence stem carefully and predict what you think the answer could be without looking at the options. Scan to locate the section of the text where the answer can be found. There will be word clues, such as synonyms (words with the same meaning as key words), to help you. Read that section carefully to check if your prediction about the answer is correct. Now read the four options and select the one that matches the answer in the text.

Another approach is to read the options straight away after reading the question or stem, identify the correct section of the text and find the option that best matches the information in the text.

▼ Watch out for synonyms and remember that the correct answer may paraphrase or summarise the information in the text.

▼ Check each of the possible answers for words that qualify or change the meaning of nouns or verbs (for example, *all*, *never*, *some*) and also for logical connectors (for example, *and*, *or*, *not*) that change meaning.

Global multiple-choice questions test your understanding of the whole text. You will not find the exact answer written in the text, but it will be inferred. Make sure you are familiar with the whole text before answering global multiple-choice questions. Use one of the above approaches.

Read the following text and answer the questions that follow.

Seven ways to fast track success

1 **Optimism:** Simply put, if you do not believe that some things can get better, you will have no reason to try wholeheartedly. The idea of 'positive psychology' has been around at least since the 1950s and we are in the grip of it once more, but don't let that put you off. Aside from some of the overblown claims and simplicities, learning how to reframe your thinking into a positive cast of mind is a useful skill.

2 **Openness:** The curse of clever people is they too readily analyse new information and categorise it into their existing schemas and frameworks. In this way they can be blind to nuances and nuggets that can change their lives. The curse of stupid people is that they don't bother analysing new information in the first place. The result in both cases is a kind of content and complacent maintenance of the status quo.

3 **Self-efficacy:** This is a concept pioneered by psychologist Albert Bandura and relates to one's belief that you can do something or achieve something. People who believe they can successfully complete a training course or diet are more likely to do so than those without this self-belief. Self-efficacy is not just about positive self-talk (though this can help) but also about engaging in action steps set out, to provide the proof to yourself that you really can do it.

4 **Vision:** Vision has received bad press because it has been overused and devalued in numerous vision statements. However, vision is creating something akin to a mental movie in which you can see yourself doing whatever it is you seek. Can you see yourself acting and interacting with the other people in this desired domain? Are you succeeding? The other point to make is I am not advocating some form of visual goal-setting. The purpose of envisaging is to create some active engagement that may lead to other opportunities as you act.

5 **Playfulness and risk:** Children will often test their toys to destruction, or use them in 'inappropriate' ways. It means coming to an idea without preconceptions to see it for what it is. It is a bit like throwing away the instruction manual. The Zen Buddhist term for this concept is Shoshin.

6 **Flexibility:** This is perhaps best summed up by Groucho Marx's quote: 'These are my principles and if you don't like them, don't worry, I've got others!' It means most diamonds have flaws as well as brilliance and it depends on how you hold them up to the light as to what you will see.

7 **Persistence:** I'll bet the most important things you've done in your life involved a degree of risk that met with resistance from some quarters. It is amazing how many people fail simply because they lose the courage of their convictions. It's therefore important to recognise that giving in is ultimately your choice and yours alone.

continued ▶

Questions 1–9

*Choose the correct letter, **A**, **B**, **C** or **D**.*

1   The author believes that 'positive psychology'   ....

    A   has been around for too long.

    B   is effective if caution is taken.

    C   is far too simple to be good.

    D   detracts because of overblown claims.

2   It is suggested that the difference between the most and the least
    intelligent people relates to   ....

    A   their analysis or non-analysis of information.

    B   their blindness to nuances and life-changing nuggets.

    C   the different ways that they change and hope.

    D   one group being more content with the status quo.

3   Albert Bandura's concept for self-efficacy encourages people to   ....

    A   commence a training course or diet successfully.

    B   engage predominantly in positive self-talk techniques.

    C   develop a positive self-belief in achieving success.

    D   engage in several steps including the provision of proof.

4   Vision relates to   ....

    A   creating opportunities through being actively engaged.

    B   developing forms of visual goal-setting in a desired domain.

    C   making positive statements of honesty and integrity.

    D   feeling comfortable and successful through interaction.

5   Children are mentioned because they   ....

    A   use their toys inappropriately.

    B   throw away the instruction manual.

    C   engage in spontaneous play.

    D   have preconceptions about their toys.

6   Flexibility relates to   ....

    A   maintaining the principles one has learnt.

    B   looking at issues differently.

    C   assessing how diamonds are valued.

    D   seeing the flaws in brilliance.

7 The idea of persistence suggests that ....

    A there is usually widespread opposition to an idea.

    B failing to achieve has a number of causes.

    C taking responsibility for one's own convictions is key.

    D giving in has some element of resistance from others.

8 The writer's overall purpose is to ....

    A suggest methods of becoming successful.

    B warn about potential negative factors.

    C give information about the idea of action steps.

    D identify the mind steps that aid success.

9 From this list of qualities, *A–E*, select two qualities that the author of this text believes are important.

....

A Positively reframing thinking	**D** Making mind-movies
B Acting impulsively	**E** Coming fresh to ideas
C Being influenced by others	

Identifying information

What do I have to do?

For questions that require you to identify information, you need to decide whether a statement is true or false according to the information given in the text, or whether no information about the statement is given. Your answer will be either 'true', 'false' or 'not given'. True statements agree with the information in the text. False information contradicts or is the opposite of the information in the text. If there is no information about the statement in the text, or if it neither agrees with nor contradicts the information in the text, the correct answer is 'not given'. It is particularly important not to confuse 'not given' statements with 'false' statements.

This question type tests your ability to identify specific information.

How do I approach identifying information?

▼ Identifying information questions will be presented in the order the answers appear in the text, so make sure you answer the questions in order to save time.

▼ The questions will relate to two to five paragraphs.

▼ Read the statement and underline key words. Try to predict synonyms of these words which may be used in the text.

- ▼ Scan to the section where the information related to the statement begins by identifying key information.
- ▼ Read that section carefully to check whether the statement:
  - – agrees with or supports the information in the text (using synonyms)
  - – disagrees with or contradicts the information in the text
  - – neither agrees nor disagrees with the information in the text because the relevant information is not present.
- ▼ Remember that the question may paraphrase the relevant information.
- ▼ If the correct answer is 'false', the statement will explicitly contradict the information in the text (possibly using a paraphrase).
- ▼ If you can't find the information in the text, the correct answer is probably 'not given'.
- ▼ It is unusual for the first question to be 'not given'.

Exercise 2 Identifying information

Read the following text and answer the questions that follow.

The world the box made

On April 26, 1956, a crane lifted fifty-eight aluminium truck bodies aboard an ageing tanker ship moored in Newark, New Jersey, USA. Five days later, the *Ideal-X* sailed into Houston, where fifty-eight trucks waited to take on the metal boxes and haul them to their destinations. Such was the beginning of a revolution.

Decades later, when enormous trailer trucks hauling nothing but stacks of boxes rumble through the night, it is hard to fathom just how much the container has changed the world. In 1956, China was not the world's workshop. It was not routine for shoppers to find Brazilian shoes and Mexican vacuum cleaners in stores in the middle of Kansas. Japanese families did not eat beef from Wyoming, and French clothing designers did not have their clothes sewn in Vietnam. Before the container, transporting goods was so expensive that it did not pay to ship many things halfway around the world.

What is it about the container that is so important? Surely not the thing itself – an aluminium or steel box with two enormous doors at one end. The value of this utilitarian object lies not in what it is, but in how it is used. The container is at the core of a highly automated system for moving goods from anywhere to anywhere with a minimum of cost and complication.

The container made shipping cheap and by doing so changed the shape of the world economy. The thousands of ill-paid workers who once made their livings loading and unloading ships in every port are no more, their tight-knit waterfront communities now just memories. Cities that had been centres of maritime commerce for centuries, such as New York and Liverpool, saw their waterfronts decline with startling speed. At the same time, the manufacturers located near them for convenience moved away. Venerable ship lines were crushed by the enormous cost of adapting to container shipping. Merchant mariners, who had shipped out to see the world, had their shore leave reduced to a few hours ashore in a remote parking lot for containers, their ships ready to leave as soon as high-speed cranes finished moving the giant boxes off and on the ships.

Even as it helped destroy the old economy, the container helped build a new one. Sleepy harbours such as Pusan and Seattle moved into the front ranks of the world's ports and massive new ports were built in places like Felixstowe in the UK and Tanjung Pelepas in Malaysia, where none had been before. Small towns with cheap land and low wages enticed factories away from the old harbours. Sprawling industrial complexes employing thousands to manufacture products from start to finish gave way to smaller, more specialised plants that shipped half-finished goods to one another in ever-lengthening supply chains. Poor countries could realistically dream of becoming suppliers to wealthy countries far away. Huge industrial complexes mushroomed in places like Los Angeles and Hong Kong only because the cost of bringing raw materials in and sending finished goods out had dropped like a stone.

Do the following statements agree with the information given in the reading passage?

Write:

TRUE   if the statement agrees with the information

FALSE   if the statement contradicts the information

NOT GIVEN   if there is no information on this

1   In the mid-1950s, the transportation of metal containers using vessels and heavy vehicles was common.   ....

2   Containers, like many other goods, are made in China.   ....

3   The container enabled trade in goods that were previously too expensive to sell in distant countries.   ....

4   The value of the container lies in its efficient structure.   ....

5   The container allowed the continuing employment of armies of waterside workers.   ....

6   Sailors hoping to visit exotic locations found that this did not happen in the way they expected.   ....

7   Singapore, like other Asian ports, expanded from a sleepy harbour to a massive new port.   ....

8   There was considerable downsizing of factories, as supply chains altered in size.   ....

9   Los Angeles and Hong Kong are given as examples of industrial complexes with mushrooming costs.   ....

Identifying writer's views/claims

What do I have to do?

For identifying writer's views/claims questions, you need to decide whether a statement agrees with the views or claims the writer makes in the text. Your answer should be either 'yes', 'no' or 'not given'. You answer 'yes' if a statement agrees with the opinions or claims of the writer. You answer 'no' if the statement contradicts the writer's opinion or argument. If the text gives no information on what the writer thinks about the statement, the correct answer is 'not given'. Be careful to distinguish between 'no' and 'not given'.

This question type tests your ability to identify views or opinions.

How do I approach identifying writer's views/claims?

▼ Identifying writer's views/claims questions will be presented in the order the answers appear in the text, so make sure you answer the questions in order to save time.

▼ Read the statement and underline key words.

▼ Scan to the section where the information related to the statement begins.

▼ Read that section carefully to check whether the statement:

  – agrees with the opinions or claims of the writer (using synonyms)

  – disagrees with or contradicts the opinions or claims of the writer

  – neither agrees nor disagrees with the opinions or claims of the writer because the relevant information is not present.

▼ Remember that the question may paraphrase the relevant information.

▼ If the correct answer is 'no', the statement will explicitly contradict the views of the author presented in the text (possibly using a paraphrase).

▼ If you can't find a statement giving the author's opinion on the subject in the text, the correct answer is probably 'not given'.

▼ Remember to write 'yes' or 'no', and not 'true' or 'false' on the answer sheet.

Exercise 3 Identifying writer's views/claims

Read the following passage and answer the questions that follow.

The pursuit of happiness

One way or another, everything we do is motivated by our desire to be happy. You're reading this because you hope it will be a pleasant experience. If you read the business section to track your investments, you're hoping for news that they're doing well, which will make you feel good.

If you're working hard in pursuit of

promotion and a pay rise, you're doing it because you believe the extra status and money will make you happier.

The philosopher Blaise Pascal said: 'All men seek happiness. This is without exception. Whatever different means they employ, they all tend to this end. The cause of some going to war, and of others avoiding it, is the same desire in both, attended with different views … This is the motive of every action of every man …'

The Harvard psychologist Daniel Gilbert puts it the opposite way: 'If there has ever been a group of human beings who prefer despair to delight, frustration to satisfaction and pain to pleasure, they must be very good at hiding because no one has ever seen them.

'People want to be happy, and all the other things they want are typically meant to be means to that end. Even when people forgo happiness in the moment – by dieting when they could be eating, or working late when they could be sleeping – they are usually doing so in order to increase its future yield.'

If *all* of us want to be happy all the time, the explanation for this has to be in the way humans have evolved as a species. According to David Nettle, a British psychologist, we're biologically programmed not to be happy but merely to *pursue* happiness. We're programmed to pursue it in ways that contribute to our biological fitness. Whether we actually achieve it, nature doesn't much care.

The pursuit of happiness is humans' basic motivating force, the drive that keeps us doing and striving. Thus we've evolved never to be completely happy (or never for long) and to quickly adapt to whatever we've managed to attain and soon be hankering for something we imagine will be better.

The good news, however, is that most of us do achieve a fair bit of happiness. Surveys unfailingly show that most people are quite happy most of the time. We are programmed to believe we'll be happier if we're physically and materially secure, if we have a mate, if we have high social status, and many other things. All these are things that, in our primitive state, would have contributed to our fitness.

Do the following statements agree with the claims of the writer in the reading passage?

Write:

YES   if the statement agrees with the claims of the writer

NO   if the statement contradicts the claims of the writer

NOT GIVEN   if it is impossible to say what the writer thinks about this

1   All of our everyday activities have the same underlying motivation.   ....

2   It would appear that young people are less able to resist forgoing happiness.   ....

3   Research shows there is no difference between being happy and the desire to be happy.   ....

4   Other research shows that there are measurable differences in happiness levels in apparently similar cultures.   ....

5   Striving for greater material security has improved our ability to survive.   ....

Matching information

What do I have to do?

For matching information questions, you need to match specific information stated in the question with the relevant section or paragraph of the text where the information is located. Sections or paragraphs will be labelled **A, B, C,** etc. You write the letter corresponding to the correct paragraph or section on the answer sheet. The instructions will indicate that you can use a letter more than once.

This type of question tests your ability to identify specific information that might not be in the same order in the text as in the questions.

How do I approach matching information?

▼ If you have not already done so, skim the whole text quickly to get an overview of what it is about. You could also read the topic sentence of each paragraph to identify what each paragraph will cover.

▼ Read the question, underlining key words so that you know what you are looking for: for example, a date, quantity, place name or other information.

▼ Scan very quickly back and forth through the whole text to find the relevant information.

▼ As usual, be aware that key words may be expressed as synonyms.

Exercise 4 | Matching information

Read the following passage and answer the questions that follow.

Eco-tourism and the tropics

A The world's tropical zone extends over a very large distance – 4000 km north of the Equator and 3500 south – and in fact covers one-third of the world's surface, 50 million square kilometres in total. With a total global coastline of 60,000 km, tropical areas are attracting tourists in increasing numbers. This large increase in tourism means that there is a need for quality tourist resorts in previously undeveloped areas.

B Up until the 1980s, the drawcard for tourists was beach and sea – simple attractions that did not necessitate quality accommodation. In fact, this aspect of the tropical holiday experience was sadly neglected and resorts were often very basic in their facilities. However, in recent years with the arrival of more affluent and discriminating tourists from developed countries, quality accommodation facilities that cope with the climatic stress of the tropics have become a priority.

C This situation, where tourists from developed countries vacation in developing tropical countries with expectations of quality at a low price, has resulted in some undesirable effects. At the same time, however, a new type of tourist has emerged – those who wish to get closer to the nature and culture of the region they are visiting while at the same time wanting to preserve what is left of it. This trend led to the development of the eco-tourism movement thirty years ago; today it is the fastest-growing segment of the tourist industry, and this trend is a reflection of many tourists' environmental concerns.

D Throughout tropical regions, efforts to develop tourist resorts in environmentally sensitive areas have resulted in heightened awareness of potential damage, and with it protests from the general public. This occurred in the Australian state of Queensland when islands in the Whitsunday Passage were to be developed to the possible detriment of the Great Barrier Reef. Protests have also occurred in many other tropical areas, for example, Borneo, the Bahamas and the Amazon Basin.

E One way in which tourist resorts can be made environmentally friendly is to make use of passive climate control. This involves providing indoor environmental comfort at a resort without the need for powered means such as air-conditioning or even electric fans. Most eco-tourists would be happy to adjust to the climate of their tropical resort if the extremes of heat and humidity were reduced. It can also be argued that adaptation to the local climate is healthier than the constant low temperatures provided by air-conditioning.

F As well as being environmentally friendly, new tourist developments need to take an environmentally conscious stance with local communities if they do not want to undermine the base on which they operate. Thus, they need to be integrated more with the heritage of the local community, its customs and social fabric; this will assist in maintaining the integrity of the local community. Another factor to consider is the fact that tourists on holiday want to relax and experience something different. Experiencing the tropics for what they are – humid and sometimes rainy – is important for them. Even so, it must be acknowledged that tourists are different in their needs and expectations from the local people and resort planners needs to take this into account.

Questions 1–6

The text has six paragraphs, A–F.

Which paragraph contains the following information?

Write the correct letter, A–F, for each. You may use each letter more than once.

1   The necessity of working more closely with nearby residents   ....

2   Location of disputes related to possible harm to local areas   ....

continued ▶

3	The geographic range of these areas	....
4	Responding to changes in requirements of guests' lodgings	....
5	A suggestion for providing an alternative cooling system	....
6	Current directions in tourism preferences	....

Matching headings

What do I have to do?

In matching headings questions you have to identify the main idea of each paragraph or section in the text by selecting the correct heading from a list of possible headings. Sections or paragraphs will be labelled **A, B, C**, etc. There will be more headings than paragraphs, so you won't use all the headings. Sometimes an example will be given for you to follow.

This question type tests your ability to identify the main idea of a paragraph and to distinguish it from supporting ideas.

How do I approach matching headings?

▼ If you haven't already done so, skim the text for a general idea of what each paragraph is about.

▼ Because there are fewer paragraphs than headings always start with the paragraphs, not the headings.

▼ Read the first paragraph and identify what you think the main idea is – it will be found in the topic sentence, which may not be the first sentence. Underline key words. Note: The main idea may extend over more than one sentence.

▼ Scan the boxed list of headings and choose the one that best matches what you the topic of the paragraph.

▼ The headings will be summaries or paraphrases, but there will be clues to help you make your choice – for example, synonyms or rephrasings.

▼ Repeat this process with each paragraph until you have selected a heading for each of them. Remember that there will be leftover headings that won't match any paragraphs.

Exercise 5 Matching headings

Read the passage in Exercise 4 and answer the questions that follow.

Questions 7–12

*Choose the correct heading for paragraphs **A–F** from the list of headings below.*

*Write the correct number, **i–ix**.*

i	Health concerns	vi	Utilising an environmental advantage
ii	Fitting in with non-tourists	vii	Government initiatives
iii	Balancing the effects of tourism	viii	Concerns lead to action
iv	Adjustment needs of staff	ix	Changes in accommodation needs
v	Background information		

7 Paragraph A   ....

8 Paragraph B   ....

9 Paragraph C   ....

10 Paragraph D   ....

11 Paragraph E   ....

12 Paragraph F   ....

Matching features

What do I have to do?

For matching features questions, you are given a number of statements, which you need to match to items or options in a box. This list of options may include, for example, types of architecture, historical time periods, different scientific theories or the names of researchers. Both the statements and the options may be synonyms or paraphrases of the information in the text. Matching features questions will not be presented in the same order as the information in the text. Be aware that technical vocabulary may be used – for example, words associated with a specific discipline, such as architecture, or with a branch of science.

This question type tests your ability to see relationships in a text and identify theories and opinions.

How do I approach matching features?

▼ Skim the whole text first to get an overview of where information is located and how the text is organised.

▼ Start with the first statement and underline key words.

▼ Be very clear about what you are looking for – for example, a name or a date.

▼ Skim and scan quickly backwards and forwards through the text until you locate and match the information you need.

Read the following passage and answer the questions that follow.

The United Nations in summary

The United Nations (UN), an international organisation with a number of aims, was founded by 51 countries in 1945 after the Second World War. Through the powers vested in its founding Charter, it can take action on a wide range of issues, and provide a forum for its 192 Member States to express their views, through the General Assembly, the Security Council, the Economic and Social Council and other bodies and committees.

The work of the UN reaches every corner of the globe. Although it is best known for peacekeeping, conflict resolution and humanitarian assistance, the UN and its specialised agencies operate many other programs that affect our lives and make the world a better place. Some of these areas include sustainable development, environment and refugees protection, disaster relief, counter terrorism, disarmament and non-proliferation.

Today, nearly every nation in the world belongs to the UN and membership totals 192 countries. When States become Members of the United Nations, they agree to accept the obligations of the UN Charter, an international treaty that sets out basic principles of international relations. According to the Charter, the UN has four purposes: to maintain international peace and security; to develop friendly relations among nations; to cooperate in solving international problems and in promoting respect for human rights; and to be a centre for harmonising the actions of nations.

The UN is not a world government and it does not make laws. It does, however, provide the means to help resolve international conflicts and formulate policies on matters affecting all of us. At the UN, all the Member States large and small, rich and poor, with differing political views and social systems, have a voice and a vote in this process.

The General Assembly is the main deliberative organ of the UN and is composed of representatives of all Member States. There are a number of committees (for example, one related to the peaceful use of outer space), programs and funds, and research and training institutes, as well as other UN entities.

The Security Council has primary responsibility, under the UN Charter, for the maintenance of international peace and security. It consists of five permanent members and ten non-permanent members; the non-permanent members each hold the position for one year. A number of UN bodies, including the Department of Peacekeeping Operations, the Counter-terrorism Committee, the Sanctions Committee, and a number of ad hoc committees, report directly to the Security Council

The Economic and Social Council (ECOSOC), established by the UN Charter, is the principal organ coordinating the economic, social and related work of the United Nations and its specialised agencies and institutions. It also operates the International Narcotics Control Board. Voting in ECOSOC is by simple majority of all members; each member has one vote.

The Trusteeship Council, which comprises the five permanent members of the Security Council, was established in 1945 by the UN Charter to provide international supervision for 11 Trust Territories placed under the administration of seven Member States, and to ensure that Territories were prepared for self-government and independence. By 1994, all Trust Territories had attained self-government or independence.

The International Court of Justice, located at The Hague in the Netherlands, is the principal judicial organ of the United Nations. It settles legal disputes between states and gives advisory opinions to the UN and its specialised agencies. It gives advisory opinions on legal questions referred to it by authorised UN organs and specialised agencies.

Questions 1–6

Look at the following statements (questions 1–6) and the list of UN responsibilities.

*Match each statement with the correct responsibility, **A–C**.*

*Write the correct letter, **A–C**, beside the statement.*

***NB** You may use any letter more than once.*

1   Providing legal assistance in several areas   A   ....

2   Peace and security issues   B   ....

3   Drafting laws   C   ....

4   Non-military space issues   A   ....

5   Illicit drug control and coordination of social issues   A   ....

6   Establishing governments   C   ....

> **UN responsibilities**
> **A** The responsibility of organs composed of all members
> **B** The responsibility of organs composed of some members
> **C** Not a UN responsibility

Matching sentence endings

What do I have to do?

For matching sentence endings questions, you are given sentence stems and you need to select the correct sentence ending from a list of options. The correct combination will correctly reflect specific information in the text. There will be fewer sentence stems than options, so some options will not be used. The sentence stems will be in the same order as the information in the text.

This question type tests your ability to identify specific information.

How do I approach matching sentence endings?

▼ If you haven't already done so, skim the whole text first to get an overview of where information is located and how the text is organised.

▼ Read the sentence stem and underline key words.

▼ Predict what you think the answer might be.

▼ Scan to where the information related to the sentence is. Look for synonyms.

▼ Read this section of the text for meaning.

▼ Read each of the options and choose the one that best reflects the information in the text, remembering that the option may be a rephrase.

▼ Make sure that the grammar of the sentence is correct once the two parts are joined.

▼ Move to the next question, remembering that the new information will appear after the information related to the previous question in the text.

▼ Remember that there will be options left over.

Exercise 7 Matching sentence endings

Read the passage in Exercise 6 and answer the questions that follow.

Questions 7–9

*Complete each sentence with the correct ending, **A–F**, below.*

7   The UN was initially founded in order to   C   ....

8   The UN is known mainly for its ability to   F   ....

9   The Charter of the United Nations obliges it to   E   ....

A involve itself in bi-nation politics.
B organise the legal requirements of new nations.
C take action in many areas of international concern.
D formulate policy of member states.
E operate in relation to four main principles.
F organise assistance in areas such as peacekeeping.

Sentence completion

What do I have to do?

For sentence completion questions, you have to find a word or phrase in the passage that correctly completes a sentence. You will be told how many words you can use. You may have to write one, two or three words and/or a number. You will be penalised if you use more than the stated number of words and/or numbers. You will not need to use contractions (such as *won't*). Hyphenated words count as one word. The questions will be in the same order as the information in the text.

This question type tests your ability to locate specific information in the text.

How do I approach sentence completion questions?

▼ If you haven't already done so, skim the whole text first to get an overview of where information is located and how the text is organised.

▼ Read the instructions carefully to make sure you know what you are looking for.

▼ Read the sentence stem and underline key words. Identify what type of words you are looking for: for example, a noun group or an adjective and a noun.

▼ Scan the text to locate where the answer is, using clues from the sentence stem.

▼ Remember you will be looking for exact words and/or numbers that will complete the sentence, both for meaning and grammar.

▼ Work through each of the sentences in turn.

▼ Make sure you are accurate when you transfer your answers to the answer sheet, and check your spelling.

Exercise 8 Sentence completion

Read the passage in Exercise 6 and answer the questions that follow.

Questions 10–13

Complete the sentences below.

*Choose **NO MORE THAN THREE WORDS** from the passage for each answer.*

10 The UN is able to operate in the way it does because of the authority of
its founding charter

11 Areas such as sustainable development and disaster relief are managed by some of the UN's specialised agencies

12 To belong to the UN, member states are obliged to agree to accept its Charter requirements.

13 While the UN cannot govern internationally, it does have the ability to assist in the resolution of international conflicts and to work to improve areas of universal concern.

Summary/note/table/flow-chart completion

What do I have to do?

For summary/note/table/flow-chart completion questions, you have to fill in gaps in a short summary, set of notes, flow-chart or table. The information needed to fill the gaps will come from one section of the text. You may have to write one, two or three words and/or a number. You will not need to use contractions (such as *won't*). Hyphenated words count as one word.

There are two forms of this question type:

1 Choosing answers from a list or bank of options. There will be more options than there are gaps.

2 Selecting information directly from the text. In this form of question, the number of words and/or numbers you are to use will be specified.

This type of question tests your understanding of the main ideas or details of a part of a text.

How do I approach summary/note/table/flow-chart completion questions?

If you haven't already done so, skim the whole text first to get an overview of where information is located and how the text is organised. For summary/note/table/flow-chart completion questions that offer you a list of options to choose from:

▼ Locate the section of the text where the relevant information can be found.

▼ Identify synonyms that will help you.

▼ Read the sentence or notes containing the first gap.

▼ Look at the words before and after the gap to decide what type of word you need e.g. a noun or adjective.

▼ Look after the gap for information on the grammar of the word e.g. singular or plural.

▼ Read the section of text to check the correct meaning.

▼ Scan through the list of options to choose the one that fits both the meaning and grammar of the gap.

▼ Move through each of the gaps.

▼ Remember that each option is used only once.

Exercise 9   Summary/note/table/flow-chart completion

Read the text in Exercise 6, and answer the following questions.

Questions 14–18

The organisation of the United Nations in brief

The UN is composed of six main organs. Of these, the **14** .... decision-making body is the General Assembly, composed of all members. The organ responsible for **15** .... bodies and a number of ad-hoc committees is the Security Council. Another organ manages **16** .... and social areas and a further one has **17** .... responsibility for Trust Territories, all of which have become independent. Another important area relates to the managing of legal advice and **18** .... between members.

A	legal	D	supervisory	G	Narcotics	J	principal
B	peacekeeping	E	important	H	trade	K	principles
C	disagreements	F	supervised	I	economic		

For summary/note/table/flow-chart completion questions requiring you to select information directly from the text:

▼ Read the instructions carefully so you know how many words you can use.

▼ Skim through the summary, note, table or flow-chart for an overview of what it is about and to understand what you need to look for.

▼ Identify where in the text this information is found.

▼ Read the sentence with the first gap. Underline the key words before the gap and check the words after the gap to see what part of speech is needed: for example, a noun/nouns or a number.

▼ Scan to find the relevant section of the text, remembering that it may be a paraphrase. Read the appropriate section carefully for meaning. Look for synonyms of key words.

▼ Look for a word group that fits into the gap and has the correct meaning.

▼ Remember that the grammar in the summary, note, table or flow-chart may be altered. For example, it may be worded in the passive rather than the active voice.

▼ Be aware that contractions *won't* be used and hyphenated words count as one word.

▼ Work through the exercise in the order of the gaps.

Exercise 10 Summary/note/table/flow-chart completion

Read the following text and answer the questions that follow.

Building the Sydney Harbour Bridge

One of the world's most recognisable and admired engineering structures is the Sydney Harbour Bridge. Its great arch, soaring above the blue water of Sydney Harbour, dominating the skyline, is a truly impressive sight. Even more astounding is the fact that the bridge was built in a low-technology era by hundreds of manual workers, operating high in the air above the watching population of Sydney. Today, many people who use the bridge may not think much about those workers, but they should appreciate

continued ▶

the fact that the workmanship was of such expertise that no major component has needed to be replaced since the bridge's opening in 1932.

The challenges of building a bridge on this site were enormous because of the width of the harbour – almost 1 kilometre at the chosen point. Even so, because the growing city was bisected by water, there had been calls for a bridge crossing from 1815. In fact, it would be almost 120 years until the dream was realised and the northern and southern sides of the city were finally connected.

How was the bridge actually built? The citizens of the era, who watched its progress over six years of construction, would have been able to describe the process in detail, but we in the modern age may not quite appreciate how it was done. It is necessary to understand the basic structure first. The main components are:

- four decorative pillars or pylons (hollow structures which actually carry no weight)
- a soaring double arch, formed of higher and lower sections known as chords
- a series of connected cross girders, supporting the busy roadway
- two rows of elegant vertical hangers, linking the arch and roadway.

It might be thought that the pylons came first, but in fact each of the arches was built first, in sections. During construction, each new chord was attached to the previous one by cables secured to the ground. As each new chord was added, the arches could be seen cantilevered out into the air above the water. Each side of the bridge was not started at the same time – the southern part was started first and the northern part followed seven months later, so any problems that became evident could be rectified. Each side of the arch was added to until they each rose into the air to the point of meeting. Sitting on top of the two top arches throughout were the two creeper cranes that lifted workers and essential materials from pontoons on the water below.

The final point of the arches meeting was achieved in 1928 when first the lower arch and then the upper arch were manoeuvred and then riveted into position. After this came the hazardous operation needed to create the roadway. First, pairs of hangers, up to 60 metres long, had to be lifted up one by one from pontoons by the cranes (with workers riding them up into position) and then attached to the arch. Once each pair of these was safely installed, a 100-ton cross girder was lifted and attached to the hangers so that the road and railway could be constructed. Only after all this was complete were the pylons constructed and then faced with granite by Italian stonemasons. In early 1932, the road and railway bridge was tested for strength by driving 30 trains onto the track. Finally, on 10 March 1932, in front of dignitaries and the general public, the big wait was over and the bridge was officially opened.

Questions 1–5

Complete the summary below.

Choose **NO MORE THAN TWO WORDS FROM THE PASSAGE** *for each answer.*

Background to the Sydney Harbour Bridge

The Sydney Harbour Bridge, one of the world's most distinctive structures, is an astonishing feat of engineering because of its very public construction in a **1** ...low technology... . However, despite its being built mainly by manual labour, there has been no need for replacement of any **2** ...major component... since its completion in 1932. In the 120-year period until then, Sydneysiders had long dreamt of a **3** ...bridge... to join both sides of the waterway. They were able to watch the progress of construction in a way that those in the **4** ...modern age... are not able to. They knew the names also of the **5** ...components..., namely, pylons, chords, cross girders and hangers.

Questions 6–11

Complete the flow-chart below.

*Choose **NO MORE THAN THREE WORDS** for each answer.*

How the bridge was built

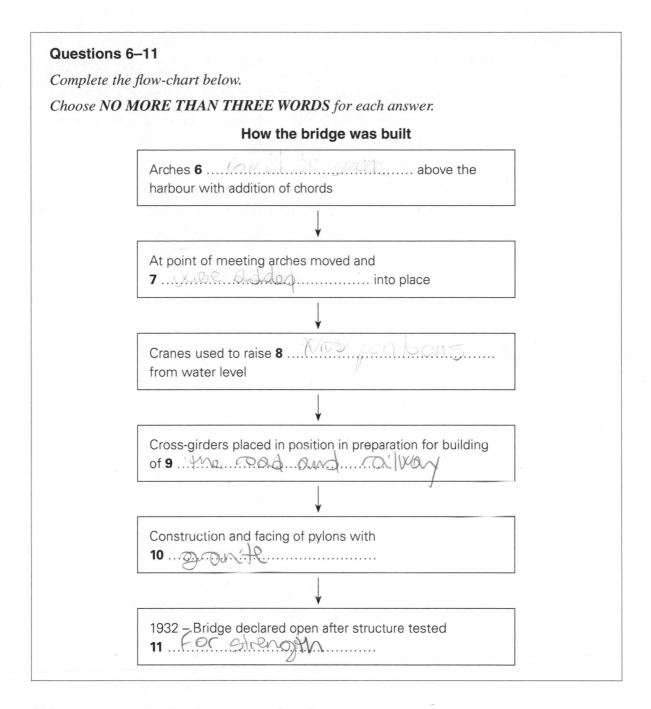

Arches **6** ....could be seen.......... above the harbour with addition of chords

↓

At point of meeting arches moved and **7** ....were added.................. into place

↓

Cranes used to raise **8** ....was pontoons....... from water level

↓

Cross-girders placed in position in preparation for building of **9** ...the road and railway

↓

Construction and facing of pylons with **10** ...granite...........

↓

1932 – Bridge declared open after structure tested **11** ...for strength...........

Diagram label completion

What do I have to do?

For diagram label completion questions, you have to use words or phrases from the text to complete labels on a diagram. You will be told how many words you can use. You may have to write one, two or three words and/or a number. You will be penalised if you use more than the stated number of words and/or numbers. You will not need to use contractions (such as *won't*). Hyphenated words count as one word. The information will usually come from one section of the text and is often in the form of a description.

This question type tests your ability to follow a detailed description and then transfer the required information into another form, i.e. a diagram.

How do I approach diagram label questions?

▼ If you haven't already done so, skim the whole text first to get an overview of where information is located and how the text is organised.

▼ Look at the diagram and try to understand what is being represented.

▼ Be clear about what you have to complete and check the word limit.

▼ Scan to the section of text where the relevant information can be found. Read this section carefully for meaning and see how it relates to the diagram. Look for word groups.

▼ Work through each missing label one by one, making sure you complete all gaps.

▼ Use vocabulary and other clues to help you.

▼ Be aware that there may be alternative information designed to test your understanding.

Exercise 11   Diagram label completion

Read the following text and answer the questions that follow.

How Locks Work

The little town of Bobcaygeon on Pigeon Lake in Ontario, Canada, shares a historic mechanical device with many other river and lake communities throughout Europe and other parts of the world. This device once aided these areas economically, in the days before railways took over, and it is still in use today for recreational sailors.

What these areas have in common is a working lock system on their rivers or canals. Locks are interesting structures, providing an extremely efficient way for rivercraft to travel along waterways of different levels or to bypass obstructions such as mill weirs, rapids and dams that alter the water height.

Even though they may seem complicated, locks are actually quite simple in their operation. Early attempts to build locks, over a thousand years ago, involved managing different water levels with one lifting gate or weir, known as a flash lock, and opening this for a vessel to pass to a lower level. However,

the pressure on the single gate was great and upstream traverses were difficult.

In the fourteenth century, a Chinese invention provided for two opening gates, enclosing a watertight chamber where water was impounded: the pound. This basic structure is still in operation today. One variation involves a pair of lifting gates called guillotine gates, a type still used on narrower canals today. However, the most common method consists of pairs of angled, opening gates of different heights, known as mitred gates, enclosing the pound. A third essential element of the system is the need for lock gear, such as vertical panels or valves to fill and empty the chamber.

One type of lock operates in this way: on the high side of the river or canal the mitred gates, angled outwards, are kept closed by water pressure. When the water in the pound reaches the same height as the high side of the river, the pressure releases naturally and the gates open easily outwards so that the vessel can sail into the chamber. After the gates are closed, water is then discharged from the pound by closing the upper valve and opening the lower valve until the water level drops to that of the lower part of the river, carrying the boat with it. At this point, the lower gates open and the boat exits. The reverse occurs for vessels moving upstream.

There are several methods of removing or adding water to the pound. The usual one involves a valve system, as described, which is operated either mechanically or electrically, and which allows water to either drain or fill. One method of doing this is through a series of holes (called wall ports) in the walls of the pound connected to tunnels. Closing the lower valve allows water to enter the chamber through these wall ports. Another method of adding or removing water is used in the non-mitred gate system where vertical panels or 'paddles' are inserted through each gate and are manually lifted or lowered, using a rack and pinion mechanism.

While many locks need to be professionally operated by trained staff at a control post, such as at Bobcaygeon, some can be easily managed by boat operators, adding to the fun of pleasure boating on the many intact canal systems in different parts of the world.

Questions 1–5

Complete the diagram below.

*Choose **NO MORE THAN THREE WORDS** from the text for each answer.*

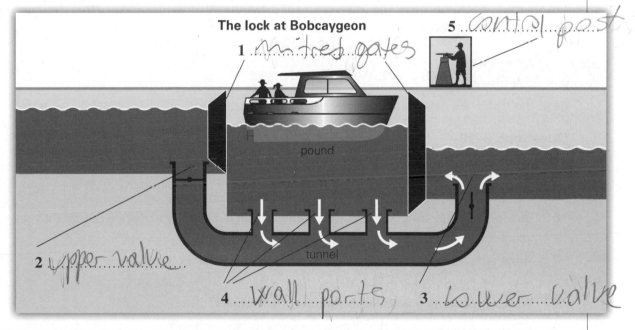

The lock at Bobcaygeon

1 *mitred gates*
5 *control post*
2 *upper valve*
4 *wall ports*
3 *lower valve*
pound
tunnel

Short-answer questions

What do I have to do?

For short-answer questions, you have to answer brief questions about information in the text. You need to find the answer in the text and write the correct number of words. You will be told how many words you can use. You may have to write one, two or three words and/or a number. You will be penalised if you use more than the stated number of words and/or numbers. You will not need to use contractions (such as *won't*). Hyphenated words count as one word. If you write more words than asked for you will receive no marks. Short-answer questions are given in the order of the text.

This type of question tests your ability to identify and understand precise factual information.

How do I approach short-answer questions?

▼ Read the question carefully to identify what you need to locate and what the word limit is.

▼ Try to predict the answer—this will improve you focus as you scan and read the text.

▼ Scan to the relevant part of the text, using word clues to help you.

▼ Be aware of the type of words you are looking for (for example, numbers, a noun or a prepositional phrase) and the word limit.

▼ Identify key words (often grouped) and their synonyms.

▼ Short-answer questions will be presented in the order the answers appear in the text, so make sure, to save time, you answer the questions in order. You do not need to scan the whole text again, because the answer to the next question will appear *after* the answer to the previous question.

Exercise 12 Short-answer questions

Read the text in Exercise 11 and answer the following questions.

Questions 6–10

Answer the following questions.

*Write **NO MORE THAN THREE WORDS** for each question.*

6 In what way did small communities benefit from a mechanical device before the invention of railways? ....

7 What type of early lock was considered to lead to pressure problems? ....

8 Which type of lock is useful for more narrow canals? ....

9 What necessary part of the system manages the water flow? ....

10 What happens to water pressure in the pound when it achieves maximum volume? ....

1.4 The reading strategies and skills you need

Strategies

The IELTS Reading Test requires you to read effectively and efficiently. Being an effective and efficient reader means more than knowing what each word in the passage means. It means being able to read using different strategies depending on your purpose for reading.

Successful candidates use three ways of reading. They:

▼ **skim** the passage to get a general understanding of the main points

▼ **scan** the passage to locate the specific information needed to answer the question

▼ **read** this information intensively to decide on the answer.

By using these strategies, you move from a general overview to increasingly detailed, focused reading depending on the question being asked and your purpose.

When you start to read a passage you need to ask yourself these three questions:

▼ *What* sort of text am I reading? (What is its purpose?)

▼ *Why* am I reading it? (What is my purpose?)

▼ *How* am I going to read it? (What techniques should I use?)

The following table gives some examples of how you might respond to these questions for different text types.

What?	Why?	How?
A letter from a friend	For pleasure and information	*Read* the letter *intensively*; that is, read it from the first word to the last word.
A magazine	For pleasure and information	*Skim* the magazine; that is, glance at the headings and photos. If an article seems interesting, read more until you finish the article or you lose interest. Move on to the next heading or photo.
An airline ticket	For information, e.g. the flight number	*Scan* the ticket; that is, look over it quickly until you find the information you need. Ignore the other information.
A travel brochure	For information and interest	*Skim* for an overview; *scan* to identify relevant information; *read* parts *intensively* for information or interest.
An academic text	To follow an argument	*Skim* for an overview to see if the text is appropriate; *read* all or parts *intensively* to follow the argument.

You can use these three strategies for reading (skimming, scanning and reading intensively) together as a three-step approach to the Reading Test. This is described in more detail below.

Step 1: Skimming

To skim text, your eyes should move methodically across lines and downwards, taking in groups of words, rather than individual words, if possible. It takes practice to develop confidence with this skill.

In the Reading Test, skim the passage so that you have a general understanding of the main points of the text without looking at each word – that is, read it to get an overview. Try to find the main point of each paragraph. This is often, though not always, the first sentence. The sentence with the main point is called the topic sentence. Read together, all the topic sentences of a passage should provide a reasonable summary of the passage.

Topic sentences have two parts:

▼ the **theme** or topic (usually called the subject)

▼ the **rheme,** or new idea (the main verb and what follows it).

Consider the following topic sentence:

The *widespread use of computers* has resulted in enormous changes in all areas of business.

You can guess that 'the widespread use of computers' is the theme. The rest of the sentence gives information (new ideas) about this theme. It forms the rheme of this sentence, and it will be discussed further in the rest of the paragraph.

Other sentences also have themes and rhemes. Some sentences may also have subordinate clauses (that is, the supporting information) – you can ignore these when skimming. Concentrate only on content words to get a general idea of the text, and ignore less important information. For example, consider this example of a sentence with a subordinate clause:

A hard durable mineral called zircon, which is found in most sands, is used for abrasive and insulation purposes.

While skimming, it is enough to understand that '(This mineral) *is used for* (something)'. The subordinate clause 'which is found in most sands' is not important at this stage.

Or, say you are skimming this sentence:

A *recent study* by Jerome Hagan found that there was a correlation between how *babies reacted* to new experiences and their *behaviour* as teenagers.

It is enough to understand that a study showed something about babies and teenagers. If you later find a question that relates to this sentence, you can come back and read it more intensively.

When you have finished skimming the passage, skim the questions. You need to know how many questions there are and approximately what the questions are about.

Exercise 13 gives you practice at skimming. To encourage you to skim as quickly as possible there is a suggested time limit.

Exercise 13 Skimming

1 Skim the following passage as quickly as possible and underline the topic sentence in each paragraph. Identify the theme and new idea in each topic sentence. Remember to ignore subordinate clauses or supporting information. (Time limit: 1 minute)

Computers

A Computers are now a commonplace feature of daily life and it is hard to imagine a world without them. Used extensively in government, commerce, education, medicine, security, aviation and in the domestic sphere, to name but a few areas, they have transformed the way that daily life is transacted.

B For all their apparent modernity, however, the idea behind computers is surprisingly ancient. After all, *to compute* means 'to calculate', and mechanical methods of calculation have been in existence for much of recorded history. In fact, the Romans used a type of abacus over 2,000 years ago. However, it is only since the mid-1940s that electronic means of computation have developed into the highly sophisticated compact machines and devices that we are familiar with today. These developments are still continuing.

C The history of the modern computer can be divided into distinct generations, each distinguished by extreme changes in three areas: namely, the technology used in the manufacturing process, the internal organisation of the systems and the different languages used in the program. The first generation, known by its acronym ENIAC, was distinguished by its size,

its use of vacuum tubes and its restricted purpose. The second generation, with its use of transistors, led to a remarkable reduction in size and opportunities for applications in previously unimagined areas. The third generation, with the introduction of integrated circuits, resulted in remarkable miniaturisation of functions and increasing capability and efficiency. The fourth generation used microprocessors and this further pushed the functions of computers into new areas of utility. The fifth generation is defined by its use of artificial intelligence and through this has come a constantly evolving range of applications, some of which were previously thought to be fanciful.

D The changes that have taken place in less than a century have been astonishing. For instance, to name but a few applications of computers, today it is taken for granted that we communicate on the move via tiny handheld devices, that in the office we communicate via emails rather than in person, that we access news and messages via computers, that students prepare homework on a personal computer, that we drive vehicles with computer-aided location devices, and that we use 'intelligent' household appliances in the home.

continued ▶

2 Now summarise the main idea of each of the four topic sentences using no more than four words for each answer. (Time limit: 1 minute)

a ....

b ....

c ....

d ....

Step 2: Scanning

The next strategy to use in your three-step approach to the Reading Test is scanning. Scan the passage to locate the *specific information* you need to answer each question. With scanning your eyes move around – up and down, backwards and forwards to locate where the answer to a question will be. Remember: not all questions are in the order of the text. When you are scanning to locate some specific information, it is not necessary to read and understand every word in the passage; just look for things related to the main idea of the question. These will often be the key words of a sentence, for example the subject, main verb and object. As you look at each sentence in the text, you need to understand only enough to answer the question: *is this what I am looking for or not?* For example, if you were trying to locate a section about shoes, you would scan the sentence below and know that it is not about shoes so you should move on.

> Like perfumes, *cosmetics* were originally used as a support in religious ritual, the ceremonial aspects gradually being lost as both men and women adorned themselves with cosmetics.

Exercise 14 gives you practice at scanning text to find where answers are located. To encourage you to scan quickly, there is a time limit.

Exercise 14 | Scanning

In the following text, each sentence has been numbered. Read the first question before reading the text, then scan the text to find which sentence contains the information you need to answer this question. Write the number of the relevant sentence from the passage next to it. Then move on to the second question. Questions are *not* presented in the same order as the information. The first one has been done as an example for you to follow. (Time limit: 2 minutes)

1 Computers are now a commonplace feature of daily life and it is hard to imagine a world without them. 2 Used extensively in government, commerce, education, medicine, security, aviation and in the domestic sphere, to name but a few areas, they have transformed the way that daily life is transacted.

3 For all their apparent modernity, however, the idea behind computers is surprisingly ancient. 4 After all, *to compute* means 'to calculate', and mechanical methods of calculation have been in existence for much of recorded history. 5 In fact, the Romans used a type of abacus over 2,000 years ago. 6 However, it is only since the mid-1940s that electronic means of computation have developed into the highly sophisticated compact machines and devices that we are familiar with today. 7 These developments are still continuing.

8 The history of the modern computer can be divided into distinct generations, each distinguished by extreme changes in three areas: namely, the technology used in the manufacturing process, the internal organisation of the systems and the different languages used in the program. 9 The first generation, known by its acronym ENIAC, was distinguished by its size, its use of vacuum tubes and its restricted purpose. 10 The second generation, with its use of transistors, led to a remarkable reduction in size and opportunities for applications in previously unimagined areas. 11 The third generation, with the introduction of integrated circuits, resulted in remarkable miniaturisation of functions and increasing capability and efficiency. 12 The fourth generation used microprocessors and this further pushed the functions of computers into new areas of utility. 13 The fifth generation is defined by its use of artificial intelligence and through this has come a constantly evolving range of applications, some of which were previously thought to be fanciful.

14 The changes that have taken place in less than a century have been astonishing. 15 For instance, to name but a few applications of computers, today it is taken for granted that we communicate on the move via tiny handheld devices, that in the office we communicate via emails rather than in person, that we access news and messages via computers, that students prepare homework on a personal computer, that we drive vehicles with computer-aided location devices, and that we use 'intelligent' household appliances in the home.

1	What does *to compute* mean?	............4........
2	What can we access while commuting today?	....
3	When did the Romans use an abacus?	....
4	What did the second generation of computers use?	....
5	What is one example of a non-professional place of use?	....
6	What is the characteristic of the fifth generation?	....

Step 3: Reading intensively

After you have scanned for and located the information you need to answer the question, your next step is to read intensively. Unlike with skimming and scanning, where you only need to understand some key words in each sentence, with reading intensively it may be necessary to understand every word to answer the question.

Exercise 15 gives you practice in reading intensively. To encourage you to read as quickly as possible, there is a suggested time limit.

Exercise 15 Reading intensively

Answer the questions below. Scan the passage about computers in Exercise 14 to locate the sentences that contain the answers. Then read those sentences intensively. Use no more than three words or a number in each answer. (Time limit: 2 minutes)

(Remember: Hyphenated words count as one word.)

1 What kind of calculation methods have been in existence for much of recorded history?

....

2 Each generation of computers is distinguished by changes in how many areas?

....

3 What remarkable feature followed from the use of integrated circuits?

....

4 What computer feature has been integrated into cars?

....

Now practise the three-step reading approach further by completing Exercises 16 to 18, which gives you practice at IELTS-style questions. Be careful to follow the suggested time limits.

Three-step reading approach

- *Skim* the passage and the questions to get a quick general understanding.
- *Scan* the passage to locate the information you need to answer each question.
- *Read* this information *intensively* so that you can answer the questions.

Read the following passage and answer the questions on page 36. Allow no more than three minutes to skim the passage to get a quick general understanding.

Wave energy

Wave energy, which differs from tidal power and ocean current energy, is the energy generated by surface ocean waves. These waves are caused by a number of forces, including the gravitational pull of the Sun and Moon, earthquakes, and especially the wind moving at a higher speed across the surface of ocean water. A feature of wave energy is that it is irregular and oscillating – that is, vibrating.

Interest in renewable, non-polluting forms of energy has led to the development of new technologies to harness the energy of waves. Although attempts have been made to do this since the 1890s, it is only in recent years that fledgling energy technologies have been developed that could generate commercially viable amounts of electricity on a greater scale in the future. This electricity could be used for domestic and commercial energy generation, water desalination and the pumping of water into reservoirs.

There are several methods of harnessing wave energy. It may be taken from locations either at or near the shoreline or further out to sea and either from the surface of the ocean or from pressure fluctuations below the surface. There are three main methods of doing this: floats on the surface, wave surge devices and oscillating water columns. The latter are the most common currently being used.

There are a number of advantages to this source of energy. The first is that there are a large number of locations capable of being exploited. These include the western seaboard of Europe, the north coast of the United Kingdom, the Pacific coastlines of North and South America and the western coasts of South Africa, Australia and New Zealand. The presence of strong, reliable westerly winds is a significant factor. Other advantages include the fact that the energy source is free, with no waste and with significant amounts of energy being able to be produced.

However, there are a number of disadvantages. The cost of installing the technology and capturing the energy over a large area is a significant factor. The energy levels tend to fluctuate, making it difficult for power generators, which need a constant steady flow of power. The devices installed need to survive the storm and saltwater damage. Noise and visual pollution may have a negative impact on coastal communities, and the fishing industry may be affected.

While this technology has enormous potential to provide large amounts of electricity, its use may be restricted by the above factors as well as by the competitive disadvantages it faces in an energy market dominated by subsidised low-cost fossil fuels and nuclear generation facilities.

continued ▶

Questions 1–7

Complete the sentences below.

*Choose **NO MORE THAN THREE WORDS** from the passage for each answer.*

1 A characteristic of wave energy is that it is …… *irregular and oscillating* ……

2 Original attempts were made to harness wave energy in …… *the 1830s* …… .

3 The most common method to harness wave energy is through using …… *oscillating wave columns* ……

4 For successful generation of energy from waves, the best wind direction is …… *westerly* …… .

5 One disadvantage of the energy levels is that they may …… *fluctuate* …… .

6 An activity in coastal communities that may be disrupted by wave energy technology is …… *fishing* …… .

7 One source of competition comes from …… *low-cost fossil fuels* …… .

Questions 8–12

*Match each sentence with the correct ending, **A–G**, below.*

8 The electricity generated by wave energy …… *A* ……

9 One way of capturing wave energy …… *F* ……

10 One advantage of wave energy …… *G* ……

11 A significant disadvantage of using wave energy …… *E* ……

12 One source of competition for wave energy …… *D* ……

A is easily diverted to a number of uses.

B is that it has been used since the 1890s.

C shares similarities with other ocean energies.

D is a subsidised form of energy.

E is the financial expenditure required.

F is from below surface pressures.

G is that it is free and available everywhere.

Read the following passage and answer the questions on page 38. Allow no more than three minutes to skim the passage to get a quick general understanding.

Jatropha – a plant for the future

A *Jatropha* is a succulent plant that grows in the arid and semi-arid tropics in poorer, degraded soil and reaches heights of between three and five metres. Its name comes from Greek: *Jatros* meaning 'doctor' and *trophe* meaning 'nutrition'. From this it can be deduced that it has medicinal benefits. In fact, it has a wide range of uses, one of which has become of enormous commercial interest in recent years.

B The primary value of this plant lies in its seeds, which are extremely viscous, containing 28–30% of their weight in oil. The crushed seeds of the *Jatropha* plant are considered to be the best future source of plant-based biofuels in a world increasingly seeking alternative fuel sources to non-renewable fossil fuels. It is estimated that one hectare of this plant can produce 1,500–2,000 kilos of biofuel per year.

C It is the interest in this fuel source that has led to commercial opportunities being provided by business consortiums, NGOs and other organisations for farmers and village people in a range of tropical countries to grow this plant for biofuel. Previously grown mainly in Brazil and the Philippines, it is now being planted throughout suitable tropical areas around the world, including parts of Africa (e.g. Mali) and South-East Asia (e.g. Vietnam and Papua New Guinea).

D Its great advantage is that it can be grown in very degraded and pebbly soil – soils that may not grow much else – and thus it is useful as a soil reclamation plant. Additionally, it can be grown between cash crops such as coffee, sugar, vegetables and fruit trees. Also, apart from its use as a source of biofuel, it provides a number of other products for local communities. These include baskets (woven from the leaves), soaps and candles, and products for dyeing and tanning. It is also an excellent fertiliser. A further use is that it can be used for microcredit programs, such as those in India, where local communities can develop small industries based on the products from this plant.

E However, there are disadvantages related to the use of this 'wonder plant'. It is highly toxic, being both poisonous and a skin irritant. Being hardy and both drought- and pest-resistant, it can also be highly invasive and in fact has been banned in Western Australia, where it took over prime farming land when introduced.

F However, despite these drawbacks, interest in this plant has been growing enormously, with very positive expectations for the future. Such is the confidence in its financial viability that, in 2008 and 2009 respectively, two airlines, Air New Zealand and Continental, made test flights using biofuels processed from *Jatropha*.

continued ▶

Questions 1–4

*Choose the correct letter, **A**, **B**, **C** or **D**.*

1   The name *Jatropha* relates to   ....

   A   succulence.

   B   medicine.   *(circled)*

   C   viability.

   D   profitability.

2   Its fuel benefits are related to its   ....

   A   growth.

   B   weight.

   C   viscosity.   *(circled)*

   D   adaptability.

3   Today *Jatropha* is grown   ....

   A   in tropical regions.   *(circled)*

   B   mainly in Brazil and the Philippines.

   C   throughout North and South Africa.

   D   in suitable temperate areas.

4   An advantage it has over other plants is that *Jatropha*   ....

   A   grows well in poor soil.   *(circled)*

   B   is an alternative to coffee.

   C   prefers reclaimed soil.

   D   needs additional fertiliser.

Questions 5–10

*Which paragraph, **A–F**, contains the following information?*

NB You may use any letter more than once.

5   How Jatropha can be used to improve environmentally damaged land   ...D...

6   An explanation and description of Jatropha   ...A...

7   How Jatropha can threaten other agriculture   ...E...

8   An energy-related environmental reason for the current focus on Jatropha   ...B...

9   A transport experiment using a Jatropha product   ...F...

10   The range of benefits of Jatropha   ...D...

Read the text and answer the questions that follow.

PACIFIC ISLAND HOLIDAYS

A Lake Holiday Resort $1545 8 nights + $800 extras package

Your package includes:

- Return airfares from Auckland or Sydney
- All flight taxes and upgrade based on availability
- 8 nights in a Superior resort
- Concierge service and VIP upgrades to Deluxe rooms
- BONUS upgrade to Lake View room
- BONUS massage/spa
- With upgrade you will receive free welcome cocktails, butler service and afternoon tea
- Discount shopping, dining and touring

B Fabulous Island Resort $1595 10 nights + 3-day cruise

Your package includes:

- Return airfare, economy class, from any major Australian or New Zealand city
- All flight taxes
- 8 nights share accommodation in Tropical Room
- Free continental breakfast
- Upgrade to Island Villa room for $50 per night
- Free use of gym, all 7 pools and spa
- Lovely sights cruise – 2 nights including all meals and transfers
- Discount shopping, dining and touring
- Special holiday discounts

C Dream Island Resort $1760 10 nights + $1200 extras

Your package includes:

- Return airfares ex Sydney
- All flight taxes and upgrade based on availability
- 10 nights for the price of 7
- Upgrade to premier suite for $200
- Full buffet breakfast
- BONUS sailing trip with snorkelling and gourmet lunch
- BONUS jet ski adventure
- Complimentary champagne

continued ▶

Classify the following information as referring to

> **A** Lake Holiday Resort
> **B** Fabulous Island Resort
> **C** Dream Island Resort

*Write the correct letter, **A**, **B** or **C**, next to each of the questions. (Note: the questions are not in order.)*

Identify the resort that offers:

1 free exercise equipment ....
2 the best-value breakfast ....
3 a choice of welcome drinks ....
4 a free bottle of wine ....
5 a free room upgrade ....
6 overnight stays away from the hotel ....
7 the highest-value extras ....
8 return flights from two cities only ....
9 flight taxes only ....
10 additional free water sports ....

Skills

There are a number of skills that will help you when you do the IELTS Reading Test. These are:

▼ identifying question types

▼ dealing with vocabulary (including recognising paraphrases and summaries)

▼ recognising text types and text organisation (including identifying the writer's purpose).

You will find some of these skills useful for your general reading, as well as for specifically practising for the IELTS test. We explore each in more detail in the following pages.

Identifying question types

Identifying the eleven different question types and knowing what each requires is an important skill. It will help you to apply your strategic reading. If you have not already done so, review the different question types covered in 1.3.

Dealing with vocabulary

When you skim and scan texts, it is not necessary to understand every word. Usually, however, you must know more than half the words if you want to understand the main points. When considering vocabulary, you should think about two situations:

1 in the test: guessing the meaning of unknown words from the context.

2 outside the test: building up your vocabulary and understanding how words relate to each other in sentences.

Expanding your vocabulary is important not only for your reading, but also for your writing, speaking and listening.

Guessing the meaning of unknown words

When you encounter an unknown word in the Reading Test, ask yourself whether it is needed to answer a question. If it *is* needed, use the strategy described below to help you guess how the word fits into the passage. If it is *not* needed, you can simply ignore it.

Consider this sentence from a passage about the use of computers in crime:

Since 1958, when the first cases of computers used for criminal purposes were reported, computers have been used in most kinds of crime, including fraud, theft, larceny, embezzlement, burglary, sabotage, espionage, murder and forgery.

Many of the words after 'crime' will be unknown to you. In an exam, this can lead to panic. However, look what happens when they are removed from the sentence:

Since 1958, when the first cases of computers used for criminal purposes were reported, computers have been used in most kinds of crime, including _____, _____, _____, _____, _____, ____, _____, murder and _____.

You can still see that the sentence is listing different kinds of crime in which computers are used. Using your general knowledge, you can guess that the unknown words are types of crime; that is enough for you to be able to answer the question.

Guessing is an important strategy when reading at university or college, as well as in the Reading Test. Remember:

▼ Skim the passage quickly. If there are words you don't know, don't stop and don't panic. Keep moving forward.

▼ Look at each question and then scan for the location of the answer.

▼ If there are questions that relate to the words that you don't understand, read intensively – look at the nearby words and sentences and then guess the meaning of the unknown words.

Complete Exercise 19 to practise guessing the meaning of unknown words.

Exercise 19 — Guessing the meaning of unknown words

Read the following short paragraph containing many unknown words and answer the questions that follow.

> Diabetes is a disorder of the pituitary gland leading to a malfunction of the kidneys. It is characterised by abnormally high glucose levels in the blood. At least 171 million people are registered as diabetes sufferers and this number is increasing, possibly due to the modern lifestyle.

1 Diabetes sufferers tend to come from European countries. True, false or not given?

....

2 This paragraph presents

    A some examples of diabetes.

    B a definition of diabetes.

    C different types of diabetes.

    D the treatment of diabetes.

It is possible to answer the questions in Exercise 19 without understanding any of the difficult words. Of course, this is not always the case, which is why it is important to understand what the question requires. If you do not understand an important word needed to answer a question, guess the answer from the context.

Exercise 20 — Guessing the meaning of unknown words

Guess the meaning of the italic word in each sentence from the context given.

1 Their boss was very *amenable* to them making the decision on their own and had no problem with this happening.

....

2 She is very *contrite* about what she did and the trouble that she caused to us all by her actions. She says she won't do it again.

....

3 The growth in the city's population was *exponential* and was much faster than anyone had expected.

....

4 The prisoner was put into *manacles* by the police so that he couldn't move his arms around or run away.

....

5 People become very *resilient* in hard or dangerous conditions where they have to learn to cope with the difficulties.

....

6 The horse was very *skittish*. It was obviously very hard to control because of the noisy traffic.

....

Building up your vocabulary

There are many different ways of learning new words and some ways will be more effective for you than others. Keep experimenting to decide which approaches work best for you. Here are some suggestions:

▼ Write the word you want to learn in a sentence so that you understand the context in which it is used.

▼ Say new words aloud many times, making sure you can pronounce them correctly (check your dictionary for a pronunciation guide).

▼ Create your own dictionary for new words, bearing in mind that sometimes it is necessary to accept an approximate meaning of some words. For example, it would be better to know the approximate meaning of 2,000 words than the precise meaning of only 1,000 words.

▼ Don't look up every word you don't know immediately: try and guess its meaning from context, and check whether you are correct later on.

You cannot and should not try to learn every word you encounter. Instead, you need to learn the most useful (or versatile) words; that is, those words that can be used in a wide range of contexts and texts.

Distinguishing between versatile and specific words

Versatile words are words that can be used in many different contexts. Compared with versatile words, specific (or technical) words have very limited use, as they are usually used in one field or context only.

Look at the following example taken from a newspaper article. Versatile words (which you might find useful to learn) have been underlined. Specific words are in italics.

Australia were now <u>reeling</u> at 8-137 at *stumps* but <u>believe</u> they <u>will be able to defend</u> their <u>eventual lead</u>, which presently stands at *345 runs*. A <u>spellbinding</u> *bowling* <u>display</u> by the Windies <u>invoked memories</u> of <u>last year's loss</u> to South Africa at the same *ground* when a *second-innings* lead of 410 was <u>not enough</u>.

The underlined versatile words can be used when talking about other topics, not just cricket, but the words in italics are specific to cricket and so are less useful to you.

Read the following short passages and:

▼ underline the *versatile* words or phrases

▼ circle *specific* words or phrases.

A Weather holds the key to which of the maxis will win this race. Facing stiff competition and challenging weather conditions, including a brisk 35-knot southerly, skippers will need to be on their mettle to fend off other contenders for line honours. All yachts will be under spinnaker at times, and at others will have to tack back and forth into the wind to outmanoeuvre their rivals.

B We specialise in high-integrity stainless steel casting and are seeking someone with extensive experience in moulding and casting heat treatment of steel castings to oversee our production line, the general operation of the foundry and implementation of policy. We seek a motivated individual who will assist us with our organisational goals.

Write down any of the versatile words and phrases that you do not already know but would like to learn. Write them in a context (for example, a sentence) that will help you remember their meaning.

Identifying how words relate to each other

Understanding how words relate to each other, within the structure of a text, will help you identify meaning and decide which words are important. You may understand the overall meaning of a sentence or text, but not specific words or examples of what is being discussed – or vice versa.

Words can be divided into the following categories: **content words** and **grammar words**.

Content words are words that give information. They may be nouns (for example, *dog*, *concept*), verbs (*to act*, *to go*), adjectives (*awake*, *considerable*) or adverbs (*very*, *unusually*). Content words may form a group of words.

Grammar words are words that show grammatical structure and indicate how other words in a sentence relate to one other. They can be helpful for understanding meaning, but they do not directly give information themselves. They may include prepositions (for example, *up*, *under*), pronouns (*he*, *her*) determiners and articles (*some*, *many*, *few*, *the*, *a*, *an*) or auxiliary verbs (*is/are*, *have*).

In order to identify meaning and work out which words are important to learn or know, it is also helpful to understand the relationship between words. Words can relate to each other in several different ways, including:

1 class/sub-class

2 whole/part

3 collocations.

Class/sub-class

In the following examples, the words in bold name a *class* of things and those in italics name a *sub-class* of those things. You can see that sometimes the class can either be named *before* or *after* the sub-class(es).

Examples

A *ferry* is a type of **boat**.

There are many types of **boats**, for example, *ferries*.

Cybercrime and *identity theft* are **issues** that concern national authorities.

Issues such as *cybercrime* and *identity theft* concern national authorities.

This diagram shows the relationship between a class of things (boats) and some of its sub-classes.

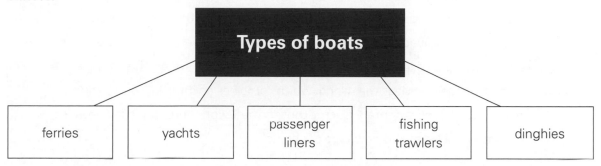

Types of boats

| ferries | yachts | passenger liners | fishing trawlers | dinghies |

Whole/part

Words can also be divided into words that describe the whole of something and words that describe a part of something. As with classes and sub-classes, note that the order of information can vary.

Examples

A **donkey's** *ears* are long.

The *ears* are the most distinctive part of a **donkey**.

A large **organisation** will have its own *accounting department* and may also have a separate *advertising department*.

An *accounting department* and possibly an *advertising department* are part of the structure of a large **organisation**.

In the IELTS exam you will be expected to see relationships between ideas and classify information according to different categories or in a summary. The ability to see relationships will also be a crucial skill for your university or college studies. Exercise 22 provides some practice at identifying relationships between ideas and classifying information.

1 Read the following passage and underline the content words.

Throughout their 130-year history, motor vehicles have been classified according to the type of fuel they use for locomotion. One type of alternative-fuel vehicle that originated in the earliest period of the automobile is the electric car. The original electric automobile, termed a Battery Electric Vehicle (BEV), was powered by an on-board battery pack consisting of cells storing chemical energy. In the early twentieth century, advances in another form of motor, the internal combustion engine (ICE), led to the rise of the gasoline or petrol vehicle, especially the Ford motor car. However, with concern about the environmental impact of petrol cars, a modified electric vehicle enjoyed a short revival in the 1990s, partially due to GM's EV1 electric car. Today, the principle alternative-fuel vehicle is the hybrid, which combines an internal combustion engine with a supplementary electric motor. The Toyota Prius and the Chevrolet Volt are examples of this new type of vehicle.

2 Fill out the following classification chart with information from this passage. Notice that you don't need to understand every word to be able to fill in this chart.

Types of motor vehicles according to fuel use

a .....motor vehicles.....

Internal combustion engine (ICE)

Electric car

Hybrid

b .....petrol vehicle.....

BEV

Modified electric car

Toyota Prius

c .....Ford.....

d .....GM EV1.....

e .....Chevrolet Prius.....

Collocations

Another type of relationship between words is collocation: the relationship between two words that are commonly used together. For example:

In the lecture tomorrow, I am going to *ask a question*.

In this sentence, the verb *ask* collocates with the noun *question*. Learning these words together is useful because they often collocate.

As another example, in Exercise 16 you read:

Weather *holds the key* to which of the maxis will *win this race*. *Facing stiff competition* ...

Each of the underlined expressions – *holds the key*, *win this race* and *facing stiff competition* – is an example of collocating nouns and verbs. Some collocations are used more frequently than others. You should keep a record of versatile collocations.

It is not just verbs and nouns that collocate. It is also common for nouns to collate with adjectives, adverbs and prepositions. For example, we say *Happy Birthday* and *Merry Christmas*, not *Merry Birthday*, and we say *interested in* and *concerned about*, not *interested about* or *concerned in*. Adverbs and adjectives can also collocate with each other, for example *absolutely fabulous*.

Improve your knowledge of collocations by reading widely, especially from media and online sources such as newspapers, magazines and journals, and noticing the way words clump together. Learning collocations as you come across them in different contexts will help you develop accuracy and improve your language level, especially in your reading but also in speaking, listening and writing.

Exercise 23 Collocations

Underline the collocations in the following passage.

A late surge in consumer demand has pushed up retail profits to new highs, especially in the electronics and white goods sectors. Heavily discounted bargains accounted for the highest sales of the holiday season, and the stampede to the checkout helped create a bonanza for retailers after one of the worst profit downturns in recent history. Never-to-be-repeated specials competed with discounted luxury items, which was ultimately to the consumer's advantage. Satisfied customers responded to the bargains with enormous enthusiasm.

Identifying key words

In Exercise 22 you identified all the content words. However, in any passage some content words are more important than others, and it is necessary to identify the words that are most important in each sentence: the **key words**. There are often two groups of key words – those before the main verb and those after. Key words may include word groups such as adjective + noun or noun + noun. For example:

In their 130-year history, <u>motor vehicles</u> *have been classified* according to the <u>type of fuel</u> they use for locomotion.

In this sentence *motor vehicles* is an example of an adjective and noun forming a word group. After the main verb (*have been classified*), *type of fuel* is the second group of key words.

Exercise 24   Identifying key words

Read this passage again, and this time decide which content words are key words. Underline the key words as you read. Circle the main verb in each sentence.

> Throughout their 130-year history, motor vehicles have been classified according to the type of fuel they use for locomotion. One type of alternative-fuel vehicle that originated in the earliest period of the automobile is the electric car. The original electric automobile, termed a Battery Electric Vehicle (BEV), was powered by an on-board battery pack consisting of cells storing chemical energy. In the early twentieth century, advances in another form of motor, the internal combustion engine (ICE) led to the rise of the gasoline or petrol vehicle, especially the Ford motor car. However, with concern about the environmental impact of petrol cars, a modified electric vehicle enjoyed a short revival in the 1990s, partially due to GM's EV1 electric car. Today, the principle alternative-fuel vehicle is the hybrid, which combines an internal combustion engine with a supplementary electric motor. The Toyota Prius and the Chevrolet Volt are examples of this new type of vehicle.

The ability to recognise key words is an important part of efficient reading and will be very helpful when you use the three reading strategies (skimming, scanning and reading intensively) to answer questions in the Reading Test. Remember that in the Reading Test you may be given a word limit. For example, you could be asked to use 'no more than three words', so you would be looking for groups of three words (or less) – key information.

Exercise 25 gives you practice at identifying key words in preparation for completing a summary question.

Exercise 25 | Identifying key words

1 Underline the key words in the following short passage. Circle the main verbs.

> Forgetting important things such as names, birthdays and appointments can really affect your efficiency and self-confidence. However, you can improve your memory by using a number of techniques. One of the oldest techniques is mnemonics: that is, remembering difficult information through a short rhyme. For example, music students will remember 'Every Good Boy Deserves Fruit', which is a way of remembering the notes written on the lines of the treble clef: EGBDF. Another method is to associate a person's name with a pleasant, colourful image.

2 Now complete the following summary using no more than three words from the passage for each answer.

Both how well you do things and your **a** .... can be

affected by problems associated with forgetting things. There are a number of

techniques to help you improve your memory. One of them that has been used for

a long time is **b** ...., where a short rhyme will help

you remember. Music students use short expressions to help them remember the

c .... Another way is to use the association of a pleasing

d .... with someone's name.

Identifying important grammar words

Although key words are very important, if you *only* notice key words you will miss important information. This is because important information is also carried in **grammar words.** They help you gain a clearer and more accurate understanding of a reading text.

Important grammar words can occur either before or after the key words, qualifying them. Grammar words include:

▼ determiners such as *all* and *most*

▼ prepositional phrases beginning with a preposition such as *of* or *in*

▼ negation words such as *not* and *never*

▼ conjunctions and linking words such as *however* and *such as*.

You should also watch out for **opinion words,** such as *believe* and *agree*, and expressions such as *it is usually agreed that.*

Exercise 26 — Identifying important grammar words

1 In the following passage the key words have been italicised. Underline the grammar words that you think qualify the meaning of these key words. Think about how they do this. Observe which ones come before the key words and which come after.

> All *people* need to *consume liquids* in order to survive. However, the *beverage of choice* varies in different countries according to *cultural preferences*. For example, it is often thought that all *British citizens*, and likewise all *Japanese citizens*, *drink tea*, either black or green respectively. However, in recent times in *both countries*, more *people*, especially young people, are also drinking *coffee*, *colas* and *sports drinks*. Even so, most *individuals* in these countries still tend to drink the national *favourite beverage* some of the time.

2 Complete the summary below.
Choose no more than three words from the above passage for each answer.

It is necessary for **a** .... to drink liquids to survive.

In the case of the UK and Japan, it is generally believed that every one of its

b .... enjoys the national beverage. Despite this

perception, today a greater number of **c** .... prefer

alternatives.

3 Choose **A**, **B**, **C** or **D**. The writer believes that most people in the two
countries mentioned   ....

    A   prefer the national drink at times.

    B   are changing to new drinks.

    C   drink only one type of beverage.

    D   choose equally between beverages.

Identifying synonyms and antonyms

A synonym is a word that has a similar meaning to another word. For example:

> One type of alternative-fuel vehicle that originated in the earliest period of the *automobile* is the electric *car*.

Automobile and *car* are synonyms.

Reread the passages on the electric car (Exercise 22) and identify any synonyms. Notice what word form they are: for example, noun, verb, adjective or adverb. Notice how they are used in each sentence. Did you find the following synonyms?

motor vehicle – vehicle – (electric) car – automobile
motor – engine
fuel – gasoline – petro

Being able to identify synonyms is an important skill for the Reading Test. For example, the question might use the words *rely on* and the passage contains the words *depend on*. If you do not know that these are synonyms, you will have difficulty scanning to the correct section of the passage and answering the question.

An antonym is a word that means the opposite of another: for example, *hot* and *cold*; *cheap* and *expensive*. Be careful with antonyms because a word may have many meanings and its opposite will relate to its context (e.g. *clear – cloudy/indistinct/imprecise/confusing* or *right – wrong/left*) but you can usually guess the approximate meaning from the context.

The negative or opposite form of a word can also be created using a prefix (see below for definition). For example: *well – unwell, register – deregister*.

Recognising such suffixes will help you in this area.

Identifying word families

Word families are groups of words that have the same **root** or base word. Different forms of this root word are created through the use of affixes. There are two main types of affixes: prefixes (added to the beginning of words) and suffixes (added to the end).

Prefixes usually show the opposite or a contrast. For example:

happy ⟶ unhappy

In this case, the word form remains the same (adjective).

Suffixes, on the other hand, change the word form. For example:

happy ⟶ happiness

The word form has changed from an adjective to a noun by adding the suffix *–ness*.

Building up a list of affixes and learning how they are used will help you when you are guessing the meanings of new words.

Look at the following word families:

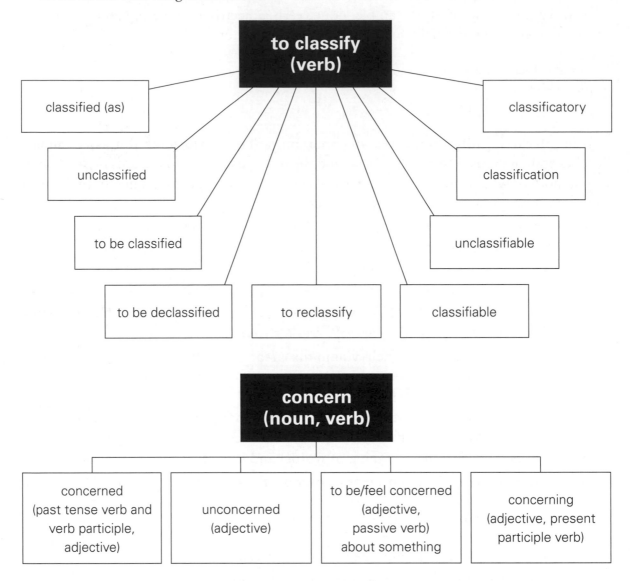

to classify (verb)

classified (as)

unclassified

to be classified

to be declassified

to reclassify

classifiable

unclassifiable

classification

classificatory

concern (noun, verb)

concerned
(past tense verb and
verb participle,
adjective)

unconcerned
(adjective)

to be/feel concerned
(adjective,
passive verb)
about something

concerning
(adjective, present
participle verb)

Note the use of the preposition *about* with *to be/feel concerned*. This is an example of a useful collocation (in this case a related preposition) to learn. Remember when you are learning new words and word families to include common collocations.

It can be difficult to identify meaning if you do not have a context. As practice, write a number of word families into your vocabulary book taken from the vocabulary of a current text you are reading, and then write sentences containing each word.

Example

The government's decision to *declassify* sensitive information about its security policy has resulted in some *concern* being expressed by both political and military leaders.

In the following passage, identify all the words in the same word family as *concern*. List them in the relevant row in the table below, indicating which row in the text they appear in.

Recently there has been increasing concern in many countries about the issue of food security, although, in fact, people have been concerned about this problem for many years. One issue is droughts, which create famine; this has especially concerned governments. However, the issue of having enough available food for all citizens concerns not only governments but also households and, as a result, some concerned individuals have suggested having more government control of resources. Additionally, there has been criticism of unconcerned citizens, those with the means to purchase food at any price who do not feel concerned about the problem. It is very concerning that these people do not seem to feel the same level of concern as the general population.

Noun	
Verb	
Adjective	

Recognising paraphrases and summaries

A **paraphrase** is a restatement of a short text or expression so that it has the same meaning but uses different words (synonyms) and grammar structure. Paraphrasing is used to avoid directly quoting the original text. A paraphrase is usually about the same length as the original piece of text and contains the same information.

A **summary** is a shorter version of the original information in the text. It contains the key information but omits details. Both of these devices are used in the Reading Test to test your reading comprehension.

The ability to recognise paraphrases and summaries is perhaps the *most important skill* that you can learn for both the IELTS test and your wider reading. This is because so many of the question types use these techniques to test you. For example:

▼ the options in matching sentence endings questions, the stems in identifying information questions, and the options in matching headings questions will be summaries of information

▼ the words around the gap in a summary completion question will be a paraphrase, which you will need to recognise when scanning.

Because both paraphrases and summaries use synonyms, reading widely and increasing your vocabulary range will help you recognise these devices. When practising for the test, use a highlighter to identify direct connections between the words and phrases in the reading passage or text and their paraphrases or summaries in the questions.

Exercise 28 Recognising paraphrases and summaries

Read the following short passage and answer the questions that follow.

Two views of mountains

Most people think they know what a mountain is; they probably do not know that there is, in fact, no universally accepted definition of a mountain. Criteria such as elevation, steepness (one factor distinguishing hills from mountains), relief and volume, among other measures, can help determine whether a particular landform is a mountain or not. In general, the idea that this elevated geographic feature stands in contrast to the surrounding landscape and has a certain elevation – usually defined as 1,000 feet or more above its base – helps determine the classification. Some definitions of mountains include such refinements as 'height over base combined with slope', for example, or 'height over base of 1,500–2,500 metres with a slope greater than 2 degrees' and 'local elevation greater than 300 m' (Wikipedia). By these, and similar definitions, 64% of Asia, 25% of Europe, 22% of South America, 17% of Australia and 3% of Africa is covered with mountains (Wikipedia). There is a further interesting and unexpected classification of mountains: the distinction between high mountains and tall mountains. The former reach into the coldest atmospheric layers and thus are subject to glaciation, whereas the latter have different climatic conditions at the base compared with the peak, which means they contain different forms of life at different altitudes.

Mountains can be discussed in terms of dry definitions and statistics, but these do not capture the lure and magic – the awesome grandeur – that spectacular mountains have always held for humankind. Their inherent mystery creates a sense of wonder and an awareness of our essential smallness in the universe, in a similar way to the way the night sky affects us as we view its infinite, distant galaxies. The majesty of the serried ranks of distant peaks, the fear engendered by encountering at close quarters the savage, unpredictable forces of nature in mountainous terrain, the glory of sunsets glowing over snow-covered ranges all contribute to a sense of our own mortality being felt against the timelessness of these giant geological landforms.

Identifying paraphrases

Read the following paraphrases and identify which sentences or clauses from the original text each is referring to. Remember that paraphrases are based on synonyms. Underline the synonyms in each paraphrase.

1 Factors such as height, gradient, outline and bulk help define a mountain's status.

....

....

....

2 Classification also relates to the mountain's height compared to the neighbouring topography.

....

....

....

3 (this type) ... has contrasting climatic features between its lowest and highest points that lead to varied biological forms at different levels of elevation.

....

....

....

4 The mysterious nature of mountains means that we feel tiny in relation to our place in the universe.

....

....

....

5 When coming too close to the hostile mountain environment, we can feel frightened.

....

....

....

Identifying summaries

6 Indicate which of the following sentences best summarises each paragraph and state why it is the best choice. What is wrong with the other summaries?

Paragraph 1

   1 There are a number of definitions of mountains but none is definitive.
   2 The different classifications of mountains and their features are surprising.
   3 Statistics are a useful way to categorise mountain types.
   4 More than half of Asia and a quarter of Europe are covered by mountains.

....

continued ▶

Paragraph 2

1 Mountains have a mystery that always makes us feel small.

2 The grandeur of mountains has been a powerful force on humanity over time.

3 Mountains can be compared favourably to distant galaxies.

4 The effect of mountains on humans is invariably negative.

....

....

7 Choose the best heading for each paragraph.

Paragraph 1

1	High and tall mountains	**3**	Height and slope
2	Where mountains are found	**4**	Definitions of mountains

....

Paragraph 2

1	Fear in the mountains	**3**	Awesome mystery
2	Mountains and weather	**4**	Close encounters

....

Questions 8–10

Do the following statements agree with the claims of the writer?

Write

YES   if the statement agrees with the claims of the writer

NO   if the statement contradicts the claims of the writer

NOT GIVEN   if it is impossible to say what the writer thinks about this

8   Scientists have recently defined what exactly a mountain is.   ....

9   The relationship between several different measures assists in deciding whether an elevated landform is a mountain.   ....

10 North America has a proportionately greater area of mountainous regions than South America.   ....

Recognising text organisation and features

In both the Academic and General Training reading tests you will be working with a number of different types of texts. Each of these uses different ways of organising and linking the information in the text. Being able to recognise text types and their features will assist you in your reading, both in your general studies and in the Reading Test.

Before looking at the different text types in more detail, let's consider the different ways in which information in a text can be organised or presented, and the different features of texts that you may encounter in the test.

Identifying theme and rheme

You will recall that when we discussed the strategy of skimming (page 30), the two parts of a topic sentence were identified as:

▼ the **topic** or theme (up to the main verb – usually called the subject). This is the overall topic.

▼ the **rheme**, or new idea (the main verb and what follows it). This limits the topic or adds new information that will be expanded on in the paragraph.

The key words will be within each of these parts.

The body sentences that follow the topic sentence in a paragraph will provide extra information related to the topic sentence. However, because they are adding to or clarifying information, the parts have different names:

▼ The **theme** is also called *known information* in non-topic sentences.

▼ The **rheme** is also called the *new information* in non-topic sentences.

These two parts of body sentences can also be referred to as *known–new*.

In a well-organised paragraph, the theme of each new sentence may relate back to either the theme or the rheme of the previous sentence or to the main theme of the topic sentence. However, it can also refer to information outside the text or new information. Identifying the theme and rheme of the body sentences will help you track information.

Forgetting important things such as names, birthdays and appointments can really affect your efficiency and self-confidence. However, you can improve your memory by using a number of techniques. One of the oldest techniques is mnemonics: that is, remembering difficult information through a short rhyme. For example, 'Every Good Boy Deserves Fruit' is a way for music students to remember the notes written on the lines of the treble clef: EGBDF. Another method is to associate a person's name with a pleasant, colourful image.

Theme (known information)	Rheme (new information)
Topic sentence	
Forgetting important things such as names, birthdays and appointments	can really affect your efficiency and self-confidence.
Body paragraph sentences	
However, you	can improve your memory by using a number of techniques.
One of the oldest techniques	is mnemonics: that is, remembering difficult information through a short rhyme.
For example, 'Every Good Boy Deserves Fruit'	is a way for music students to remember the notes written on the lines of the treble clef: EGBDF.
Another method	is to associate a person's name with a pleasant, colourful image.

Notice in this example how the themes allow you to track the information easily. Some themes relate back to previous new information (rhemes). For example, the theme of the third sentence ('One of the oldest techniques') refers back to the rheme of the second sentence ('a number of techniques'). Some themes relate back to previous themes, for example, 'Another method', where 'method' is a synonym for 'techniques' and refers back to the rheme of sentence 2.

Exercise 29 — Identifying theme and rheme

Read the following short passage and underline the theme (or new idea) of each sentence.

> The term *food security* refers to the availability and accessibility of food to a population, both households and individuals. Contained within this definition is the expectation that food is both physically available and priced to be accessible to local people. One definition, from the World Resources Institute, couches food security in negative terms: that is, a household is considered to be food secure if its occupants do not live in hunger or fear of starvation or need to acquire food in socially unacceptable ways such as scavenging, stealing or resorting to emergency supplies. Other definitions are more precise in that there is an expectation of more than minimum levels of food. According to the FAO, households should be able to have access to enough food for an active, healthy life. Individuals should have access to 'sufficient, safe and nutritious food to meet dietary needs and preferences'.

The value of being able to identify and understand theme and rheme in sentences is that it helps you both in skimming (by helping you identify the topic being written about) and scanning (by helping you locate and track specific information). This is important for all question types but especially for summarising, identifying information ('true, false, not given') questions, and also for matching sentence endings questions where you need to understand both parts of the sentence.

Recognising linking words

One way that information can be organised is through the use of linking words. These can be broadly divided into four main types:

1 addition and alternation
2 comparison and contrast
3 time
4 consequence.

Understanding how linking words are used will help you understand meaning, to see how one part of the information relates to other parts and to recognise how information is sequenced. Exercise 31 will give you practice at identifying these different kinds of linking words, which are explained in more detail on the following pages.

Addition and alternation

Linking words of addition introduce additional information of equal value to what has already been mentioned. They include: *and*, *besides*, *as well as* and *in addition*. They can join words, phrases, clauses or sentences. Linking words of alternation introduce an alternative option. For instance: *or*.

Examples

Criteria such as elevation, steepness, relief *and* volume determine whether a particular landform is a mountain *or* not.

Their inherent mystery creates a sense of wonder *as well as* an awareness of our essential smallness.

Mountains can be discussed in terms of dry definitions and statistics *or* they can be described poetically.

The scientific measurement of mountains needs to be accurate. *In addition*, any new statistical data needs to be updated.

Comparisons and contrasts

It is important to be able to recognise comparisons and understand them immediately when you see them in a reading passage. Examples of words often used to make comparisons include *like*, *as if* and *both*, as well as comparative and superlative adjectives.

Examples

Both your efficiency and your self-confidence can be affected by forgetting important things.

This building is easily the *biggest and most beautiful* building I have ever seen.

In the following sentences the writer is looking at the differences between two situations or events. This is sometimes called *contrasting*. Words and phrases used to contrast include *but*, *whereas*, *on the other hand*, *not only ... but also*.

Examples

Although the number of libraries multiplied, library users remained few in number until literacy levels increased during the eighteenth century.

The original alternative fuel vehicle used an on-board battery pack *whereas* today's model is a hybrid combining different power sources.

Not only your memory *but also* your confidence can improve if you practise using mnemonics.

Exercise 30 | Comparisons and contrasts

Complete the following sentences with the following linking words and phrases. You may use each one more than once.

not only ... but also	while	whereas	however
but although	even though		on the other hand

1 All people need to consume liquids in order to survive. ...., the beverage of choice varies in different countries according to cultural preferences.

2 High mountains reach into the coldest atmospheric layers .... tall mountains have different climatic conditions.

3 .... they were invented over 100 years ago, electric cars have only recently been commercially produced.

4 Daily exercise will .... improve your physical health

.... your mental well-being.

5 Warsaw has a long, cold winter .... Sydney has a short, coolish one.

6 Americans love gridiron football. ...., they are not very interested in cricket.

Time

Time linking words may be either successive (*then*, *after*, *before*) or simultaneous (*while*, *meanwhile*). Successive time words may be used to list events in chronological order (for example, in description), or they can be used to list steps in a process.

Examples

First, click on 'format', *then* 'autoformat', and *then* 'options'. *After that* you can get started.

Before logging in to get your mail, you need to check you have enough power.

While you're waiting for the program to load, you could make yourself a coffee.

Consequence

As you are reading, it is important to follow the reasons that writers give to explain events and situations.

Another term for reason is cause and another term for situations is **consequence**. Many consequence linking words and phrases describe **cause and effect**. Common examples are *so* and *because*, which link clauses, and *as a result* and *consequently*, which link sentences.

Cause–effect relationships, also called reason–result relationships, can be shown in a number of ways, including through the use of **coordinating conjunctions** such as *for* or *so*.

He bought a juice *for* he was thirsty.

He was thirsty *so* he bought a juice.

In the first example above, the effect is given before the cause. In the second example the cause precedes the effect.

Other cause and effect linking words may be **subordinating conjunctions** such as *because*, *since* or *due to*.

Because/Since he was thirsty, he bought a juice.

Due to his thirst, he bought a juice.

He bought a juice *because* he was thirsty.

Adverbs such as *therefore*, *as a result* or *consequently* are also examples of linking words of cause and effect. Notice in the examples below that they are found at the beginning of new sentences or clauses and are followed by a comma.

He was thirsty; *therefore/as a result/consequently*, he bought a juice.

He was thirsty. *Therefore/As a result/Consequently*, he bought a juice.

Linking phrases such as *so as to*, *so that*, *so ... that*, *in order to*, *in order that* (formal) are used to show **purpose**: why an action is being taken.

Their holiday was *so* enjoyable *that* they extended it by a week.

In order to save for a new car, Max took on a second job.

In order that she be seen to be trying hard, Jill did extra homework.

Linking phrases of **means** show the way in which something is done and include *by this/ these means* and *in this way*.

Work hard and, *by this means*, you'll succeed.

Read widely. *In this way*, your vocabulary will improve.

He travelled by train over several days and, *in this way*, reached home.

Linking words of **condition** are used to show what would happen if something is done or not done and include *if* and *unless*.

> ### Examples
>
> *Unless* you want to catch cold, dress warmly.
>
> *If* you want to make sure you have a good holiday, plan well in advance.

Recognising textual linkers

Textual linkers are another important group of linking devices. They are especially important for Academic Reading Passage 3, because they are used to organise information logically in a text. Understanding textual linkers will thus help you follow an argument.

Ordering words/phrases

Examples of ordering words or phrases include: *the first reason*, *the second reason*, *another reason*, *a further reason* or *first/second/third/finally*. These phrases may be used in topic sentences, or they may be used to organise information within paragraphs.

> ### Examples
>
> New tourist developments need to consider a number of factors. *First*, they need to be environmentally friendly. *Second*, they need to protect the community's integrity. *Third*, they need to remember that tourists want to have a different experience.

Referencing words

The words *this*, *these* and *their* are referencing words. They refer to something already mentioned. These devices help you track information in a text. The writer uses these to refer back to previous information (or forward to new information) and to avoid repeating information. They thus help with summarising and paraphrasing. It is important that you are clear about what is being referred to.

> ### Examples
>
> *These* devices (referring to reference words) help you track information in a text. The writer uses *these* (reference words) to refer back to previous information or forwards to new information and to avoid repeating information. *They* (reference words) thus help with summarising and paraphrasing.
>
> Throughout *their* (motor vehicles) 130-year history, motor vehicles have been classified according to the type of fuel *they* (motor vehicles) use for locomotion.

Substitution

Examples of substitution include *one such (reason)* and *to do so*. Substitution is used to replace previous information in order to avoid repetition. It is very important that you are clear about what is being referred to.

There are a number of reasons why there is increasing interest in growing Jatropha in semi-arid regions. *One such* (reason) relates to developing an industry to extract biofuels. However, *to do so* (develop an industry to extract biofuels) successfully, there is a need for greater education of farmers. It is only *in this way* (educating farmers) that efficiencies can be achieved.

Recognising evaluative language

Evaluative language is an important feature of some texts. Evaluative language means the writer has used opinion words to express his or her views on the subject being discussed. Using evaluative language helps the writer to build up a point of view over the course of the text, so that the reader is able to assess either the writer's opinion of the overall subject or his her opinion of individual topics. Here are some examples of opinion words, or evaluative language:

An *excellent* idea

An *unreliable* employee

For all their *apparent* modernity, however, the idea behind computers is *surprisingly* ancient.

The changes that have taken place in less than a century have been *astonishing*.

Recognising definitions and defining words

In many texts the writer will define the subject being discussed. Definitions often use the verb *to be*, and they may be introduced by:

▼ the linking words *that is*

▼ *who*, *which* or *that*

▼ a comma between the thing being defined and its definition (the definition forms a subordinate clause)

▼ a dash between the thing being defined and its definition.

Genetics *is* the science that studies all aspects of inherited characteristics.

Genetics – *that is*, the science that studies all aspects of inherited characteristics – has become increasingly important.

Genetics, *which* is the science that studies all aspects of inherited characteristics, has become increasingly important.

Genetics, *the science* that studies all aspects of inherited characteristics, has become increasingly important.

Genetics – the science that studies all aspects of inherited characteristics – has become increasingly important.

Another way of giving a definition is through naming or labelling something.

A type of spear <u>called</u> a *woomera* was used by Aborigines to throw further.

The Canadian city of *Vancouver was* <u>named</u> after an eighteenth century navigator.

Identifying examples

Examples are an important feature of many texts. Examples can be identified by the words *for example* or *such as*. This type of structure is also termed *general* $\longrightarrow$ *specific*. Look at the following examples.

<u>Many branches of science</u>, *such as genetics*, have become increasingly important.

<u>Many branches of science</u> – *for example, genetics* – have become increasingly important.

Identifying categories

Categories group information at a similar level together and give a name to this group. Some of the ways of showing categories include such expressions as: *types of*, *sorts of*, *can be divided into …* and *can be classified into …*

Spears, guns are knives are all *types of* weapons.

Sportspeople *can be divided into* those who earn money (professionals) and those who don't (amateurs).

Recognising text types

Different kinds of texts have different overall purposes that reflect the writer's aims. The purposes of the different text types used in the Reading Test are broadly as follows:

1 to inform
2 to describe
3 to instruct
4 to analyse
5 to persuade or argue.

Information texts

When the writer's main aim is *to inform*, *to educate* or *to pass on knowledge*, the text is an information text. Information texts cover general or semi-specialist topics and they are aimed at non-specialist readers. Their aims are:

▼ to present factual information clearly

▼ to identify key issues and define them

▼ to provide supporting information, including statistics

▼ to show a clear distinction between fact and opinion.

Information texts may contain some description but they do not usually include sustained analysis or argument. Information texts may be used in Academic Reading Passage 1 and for some of the shorter texts in Sections 1 and 2 or for Section 3 in General Training.

Information texts may be organised with sub-headings and bullet points. They generally use simple language and use linking words to indicate addition and alternation, comparison, time, cause/effect and condition.

Exercise 31 | Information texts

Read the following text and answer the questions that follow.

The London Underground

A The necessity to increase and expand London's Underground system, described as 'the nervous system of the economy' by London's Mayor, Boris Johnson, in 2010, has resulted in ambitious plans for an extensive upgrade costing billions of pounds. Already one of the most complex and efficient transportation systems in the world, currently servicing a billion passenger journeys a year, this network urgently needs investment if capacity is not to be exceeded over the next six decades due to increased population growth.

B The original purpose of this extensive system was to provide a conduit for the workers in the outer suburbs and counties to access their places of employment in Central London. Methods of constructing this underground feeder system changed because improved technology and different sources of finance became available, so that, in 1900, the 'deep level' tube system, with its tunnelling shields and segmented tunnel linings used on the Central, Waterloo and City lines, replaced the earlier 'cut and cover' methods of the 1851 Northern Line and the 1863 Metropolitan Line. This resulted in rail lines of different depths, necessitating the somewhat inconvenient long escalators and, earlier, lifts for efficient passenger access to different lines and the surface. It was during the change in construction methods that the term 'the Tube' was first used – initially only referring to the new deep-level system. Greater availability and integration of funding sources led to mergers in the system, benefitting commuters through a reduction in the competition that had previously led to inefficiencies. A consequence of this was integrated ticketing and less inconvenience for passengers.

C In recent years, with several changes in nomenclature of the controlling and funding entity and ever-present issues regarding the financing of upgrades and new lines, there has been a need for radical reinvestment in the system. London is the powerhouse of the United Kingdom, generating 25% of its income, and the Tube is its lifeblood. To prevent constriction of future growth, the Tube will need to grow by 30%. Currently, there are 3.5 million individual journeys made on the 11 lines and through 270 stations every day (compared with the 40,000 who travelled on the first day of the Metropolitan Line). In the period up to 2020, the 30% additional capacity will be realised through new lines, including the Crossrail for 2017, expansion of the Docklands Light Rail, new signalling and tracks and 191 new trains, and by rebuilding some of the hub stations such as Victoria and Tottenham Court Road, the busiest in the system, with the former alone hosting 78 million passengers a year. The busiest peak-hour station, incidentally, is Waterloo, with 51,000 passengers entering over three hours.

D Overall, Transport for London (TfL), the integrated body created in 2000 under the control of the Mayor of London, intends to expand and improve on the world-class Underground system and enhance the life and business of this vibrant and expanding city.

Questions 1–10

Paragraph A

1 What is the key issue identified in the first line?

....

2 What linking word indicates the timeframe of carrying capacity?

....

3 What linking words are used to explain why investment is needed?

....

Paragraph B

4 What was the initial reason for the underground system?

....

5 What linking word indicates reasons for alterations in initial methods of construction?

....

6 a Which came first: the 'deep level' tube system or 'cut and cover'?

....

  b What word tells you? ....

7 a Which came first: long escalators or lifts? ....

  b What word tells you? ....

continued ▶

8 What linking words show the cause and effect link between 'greater availability of funding sources' and 'integrated ticketing'?

....

Paragraph C

9 Identify linking expressions of time used and the verbs that match each of them. One has been given for you as an example.

In recent years, ... has been

....

....

....

Paragraph D

10 a What linking word indicates a summary of information?

....

b What verb gives the time frame of plans?

....

Questions 11–14

*The text has four paragraphs, **A–D**.*

Which paragraph contains the following information?

NB You may use any letter more than once.

11 The new railway line to be built   ....

12 The total number of trips taken in a year   ....

13 How early construction of the system took place ....

14 The highest number of passengers in a limited travel period ....

Questions 15–18

*Choose **ONE NUMBER ONLY** from the text for each answer.*

15 When was the second earliest Tube line completed?   ....

16 How many trips are made in a single day?   ....

17 When will the extra capacity for the system, including the Crossrail, become available?   ....

18 When was the current controlling authority incorporated? ....

19 Which FOUR of the following features are mentioned by the writer of the text?

....

A	Criticism by the Head of Operations
B	Initial justification for an Underground
C	Explanation of workers' roles in construction
D	Reasons for early passenger inconvenience
E	London's pre-eminent position in the British economy
F	Upgrading plans for the Waterloo Line
G	International sources of funding
H	A comparison of initial and current individual daily trips taken

Information texts often define and label things, as well as give examples of them or describe how information fits into categories. Definitions, examples and categories may also be used in other kinds of texts, but they are particularly common when the writer's aim is to provide information.

Exercise 32   Definitions, examples and categories in information texts

Skim the following text from a telecommunications company and complete the questions that follow.

Types of Mobile Telephone Technology

Changes in mobile phone technology have enabled us to provide a better service to you. There are basically two types of mobile phone technology: analog and digital.

Analog

In an analog system, voice messages are transmitted as sound waves; this means that when you speak into an analog mobile telephone, your voice wave is linked to a radio wave and transmitted. This is the system used in your landline telephone.

Digital

A digital system is what is known as a binary system – that is, voice messages are transmitted as streams of zeroes and ones.

However, there are also other telephone technologies (using one of the two systems above) that allow more than two people to speak to each other at the same time. Currently, these are: FDM, TDMA and CDMA.

continued ▶

Frequency Division Multiplexing (FDM)

In a FDM system, which uses analog technology, the frequency that is available is divided into different channels or routes for each user's conversation. When all channels are in use, then no more connections can be made.

Time Division Multiple Access (TDMA)

In this system, a radio-frequency channel is used to transmit your digitised voice in an assigned timeslot. There are a number of different systems that make use of TDMA including D-AMPS (which is a digital system) and iDEN systems.

Code Division Multiple Access (CDMA)

In this system your digitised voice is divided into packets, tagged with something called a *code*. The packets are then mixed with other packets of digitised voices. Only packets with attached codes will be accepted by the recipient system.

Questions 1–10

*Write **NO MORE THAN THREE WORDS** for each answer.*

1   What are analog and digital subgroups of? ....

2   What words tell you this? ....

3   What defining words are used to introduce a definition of analog? ....

4   What defining words are used to define what a digital system is? ....

5   What linking word introduces a contrasting idea? ....

6   What is being contrasted? ....

7   What linking expression of time (an adverb) indicates events occurring now? ....

8   In relation to FDM, which linking word indicates an alternative name for something? ....

9   What are the two possible names? ....

10   In relation to CDMA, what is named? ....

Questions 11–15

Look at the following statements (questions 11–15) and the list of types of technology below.

*Match each statement with the correct types of technology, **A–C**.*

*Write the correct letter, **A–C**.*

NB You may use any letter more than once.

11	Voices are parcelled together into packets.	....
12	There is a limit to the amount of information able to be transmitted.	....
13	A suitable time for a call is set up ahead.	....
14	This is the only non-digital system considered.	....
15	Several other operations use this technology.	....

Types of technology		
A FDM	**B** TDMA	**C** CDMA

Description texts

When the writer's main aim is *to describe*, the text is a description text. In this kind of text the writer does not usually include detailed evaluation of information. Both Reading Passage 1 of the Academic Test and Section 3 of the General Training Test may be description texts and may be in the style of a magazine or newspaper article of general interest or may include a description of an accompanying graph, process or other related visual.

Description texts may describe a situation (including people, animals and places), a problem, a process or the effects of an action. They may also identify the characteristics of something. Linking words used in this text may be ones of addition/alternation, exemplification, comparison/contrast, time or consequence. It is common for descriptions to:

▼ be sequenced in chronological time

▼ include causes of something

▼ have a problem–solution or solution–problem structure: that is, the problems may be listed first followed by solutions, or vice versa.

In terms of grammar and vocabulary, descriptions often include modal verbs (for example, *may*, *could*), adverbs (for example, *successfully*, *interestingly*) and adjectives, including compound or hyphenated adjectives (for example, *sure-footed*, *eye-catching*).

Complete Exercise 33 to practise identifying linking words in a description to help you understand its meaning.

Exercise 33 Description texts

Skim the following text and answer the questions that follow. The first one has been done for you as an example.

continued ▶

Bees

The most that many people know about bees is that they produce honey and they sting. This is quite true, but there is more to know about these small insects than these two facts.

Actually, very few of the 20,000 species of bees identified so far produce honey. Bee species are classified into seven to nine different types, not according to whether they make honey or not, but according to their social relations – that is, whether they are social (for example, honey bees) or solitary (for example, carpenter bees) – or according to their nesting habits (for example, ground bees, which build hives underground). Another interesting fact is that, in terms of their evolution, bees predate most other insects. Along with ants and wasps, they belong to the insect order Hymenoptera.

Besides providing us with honey, bees play an essential role in both modern agriculture and nature, as pollinators. Through their pollination of all sorts of monoculture crops, such as almonds in California, they play a vital role in fertilising the flowers that provide the fruit and seeds so necessary for large-scale agriculture to operate successfully in a populous world. They also assist nature by cross-fertilising wild plants.

There is an interesting history connected with the domestic honey bee. Native to both the Middle East and South-East Asia, including the Philippines, it was taken to the New World during the period of colonisation. After its introduction to North America in colonial times it became widespread by the mid-1800s. In fact, it became so common that 100 years ago almost half of all households kept two or three hives in their backyards, extracting honey when convenient.

In recent years, there has been widespread concern at the catastrophic decline of the European honey bee. A phenomenon known as Colony Collapse Disorder (CCD) has widely decimated hives, leading not only to concern about honey production and supply but also to concern about the reliable pollination of agricultural crops and wild flowers. The reason for CCD is not fully understood but it may be connected with bees having a monoculture diet, with unreliable weather or with a number of other factors. Arguably connected with the disorder is the presence of a small parasitic mite called *Varroa destructor*, shown to be present in a number of weakened or dying hives. Scientists are yet to provide a solution to what could be a truly devastating event. The tiny honey bee should never be taken for granted.

Questions 1–9

1 How are bee species classified? What linking words tell you?

   into seven to nine different types ... *according to* their social relations ... *or* nesting habits ...

2 What other insects are included in the same order? What linking words help you?
   Other insects: ....
   Linking words: ....

3 Fill out the following flow-chart with information from the text.

The contribution of bees

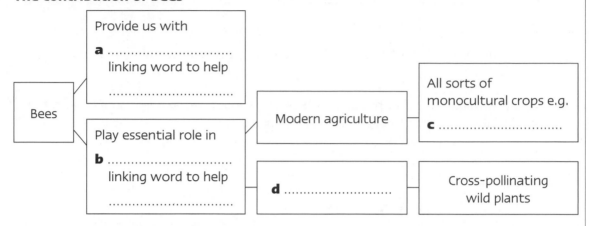

Bees

Provide us with
a ....
linking word to help
....

Play essential role in
b ....
linking word to help
....

Modern agriculture

All sorts of monocultural crops e.g.
c ....

d ....

Cross-pollinating wild plants

4 Look at the following list of events in the history of the honey bee. Put them in order. What linking words (if any) help you?

A Households kept hives
B Decline in European honey bee
C Native to Middle-East and South-East Asia
D Introduction to North America
E Taken to New World

Number	Event	Linking words
1		
2		
3		
4		
5		

5 What is the result of Colony Collapse Disorder?

....

6 What are the consequences of this?

a ....

Linking words: ....

b ....

Linking words: ....

7 What might cause this disorder?

a ....
continued ▶

b ....

c ....

d ....

8 What modal verb is used to show that scientists are not certain about causes?

....

9 What word tells you that not all scientists agree about *Varroa destructor*'s role in the syndrome? (Note: this is an adverb, not a linking word.)

....

Question 10

Choose the correct letter, A, B, C or D.

10 The types of bees are classified according to

    A several features.

    B two different characteristics.

    C their evolution.

    D their order.

Questions 11–13

Do the following statements agree with the information given in the text?

Write

TRUE   if the statement agrees with the information

FALSE   if the statement contradicts the information

NOT GIVEN   if there is no information on this

11 Bees are mainly valuable because of their contribution to agriculture.   ....

12 Honeybees are native to North America.   ....

13 Honey production and supply are causing Colony Collapse Disorder.   ....

Instruction texts

When the purpose of a text is *to teach someone how to do something or to provide knowledge in an organised way*, then it is an instruction text. Instruction texts may be used in Sections 1 and 2 of the General Training Test: for example, explaining how to use a piece of office equipment or a home appliance.

Instruction texts often:

▼ are organised with subheadings and/or numbering or bullet points

▼ present information chronologically: for example, using *first*, *then*, *after that*

- use imperative verbs: for example, *take steps to ...*, **make** *sure you ...*
- give advice: for example, *you should ..., it is important that you make sure ...*
- use linking words of addition and alternation, comparison and contrast, time, and consequence

When answering questions on instruction texts, pay attention to the sequence of information, and watch out for synonyms and rephrasing used in questions.

Exercise 34 Linking words in instruction texts

Skim the text and then answer the questions that follow.

This winter, heat your home – not the Earth

This new guide will help homes save energy, save money and also help save the environment with four simple steps. It includes a simple plan to keep your home warm while keeping costs down.

Save energy

1 Hold in the heat with insulation – for example, window treatments – and try to draught-proof your home.
2 Evaluate all your heating options so you can choose the right one for your home.
3 Take steps to be more energy-efficient while the heater is on by closing doors or wearing warmer clothes.
4 Check timers and temperature settings on your heater to make sure you're not overheating your home.

Save money

The first step in keeping your home warm takes place even before a heater is switched on. Not only will insulation help keep your home warm in winter and cool in summer but it can also help cut your energy bill by up to 40%.

Help the environment

Gas heaters produce less greenhouse emissions than electric heaters and are cheaper to run, which makes them good for larger spaces or if you're heating often. Also, in this way you can feel you are doing your part for the environment. It's important not to overheat your home. A one-degree increase in temperature can increase your heating costs by up to 10%, so you should set the temperature between 18 and 21 degrees Celsius.

continued ▶

1 Identify examples of different types of linking words. Which category and sub-category (for example, time: successive) does each fit into?

Addition and alternation		
Comparison and contrast		
Time	Successive	
	Simultaneous	
Consequence	Cause and effect	
	Purpose	
	Means	
	Condition	

Questions 2–4

Do the following statements agree with the information given in the reading passage?

Write

TRUE   if the statement agrees with the information

FALSE   if the statement contradicts the information

NOT GIVEN   if there is no information on this

2   Simple ways to save energy include dressing warmly.   ....

3   It is recommended that you purchase your heater before your house
        is insulated.   ....

4   Solar heaters are also useful to help the environment.   ....

Questions 5–7

Complete the sentences below.

*Choose **NO MORE THAN TWO WORDS** from the passage for each answer.*

5   Besides draught-proofing, you should take measures to retain heat in your home by
        using ....

6   Insulation helps you to retain .... warmth and summer coolness, and also
        save on bills.

7   One reason gas heaters are preferable to electric heaters is that the running costs are
        ....

Questions 8

*Choose the correct letter, **A**, **B**, **C** or **D**.*

8   To cut heating bills you should first   ....

    A   install insulation.

    B   buy a gas heater.

    C   evaluate options.

    D   wear warmer clothes.

Analysis texts

When the writer's main aim is *to analyse*, the text is an analysis text. Analysis texts are often used in Passage 2 of the Academic Test. They may be in the form of a semi-academic article or report, and they may include a graphic (visual) or support in the form of statistics.

Analysis texts often begin by outlining an issue, situation or problem. Then the effects, consequences or solutions are presented, followed by evaluation of these. Different points of view regarding these may be included. It is therefore necessary to identify and understand the writer's purpose and what is being analysed and to be able to separate the different viewpoints.

The text may be organised in one of these ways:

▼ problem–solution–evaluation: a problem or problems are presented, one or more solutions are provided and then these solutions are discussed and assessed

▼ cause–effect or effect–evaluation: the consequences or effects of a cause or causes are assessed or evaluated

▼ compare–contrast: different effects or solutions are discussed and assessed.

Grammatical features of analysis texts, used to convey the writer's viewpoint or the viewpoints of others, include:

▼ determiners: for example, *all*, *most*, *many*, *few*

▼ negatives: *no*, *not*

▼ opinion words such as adverbs (for example, *ideally*, *surprisingly*, *rarely*), adjectives (*ineffective*, *beneficial*, *important*) and nouns (*disadvantages*)

▼ modal verbs: *may*, *might*, *could*

▼ reporting verbs, such as *suggest* and *claim*, to report claims or arguments and possibly to indicate what the writer thinks of these.

It is important to understand the use of these features for the text to be read effectively. In matching features questions, matching headings questions and summary questions, a knowledge of how these language devices work is very helpful.

Read the following passage and answer the questions that follow.

The use of supplementary vitamins

A   There is no dispute about the necessity of vitamins for the bodily maintenance of humans and most other animals. Defined as 'organic substances essential in minute quantities to the nutrition of most animals … in the regulation of metabolic processes' (*Merriam-Webster Medical Dictionary*), these substances are essential for the correct functioning of the immune, nervous and hormonal systems. Found in natural foods and sometimes produced by the body itself, these 13 micro-substances, divided according to whether they are fat or water soluble, are needed for the avoidance of specific illnesses and subsequent mortality. Well-documented examples include scurvy and rickets, caused by insufficient amounts of Vitamin C and D respectively.

B   What there is dispute about is whether the taking of supplementary vitamins has adverse effects when an individual's basic diet is adequate. This practice has become commonplace for reasons related to perceived enhanced well-being, with *Men's Health Advisor* (2010), a reputable health magazine, reporting that 35% of American adults take an over-the-counter supplement, and the respected Canadian Public Health Association (2009) reporting that females with a higher socioeconomic status have a higher multivitamin intake and poor awareness of potential side effects.

The latter can result in possible toxic effects from overdosing on a particular vitamin, especially one of the fat soluble ones such as Vitamin A or, even more serious, interference with a prescription drug necessary for a particular medical condition. Medical authorities, therefore, suggest individuals confer with their doctor before undertaking a course of vitamins, which would appear to be sound advice.

C   Another issue relates to the use of specific vitamins in the amelioration of side effects of particular diseases or illnesses. One such example, undertaken by the Townsend Letter Group, is a study of the effects of Vitamin B supplements on migraine sufferers. Results show a fall in migraine rates from 61% to 30% over six months in the special group compared to the placebo group. However, while results are promising, further analysis appears to be needed. Another study with potentially positive results examined the use of Vitamin D in the treatment of diabetes, as reported in *Women's Health Advisor* in 2009. However, this study included only subjects suffering Vitamin D deficiency, and there is thus uncertainty regarding the effectiveness of this treatment when the micronutrient level is adequate. As in the migraine study, despite claims regarding positive results, further research is needed.

Questions 1–14

1 What issue is not disputed?

....

What words help you identify this?

....

2 How are vitamins classified?

....

What words help you identify the information?

....

3 What issue is disputed?

....

What words help you identify this?

....

4 Why do people take multivitamins when they don't need to?

....

5 What evidence does *Men's Health Advisor* provide?

....

6 What information does the Canadian Public Health Association report?

....

7 Does the writer of the text think the information from these two sources is able to be trusted? Yes or No? ....
What adjectives does the writer use to show his opinion of these sources?

....

8 **a** What are two potential side effects of taking higher doses of multivitamins?

....

b What words help you identify these?

....

9 What action do medical authorities suggest as a consequence?

....

continued ▶

10 Does the writer agree or disagree with this suggestion?

....

Which words show the writer's opinion?

....

11 What two examples are given of the benefits of using specific vitamins for specific conditions?

....

....

12 What suggestion is made by the writer regarding the potential of the first example?

....

13 What limitation is provided by the writer regarding the results of the second example?

....

14 What final recommendation is made by the writer at the end of the text?

....

Questions 15–20

Do the following statements agree with the claims of the writer?

Write

YES   if the statement agrees with the claims of the writer

NO   if the statement contradicts the claims of the writer

NOT GIVEN   if it is impossible to say what the writer thinks about this

15 The purpose of vitamins in human and animal health is yet to be proven.   ....

16 There is a direct relationship between inadequate vitamin intake and the possibility of death.   ....

17 Diseases such as scurvy are caused by inadequate quantities of specific vitamins.   ....

18 Excess amounts of water soluble vitamins appear to have a greater toxic effect than fat soluble ones.   ....

19 Studies using Vitamin E show a number of positive effects.   ....

20 Two studies of vitamin use for specific conditions, while indicating improvements in the health of sufferers, still need further assessment.   ....

Question 21

*Choose the correct letter, **A**, **B**, **C** or **D**.*

21 The writer's approach to the results of studies of vitamin use is ....
    A critical.
    B cautious.
    C optimistic.
    D confirming.

Exposition/argument texts

When the writer's main aim is *to argue* or to *present a point of view*, the text is an exposition or argument text. This text type is often used as Reading Passage 3 in the Academic Test. Exposition or argument texts may include semi-academic essays or reviews of books or theories.

In this text type, a thesis (claim) is presented at the beginning of the text and then evidence supporting this thesis is presented in the following paragraphs. This support may be other writers' claims, evidence from studies, or examples. It is necessary, therefore, to be able to identify the thesis and follow it as it develops and also to distinguish between the main ideas and the supporting ideas.

An exposition or argument text may be organised with the following features:

▼ a clear thesis, stated at the beginning

▼ clear topic sentences or main points

▼ supporting information, possibly, but not always introduced using linking words such as *first, second, finally*

▼ examples

▼ reference to previous or future points, for example, *for these reasons*

▼ repetition of main points and a summary of the writer's views to end the text.

Remember that the argument will be explained using key words, including synonyms.

Read the following passage and answer the questions that follow.

Can't save them? Move 'em

Picture an elephant in the wild, making its stately progress across the savannah, tall grass bending under its feet. Now transplant that image to the American prairie. In one of the most startling new ideas to emerge about climate change, a leading conservation biologist is calling for plants and wildlife facing extinction to be saved simply by picking them up and moving them.

Camille Parmesan, a butterfly biologist at the University of Texas, has been monitoring the effects of rapid climate change on species – particularly those threatened because they cannot adapt to, or escape from, rising temperatures – for more than a decade. But her idea for a modern take on Noah's Ark remains hugely controversial.

'The idea is that, for certain species at very high risk of extinction due to climate change, we should actively pick them up and move them to suitable locations that are outside their historic range,' she says. Her proposals, once confined to a handful of scientists, are now getting a broader airing as governments begin to grapple with the enormous problem of how to insulate animal and plant life from a warming climate.

Scientists have long believed that 20% to 30% of all known species of land animals, birds and fish could become extinct because of climate change. But recent studies, based on more elevated temperature projections, have suggested an even greater rate of 40% to 70% as heatwaves, drought and the increasing acidification of the oceans drive animals from their habitats and destroy their food supply.

The scale of threatened extinctions has forced conservationists to rethink what was once dismissed as an outlandish notion. And it's this that got Parmesan thinking about elephants. To date, there is little evidence about how climate change – rather than traditional threats such as poaching or growing urbanisation – is affecting the grasslands where elephants live in the wild.

She has been pushing to regenerate America's prairie in parts of Texas and the Midwest, by bringing in big grazing animals. There are fossils to suggest there were elephants in North America tens of thousands of years ago. So why not transplant African elephants to North America?

'With climate change, I am starting to think that, if we do get a massive reduction of Africa's grassland, then, as I am advocating restoration of the US prairie anyway, we can use the large herbivores from Africa to help that process because they are already co-adapted.'

Questions 1–18

1   What image is presented in the opening sentence?

....

2 In what new setting does the writer then ask the reader to imagine it?

....

3 What is one person's solution (the thesis) mentioned in this text? Note: there are two parts to the thesis.

....

4 What adjective tells you that the article's author thinks this idea is surprising?

....

5 Is Parmesan's idea widely accepted? Yes or no? ....

6 What adverb and adjective gives this information?

....

7 In Parmesan's quote in the third paragraph, what further detail does she provide regarding her thesis?

....

8 Choose A or B. Are Parmesan's proposals accepted   ....

    A more today?   **B** in the past?

9 What words provide the answer to question 8?

....

10 What evidence is given that discussion is extending beyond scientists?

....

11 What new scientific information given in paragraph 4 supports Parmesan's thesis?

....

12 In paragraph 5, what reason is given for conservationists adjusting their thinking?

....

13 What does *it's this* refer to (paragraph 5)?

....

14 In paragraph 6, what other idea is Parmesan promoting that relates to her thesis?

....

15 What evidence is provided to show Parmesan's idea is not new?

....

16 In paragraph 7, she expands on her thesis with more detail. What is this?

....

continued ▶

17 Parmesan uses synonyms for elephants in paragraphs 6 and 7. What are these?

....

18 Parmesan uses the reference *that process* in the last paragraph. What is being referred to?

....

Questions 19–20

*Complete each sentence with the correct ending, **A–D**, below.*

19 Camille Parmesan's ideas to relocate wildlife from Africa   ....

20 Scientists' theories about climate change   ....

> **A** have been widely accepted.
> **B** are closely connected to government concerns.
> **C** are a response to the consequences of climate change.
> **D** have changed with new evidence.

Questions 21–24

*Complete the summary below **USING NO MORE THAN TWO WORDS** from the passage for each answer.*

As a response to **21** ...., large herbivores being relocated to the American prairie is an extremely surprising suggestion according to the writer of the article. However, a prominent **22** .... has proposed just this, particularly where **23** .... prevent species adaptation or flight. Even so, this idea is still **24** ....

Questions 25–27

Do the following statements agree with the claims of the writer?

Write

YES   if the statement agrees with the claims of the writer

NO   if the statement contradicts the claims of the writer

NOT GIVEN   if it is impossible to say what the writer thinks about this

25 Scientists believe heatwaves and other factors have contributed to increased rates of climate and environmental change.   ....

26 Evidence shows that climate change has affected African grasslands more than urbanisation.   ....

27 There is evidence to suggest that elephants once roamed the American prairie.   ....

1.5 Developing an independent study program

To prepare for the IELTS Reading Test you need to devise a study program that will help you develop your listening strategies and skills independently. The first step is to identify your needs.

Identifying your needs

Think about what you need to work on in your study program and tick those items in the checklist below.

Reading checklist ✓

1 Do you need to improve your general reading? Which areas need particular attention?

Building up your vocabulary ☐

Guessing the meaning of unknown words ☐

Identifying synonyms and paraphrases ☐

Understanding the writer's purpose ☐

2 Which aspects of the Reading Test do you need to find out more about and practise?

The format of the test (length, number of sections, types of questions, etc) ☐

General Training

Section 1 (two or three short texts) ☐

Section 2 (two texts that deal with the workplace) ☐

Section 3 (general reading: a longer text that describes or instructs) ☐

Academic

Reading Passage 1 ☐

Reading Passage 2 ☐

Reading Passage 3 ☐

3 Which specific strategies and skills do you need to improve for the Reading Test?

Skimming ☐

Scanning ☐

Reading intensively ☐

Identifying question types ☐

Dealing with vocabulary ☐

Recognising text organisation and features ☐

Recognising text types ☐

When you have completed the checklist, note the section(s) where you have the most ticks, and read the relevant section below, to discover how you can develop an effective and relevant program of independent study. You can also check the Reading skills and strategies summary on page viii to make sure you have completed the relevant exercises.

Improving your general reading

The Reading Test is a test of your general reading ability as well as your ability to pass an exam. The more you read generally, the greater will be your success in the test. If you only do IELTS practice, you will not improve in leaps and bounds. Develop a consistent study program and also read widely.

Reading widely and for enjoyment will improve your speed and your knowledge of vocabulary and grammar. Choosing texts that you find interesting is important, because if your reading is enjoyable you will read more often.

Like any other skill, the ability to read a foreign language requires a lot of regular practice, especially if your goal is to be able to read accurately and quickly. As a general guideline, you should do at least 30 minutes of focused reading a day. As your study program progresses you should practise more specific exercises as suggested below. Remember that it takes a long time to become as efficient a reader in a foreign language as you are in your own.

Look for reading passages in the following:

▼ textbooks used in either high school or university, on any subject. Textbooks that contain some diagrams, tables and graphs are particularly useful

▼ textbooks that teach English, either at an intermediate or advanced level. Focus particularly on reading passages, but sections on grammar and vocabulary and writing skills can also be useful

▼ English-language newspapers, either foreign or local. There are many provided free online. Read articles that you find interesting, whether sport, politics, current events or even comic strips. Use a mix of skimming and reading intensively. Try to connect headlines to the content

▼ magazines such as *Time*, *Newsweek* and *The Economist*. Choose articles that you find interesting

▼ encyclopedias. Skim through the list of contents or index and select those entries that you find interesting

▼ novels or short stories that you think you will enjoy.

Websites

Search for relevant websites on the Internet. A useful starting point is the official IELTS site: <www.ielts.org>. Use a reliable search engine like Google, <www.google.com>, to find web-based IELTS practice resources. Search for 'IELTS reading practice online' or 'IELTS reading practice material' to bring up hundreds of sites. New websites are being created all the time (and existing websites change), so be prepared to search often and extensively.

Practising for specific sections of the test

Your first resource for finding out more about the Reading Test is sections 1.1 to 1.4 of this unit. If you haven't already done so, make sure you do all the exercises in the unit.

You can also find out more about the demands of the test by talking to people who have already successfully completed IELTS. Ask them what they did to prepare for the Reading Test and ask for their advice.

Above all, keep positive, and you'll do well if you continue to practise.

In Section 1 of the **General Training** Test, you are to read two or three short texts or several quite brief texts, such as advertisements or notices. The focus of the test is on extracting general factual information from the texts. For this section of the test you need to be able to understand information texts.

In Section 2, you are to identify and extract specific information on work-related topics.

Section 3 contains a longer reading text and tests your ability to find and follow how information is organised in a more developed text. Practise reading longer pieces, preferably about topical issues, to prepare for Part 3.

In the **Academic** Test, you are to read three longer passages, which may include description, analysis and evaluation. At least one of the passages will be an exposition/argument text.

Practice Reading Tests

If you are still not confident about the format of the Reading Test after studying Unit 1 of this book, it may be useful to complete a number of practice tests. By doing these, you can familiarise yourself with the layout and appearance of the IELTS test and practise transferring your answers to the answer sheet. You can also get used to the three different sections. There are practice tests (one for General Training, one for Academic) in 1.6, pages 89–112 of this book.

Practising specific strategies and skills

When you are practising reading for the IELTS exam, make sure you think about what strategies and skills you are using. If you need to practise the different strategies and skills required for the Reading Test, covered in 1.4, the suggestions below will help you.

▼ When practising for the Reading Test, think about what question type you are doing and what strategies and skills you are using.

▼ Keep a list of useful synonyms and word families.

▼ Highlight any expressions you see in newspapers that you think will be useful.

▼ Write example sentences for new vocabulary words so that you can learn them in context.

▼ Read actively – try to understand how information is being organised and what the writer's purpose is.

Exercises for study partners

Here are some exercises you can do with a partner.

Tell your partner what you have read

Read a short passage once only, writing a few notes as you read. Using these notes and without looking at the passage, tell your partner what you have read.

Working on vocabulary

Keep and swap vocabulary lists with definitions written in English. Quiz each other on these lists. Brainstorm topics and build up word families related to the topics. Choose texts and predict what words might be included in them before your read.

Working with texts

Separate headings and subheadings from a text and then match them to sections. Cut up a text into paragraphs and then reorganise these. Use highlighters to identify linking words and then explain the relationship between ideas to your partner. Discuss texts: what are the main ideas and what is supporting information? Meet regularly to work with reading texts.

1.6 Practice IELTS Reading Tests

Practice Academic IELTS Reading Test

ALL ANSWERS MUST BE WRITTEN ON THE ANSWER SHEET.

The test is divided as follows:

Reading Passage 1   Questions 1 to 13

Reading Passage 2   Questions 14 to 26

Reading Passage 3   Questions 27 to 40

Start at the beginning of the test and work through it. You should answer all the questions. If you cannot do a particular question leave it and go on to the next one. You can return to it later.

TIME ALLOWED: 60 MINUTES

NUMBER OF QUESTIONS: 40

READING PASSAGE 1

You should spend about 20 minutes on questions 1–13.

The Search for the Northwest Passage

For hundreds of years, the search for a convenient route by water across the North American continent, from the Atlantic Ocean in the east to the Pacific Ocean in the west, inspired explorers and sailors. This was the fabled Northwest Passage. The main reason to seek this route was that it would provide a short cut from Europe to the established markets of Asia, especially China and Indonesia. From the fifteenth century until the Suez and Panama Canals were built many centuries later, the only way for a ship to travel from, for example, Spain to the Philippines was via Cape Horn against ferocious winds and dangerous currents, or via the longer and still more dangerous Cape of Good Hope. Either way, it was a long and perilous journey.

Between the early fifteenth century and the early twentieth century, when the Northwest Passage was finally traversed entirely by sea, there were many theories regarding where such a route might be. Some believed there might be a continuous waterway across the American continent, between what is now California in the west and the Great Lakes and Saint Lawrence Seaway in the east. Others believed it would be in the far north, above Alaska and normally frozen Northern Canada. In order to locate this fabled route, expeditions set out from both the eastern Atlantic and the western Pacific coasts.

The earliest journeys from the eastern coast into the wilderness of Northeast Canada were undertaken by Greenland Vikings before the thirteenth century. Further journeys of discovery were not made in earnest until the fifteenth century, the first of which was led by Englishman John Cabot in 1497, followed by three voyages starting from 1576 led by Cabot's fellow countryman, Martin Frobisher, after whom Frobisher Bay is named. During the following three centuries, further expeditions set out, several of which suffered great hardship through their ships becoming frozen in the ice as winter set in. The most famous of these was another Englishman's expedition, that of Sir John Franklin's, whose ship disappeared without trace in 1846. This

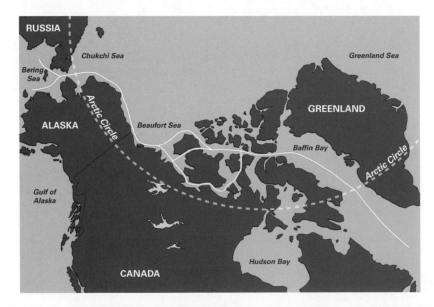

led to over 25 search parties, resulting in further exploration. However, they initially had no success in pushing beyond the bays and changing channels of Eastern Canada.

On the western coast, at the same time as English exploration was taking place in the east, Spanish seamen were attempting to find a route from west to east. In 1539, 60 years before Frobisher's epic journeys, a Spaniard, Francisco de Ulloa, explored California and his exploits created the myth of a passage across the continent from California. Further exploration by Spain continued for the next two centuries. During this time, Russia became involved in exploration further north, with Vitus Bering, a Dane working for Russia, locating and naming the Bering Strait, the waterway between Russia and Alaska.

The most famous of the western navigators was Englishman Captain James Cook, who in 1778 attempted to find the passage for a prize of £20,000 offered by the British Admiralty. Neither he nor other navigators who followed him, including compatriot George Vancouver, found any sign of a river that would lead eastwards, and in fact they were blocked by glaciers close to the coast. They concluded that there was no passage south of the Bering Strait.

Perhaps the most impressive journey was the one that finally achieved success. In the search for Franklin, the expedition of Commander Robert McClure engaged in a remarkable journey between 1850 and 1854. His ship *HMS Investigator* sailed first around Cape Horn and then, after heading north, found a route from west to east through the Bering Strait and across Northern Canada. During this time his ship was trapped in ice for three winters and his crew, despite nearly dying of starvation, completed the journey across the ice in sleds, before being picked up by another ship. However, the Northwest Passage was not finally traversed entirely by sea until 1906 when Roald Amundsen, the great polar explorer (who was also the first to reach the South Pole), achieved this feat taking the east–west route. The first successful fully marine west–east crossing was completed in 1942 by a Royal Canadian Mounted Police crew in their plucky Arctic workhorse, the converted schooner *St Roch*, which later made the return trip. Many other vessels have since made the voyage, including as late as 2008, the first commercial crossing.

Questions 1–5

Do the following statements agree with the information given in Reading Passage 1?

In boxes 1–5 on your answer sheet write

TRUE   if the statement agrees with the information

FALSE   if the statement contradicts the information

NOT GIVEN   if there is no information on this

1   European countries looked for a convenient sea route to Asia so that trade could begin.

2   Theories about a navigable passage, over many centuries, tended to concentrate on the eastern coast.

3   Norwegian seamen were exploring at the same time as the British in the sixteenth century.

4   At first, those searching for Sir John Franklin's expedition were restricted to eastern Canada.

5   The mistaken belief in a sea passage from California eastwards resulted in extensive exploration by one European country over two centuries.

Questions 6–10

Look at the following statements (questions 6–10) and the list of attempts and successes below.

*Match each statement with the correct attempt or success, **A–D**.*

*Write the correct letter, **A–D**, in boxes 6–10 on your answer sheet.*

NB You may use any letter more than once.

6 An Englishman whose name was given to a geographic feature

7 A modified local working vessel

8 A renowned navigator chasing a reward

9 An adventurer successful in other locations

10 A mysterious disappearance

> **List of attempts and successes**
>
> **A** East–west attempts
> **B** West–east attempts
> **C** Successful one-way traverses
> **D** Successful two-way traverses

Questions 11–13

*Complete the summary using the list of words and phrases, **A–G**, below.*

*Write the correct letter, **A–G**, in boxes 11–13 on your answer sheet.*

In contrast to earlier voyages, Commander Robert McClure's expedition succeeded in discovering **11** .... It was a long and difficult journey for the *HMS Investigator*. The ship was stuck for a long time and the crew were suffering from **12** .... McClure and his crew finally finished the expedition in **13** .... The passage was crossed entirely by sea in subsequent years, including a relatively recent commercial expedition.

> **A** sleds
> **B** hunger
> **C** Franklin's ship
> **D** a route from west to east
>
> **E** Amundsen's ship
> **F** disease
> **G** a timely solution

READING PASSAGE 2

You should spend about 20 minutes on questions 14–26.

Questions 14–20

Reading Passage 2 has seven paragraphs, **A–H**.

Choose the correct heading for each paragraph from the list of headings below.

*Write the correct number, **i–xi**, in boxes 14–20 on your answer sheet.*

List of headings

i	Another detection method with some warnings
ii	Parents warn schools about findings
iii	Causes, symptoms and reportings
iv	Disputes about data
v	Classification of allergies and what causes them
vi	Comparisons over a century
vii	International cooperation could yield useful information
viii	Differentiation methods and associated concerns
ix	Economic factors limit research opportunities
x	Uncertain reasons mean more research needed
xi	A common substance with deadly consequences for some

Example

Paragraph A   *x*

14 Paragraph B

15 Paragraph C

16 Paragraph D

17 Paragraph E

18 Paragraph F

19 Paragraph G

20 Paragraph H

Food allergies

A   In recent decades there has been a very real increase throughout the world in different types of allergies – that is, the over-reaction by the body's immune system to a normally harmless substance – particularly in babies and young children. The reasons for this increase are still unclear, which points to the need for more research to establish how and why this is happening and what solutions there might be to prevent and treat potentially life-threatening events arising from this medical condition.

B   There are three main types of allergies: food (the main triggers being eggs, nuts and seeds, legumes, especially peanuts, fish and dairy products – the latter because of the lactose in milk and cheese), environmental factors (grasses, grass seeds and pollens) and bites from insects (bees and wasps, among others). However, because of the increasing incidence of food allergies, and the need for health and lifestyle modification by sufferers after diagnosis, this paper will concentrate on this area.

C   Food allergies, which may result from a genetic predisposition in parents of allergic children to have eczema and other skin allergies, can be life-threatening due to the threat of anaphylactic shock: that is, severe breathing difficulties leading to death without medical intervention. In recent years there has been an increase of either 18% or 33%, depending on the source of information, in food allergies in young children. It is estimated that between 3–4% and 4–6% of adults in developed countries (for example, Canada, France, Germany, the United Kingdom and Australia) suffer from this condition. However, it does need to be emphasised that these statistics are unverified.

D   The most publicised food allergy is peanut allergy, perhaps because of the widespread prevalence of peanuts in many foods, as well as the use of peanut oil in so many products, so that a visit to a restaurant or children's party can be lethal for a sufferer. The possibility of an unexpected encounter with peanuts has resulted in extreme vigilance by parents and in many schools banning peanuts as a precaution. It is in this area, particularly, that there is a need for clearer identification of sufferers. However, a 2010 study found that many children were wrongly diagnosed as being allergic to peanuts, based on a standard test, suggesting the need for a reassessment of testing procedures or the need for a more sensitive test.

E   Some specialists believe the increase in all food allergies may be due mainly to greater awareness and therefore greater reporting, rather than to an increase in actual incidents. However, Amy Branum, a health statistician with the US Centre for Disease Control and Prevention, disputes the greater reporting theory, citing evidence that increases in the condition extend across all surveys, and thus must be the result of more than just increased awareness.

F   A number of testing tools have been developed to diagnose and distinguish between food allergies and food intolerance, a less serious condition. First, it is important for a full family history and physical examination to be undertaken. After this, a simple skin test, administered by pricking the skin, is able to detect whether an apparent allergy is related to external factors or, more seriously, to the immune system. However, even a simple skin test can be problematic. According to the *Journal of Allergy and Clinical Immunology* (2009), there is variability in the way the test is administered by physicians and this can affect results. As well, there has been no standardisation of the extracts of food products used in skin testing, and this can lead to unacceptable variations in results.

G A further diagnostic tool for asthma involves a blood test to detect the presence of antibodies in the blood for various foodstuffs. This test, known as the IgE test, is generally considered to be effective, but with reservations. In 2008, the Clinical Laboratory Standards Committee warned that the presence of antibodies did not necessarily denote the presence of an allergy; that is, there could be a false positive result. Additionally, antibody results for one food could not be used predictively for another food. An important issue, reported by Ewen and Clark (2005) is that there are a number of tests available but no 'gold standard' accurate test for all allergens. It would thus appear that more research is needed to clarify how best to identify the growing number of babies and young children with allergies.

H Because of the lack of clarity in this important area, there have been a number of initiatives and cross-country collaborations instigated. One such, EuroPrevall, launched in 2005, is a multidisciplinary project with 54 partners, which aims to use diagnostic tools and conduct long-term studies, and also look at social and cultural factors related to food allergies. Another study, based in the United Kingdom, is funding 45 projects, many ongoing, examining a wide range of factors. A recent report indicates that food allergies decrease with age. It is anticipated that further such useful results will become available in the coming years.

Questions 21–25

Complete the summary below.

*Choose **NO MORE THAN THREE WORDS** from the passage for each answer.*

Testing for allergies

There is uncertainty about the reasons for increases in food allergies. All surveys now indicate overall increases, which causes Amy Branum to question the **21** .... However, more testing tools have been developed, including a **22** .... to ascertain what an allergy is related to. Even this can have questionable validity due to several factors including a lack of **23** .... of components. Another test, the IgE test, has resulted in concerns that the presence of antibodies could lead to a **24** .... In fact, Ewen and Clark (2005) are quoted as saying that a **25** .... test that is appropriate for all triggers does not exist. Initiatives to provide greater clarity in this area include, through cross-cultural collaboration, the use of diagnostic tools and long-term studies.

Question 26

*Choose the correct letter, **A**, **B**, **C** or **D**.*

Write the correct letter in box 26 of your answer sheet.

26   The writer believes that food allergies are

    A   an over-rated issue in society today.

    B   now being studied more productively.

    C   virtually impossible to diagnose.

    D   more prevalent in adults than children.

READING PASSAGE 3

You should spend about 20 minutes on questions 27–40.

Learning the dominant language

In more and more cultures throughout the world, local languages are being displaced by the economic and educational necessity for citizens to learn one of the world's dominant languages. This impetus towards bilingualism has raised questions about when and how children from groups that speak minority languages (termed heritage languages) should best learn the second or dominant language of their country, which is essential if they are to fully be part of the dominant culture. An interesting longitudinal study, carried out over a decade, has been undertaken by Dr Stephen Wright of Simon Fraser University in Vancouver, Canada, who looked at exactly these issues. His hypothesis was that introducing the dominant language at school to children before they had consolidated their own language could permanently disadvantage them in a number of ways.

The group selected by Dr Wright for study was a community of Inuit people from Nunavut in the Canadian Eastern Arctic region. These people have strong social networks, consisting of small communities of usually 500 to 700 members, although the group studied by Dr Wright was about 1,200-strong. Despite the increasing introduction of English and French, the official languages of Canada, these communities speak a language called Inuktitut both proficiently and almost exclusively. When children begin kindergarten at the age of five, they have traditionally spoken only the heritage language. Fortuitously for Dr Wright, there had been pressure in 2000, when he commenced his study, for increased attention to be paid to the local culture and language so that these did not continue to be swamped by the teaching of the official languages in schools, despite awareness that learning these was essential for future interaction with the main culture.

In the study, children were divided into two groups randomly when entering school. For the first three years until third grade (that is, in kindergarten, first and second grade) each group studied exclusively in one of the two languages: either Inuktitut only, with native-speaker teachers, or English or French only, with teachers of those languages, as was the normal educational practice. Learning via the former method reinforced the language skills that children used at home, whereas via the latter children were exposed to a new language, including learning to speak and read English or French without family support. At the end of three intensive years, the children were combined randomly, and, from then until they finished high school, were taught only in English or French, with no further formal studies in their first language, which continued to be spoken at home.

When tested at the end of third grade, when one group had had only one

continued ▶

year of English or French and the other group four, and then again at the end of seventh grade (entry to high school), each group revealed remarkable differences that reinforced Dr Wright's belief that introduction of the dominant language too early can have negative effects. At the end of third grade, those who had only studied in Inuktitut were still conspicuously weaker in English or French than those who had been learning in the dominant language, which was hardly surprising. However, by seventh grade, according to Dr Wright, the differences between the two groups had completely disappeared, to the extent that it was not possible to identify which student had come from which stream. In other words, the Inuktitut group had caught up with no apparent ill effects.

Based on this and other evidence, Dr Wright argues that learning through the first language actually benefits young students, and introducing the dominant language too early disadvantages them in both their first and second language. Furthermore, these disadvantages extend over time. The first reason for this relates to what he terms academic thinking, which he tested in a number of ways. At the end of third grade students were each read a story and asked to summarise the moral of the story. They were also read a story and asked to extrapolate, to predict what would happen in the future, based on events in the reading. Those from the Inuktitut stream were able to perform both these tasks effectively – but in their native language. Those from the English or French stream were not able to do so – in either language. This inability to develop academic thinking

skills, which also extends to wider reading and development of vocabulary skills, extended over time to the end of seventh grade, when this group was seriously disadvantaged. The other group, however, demonstrated that they had benefitted from developing academic reasoning skills in two languages. The second reason was that the dominant language learning group had had insufficient grounding in their own language at a crucial point – they had not learnt basic reading and reasoning skills in their own language at a time when their families and school could have cooperated to provide assistance in developing these. They had remained weaker in essential academic skills, despite equivalent education after second grade.

Dr Wright believes very strongly that, when considered in relation to second language proficiency and self-esteem, two of the criteria he studied, there is no clear advantage to children learning a second language early. Taking it further, he believes that there is, in fact, an actual cost from these programs in relation to first language acquisition, based on very clear data. By not providing early formal study of the heritage language, children are disadvantaged both socially – for example, through decreased ability to interact with the elders of the community at a more proficient language level – and educationally, through restricted academic ability at later levels of high school, and thus into the future for tertiary studies and employment opportunities. His conclusion, therefore, is that the learning of the official language should be delayed in the crucial early years of education.

Questions 27–31

*Choose the correct letter, **A**, **B**, **C** or **D**.*

Write the correct letter in boxes 27–31 on your answer sheet.

27 The introduction of bilingualism is a trend

    A   benefitting all children equally over time.

    B   causing disagreements about implementation.

    C   encouraged by the government and local citizens.

    D   considered not to be essential for minority groups.

28 The study by Dr Wright looked at

    A   the problems of children studying their own language.

    B   how children who speak minority languages can integrate better.

    C   the relationship between culture and language.

    D   issues related to learning the dominant language.

29 Dr Wright was trying to prove that early introduction of another language was

    A   problematic.

    B   necessary.

    C   permanent.

    D   irrelevant.

30 The people in the community of the study generally spoke

    A   a single language well.

    B   French, English and Inuktitut equally.

    C   several heritage languages.

    D   several languages poorly.

31 Dr Wright's study began

    A   before pressure to study the local language occurred.

    B   despite the need for an official language in the future.

    C   in response to community concerns about cultural pressures.

    D   at a time when there was a focus on maintaining local languages.

Questions 32–35

Do the following statements agree with the claims of the writer?

In boxes 32–35 on your answer sheet write

YES	if the statement agrees with the claims of the writer
NO	if the statement contradicts the claims of the writer
NOT GIVEN	if it is impossible to say what the writer thinks about this

32 Some children in the study were taught by teachers who used two languages in class.

33 The disparity between the two groups after four years of school supported Dr Wright's hypothesis.

34 The experiment had a profoundly negative effect on the heritage language learners by the end of high school.

35 The government expressed interest in the results of the study.

Questions 36–40

*Complete each sentence with the correct ending, **A–J**, below.*

36 According to Dr Wright, learning the heritage language when commencing school

37 Being able to understand the moral of a story or predict the future

38 One group was disadvantaged at the end of high school because they

39 As a result of his study, Dr Wright believes that learning the official language

40 Inability to communicate with older members of the community

A	showed that students could read well.
B	benefits both groups proportionately.
C	should be delayed for a couple of years.
D	is given as an example of social disadvantage.
E	has neutral effects on both groups.
F	had missed out on crucial early learning skills.
G	has not seemed to be a problem educationally.
H	helped in distinguishing critical thinking ability between the groups.
I	had spoken their mother language at primary school.
J	has long-term benefits.

Practice General Training IELTS Reading Test

ALL ANSWERS MUST BE WRITTEN ON THE ANSWER SHEET.

The test is divided as follows:

Section 1   Questions 1 to 14

Section 2   Questions 15 to 27

Section 3   Questions 28 to 40

Start at the beginning of the test and work through it. You should answer all the questions. If you cannot do a particular question leave it and go on to the next one. You can return to it later.

TIME ALLOWED: 60 MINUTES

NUMBER OF QUESTIONS: 40

Read the text below and answer questions 1–7.

What is the best insurance?

It is important that you make sure that your home and contents insurance not only is up to date and covers important areas of concern but also is the best value for money. We looked at the premium – that is, the cost of the cover – offered by three different insurance companies for each of these areas. We also looked at their disclaimers, those areas that were excluded from cover.

Home insurance

This covers the value of your house and also fixtures: that is, fixed structures such as garages and in-ground swimming pools, and fixed domestic items such as fixed dishwashers and air-conditioners. Note that some companies (for example, Star) also provide builders' insurance – that is, cover for faulty workmanship or damage while building work is being undertaken – as well as home builders' insurance.

Contents

This covers unfixed household goods (that is, those not built-in or part of the building structure) and includes items such as electrical goods and furniture, as well as fitted carpets, clothing and personal belongings such as jewellery. Some companies – Star, again, for example – offer replacement as new. This means that no matter how old the item is it will be replaced at the new price, not at the original purchase price. Some companies (AA Budget is one example) also offer protection of items outside the home.

Home and contents insurance

We looked at packages that covered both types of insurance. Generally, bundling or choosing a package is better value, and AA Budget again is best value here.

What is covered

We looked at cover against natural calamities such as fires, explosions, rain, storms, earthquakes and falling tree branches, as well as criminal acts such as theft and malicious damage. Please note that most insurance companies do not cover flash flooding, which is flooding caused by an upswell of water rather than by direct rainfall. They also do not cover landslides occurring without accompanying rain – that is, movement of earth caused by underground water. They will also not cover tidal damage caused by ocean or river tides.

We divided our survey into high cover and low cover, and show here the annual premiums.

Company	Home and Contents		Home only		Contents only	
	High	**Low**	**High**	**Low**	**High**	**Low**
	£350,000	£140,000	£300,000	£110,000	£50,000	£30,000
Lennons	£340*	£160	£245	£160	£100	£80
Star	£300	£135	£240**	£135	£110	£92***
AA Budget	£230	£90	£190	£90	£85	£75****

* discount provided if premiums paid monthly   *** includes replacement as new

** provides home builders' insurance   **** extra cover for jewellery outside the home

Questions 1–7

Match each statement with the correct company, A–D.

Write the correct letter, A–D, in boxes 1–7 on your answer sheet.

NB You may use any letter more than once.

1   Will replace items as new

2   Has the cheapest home only insurance

3   Offers a special deal regarding payment

4   Has the highest premiums in two of the packages

5   Covers against flash flooding and landslides

6   Has an offer for valuables taken outside the home

7   Has an offer for those building their own homes

List of companies

A Lennons   **C** AA Budget

B Star   **D** None

Questions 8–14

The text on page 104 has seven sections, **A–G**.

Choose the correct heading from the list of headings below.

Write the correct number, i–x, on your answer sheet.

List of headings

i   The services of a professional

ii Specialist coffee companies

iii Height is best for quality

iv Storage of your own beans

v   Price makes a difference

vi Parts of the world where coffee grows best

vii Microwave techniques

viii Buying beans that have already been prepared

ix Preparing your own beans

x   The two categories of coffee

8   Section A

9   Section B

10   Section C

11   Section D

12   Section E

13   Section F

14   Section G

Knowing more about the coffee you drink

A Did you know there are different types of coffee beans and that where they come from determines how good your cup of coffee will be? Even though coffee grows in about 70 countries, it flourishes the most within a narrow band between 25 degrees north and 25 degrees south of the Equator.

B There are only two main types, arabica and robusta, with the main difference between them lying in the amount of caffeine each contains, with the former having half that of the latter. This means that arabica is the preferred choice of connoisseurs, being full of flavour and aroma.

C A further choice affecting quality is the altitude at which the coffee is grown. Higher altitudes are preferred for all beans, and thus arabica beans grown above 900 metres are the most desired beans.

D Beyond this, your choice of coffee bean depends on how you intend to prepare the coffee beans. If you are intending to roast your own, then you will need to choose soft, green, unroasted beans and follow techniques to bring out the best in them.

E If you're buying ready-roasted beans, then you have a wider choice, each with a different purpose. For example, there's the medium or 'American' type, which is probably the most popular; the dark or 'city' roast, favoured by those who prefer a sweeter, less bitter brew; and the darkest 'Italian' roast, used mainly in espressos and noted for its pungent aroma.

F Of course, if you're out and about, you'll be like so many others – relying on the skills of a great barista, someone who really knows his or her stuff. He'll know the right beans to choose and how to prepare them for the soothing cup that you're requiring.

G However, if you're keen to learn how to use a coffee-making machine, you'll need to look around and choose a suitable one and also learn how to keep your coffee beans for optimum freshness. You should keep them somewhere cool and dry but, counter to general perceptions, don't put them in the fridge because it's too moist there. If you're going to keep them for long periods, be aware that 12 months maximum is the use-by period of coffee beans.

Read the text below and answer questions 15–20.

Finding that ideal job

With the plethora of job opportunities available today, including a whole range that didn't exist even ten years ago, it can be very confusing for job seekers to decide on a career path, let alone get the ideal job. There are a number of factors you should think about as your plan to land that job you think you'd be great for.

Deciding what you're good at

The first consideration you need to think about is: what is your ideal job? You may have a wide range of experience and skills, which will really help you focus on a specific career, or you may be quite inexperienced compared with others. There are a number of points to consider: what are you interested in? what do you really enjoy doing that helps you lose yourself in time? Recent research shows that those who work doing what they enjoy are happier, healthier and wealthier than those who do a job solely for the money. Put aside time for introspection, thinking about what you'd really like to do – and don't forget to get advice from others.

Keeping an eye for opportunities

Check out the Internet, newspapers (including local papers), word of mouth and community noticeboards for jobs that might come up that you feel you'd like to do. Don't forget that early on in your career you could get experience through volunteer work (think about community radio, for example) and in casual jobs. If you're clear about your goals, then it's easier to see where everything fits, but this doesn't always happen, especially when you're young.

Your CV and cover letter

You see the job you'd really like and you want to apply for it. There's a knack to producing a great CV – one that the potential employer will pull out from the pile. It shouldn't be too long; two pages is ideal. Keep to relevant facts: personal details; your education qualifications (most recent first); and the experience and skills that apply to the target job (again, most recent first). Your cover letter should summarise the sections of your CV that apply directly to the job – the 'hooks'. Finally, check your CV for typing mistakes – they're very off-putting and will definitely reduce your chances of an interview.

The interview

If you're lucky enough to get an interview, then spend time preparing for it. Learn more about the company so you can ask the right question should the need arise. Think ahead about how you can contribute to the company if they take you on. Also, dress neatly and be on time – don't arrive puffing, rushed and apologetic. Don't forget to bring along identification if asked for. At the interview, be confident and clear in your responses.

If not this time ...

Remember there's a new world of opportunities out there. Check online for all the ways you could perhaps start a business, or get tips to gain additional skills. Overall, be optimistic, persistent and future-focused, and realise your ideal job might not be this one right now!

Questions 15–20

Complete the sentences below.

*Choose **NO MORE THAN TWO WORDS AND/OR A NUMBER** from the text for each answer.*

Write your answers in boxes 15–20 on your answer sheet.

15 Those looking for jobs today may have difficulty making decisions about their
....

16 In deciding what you are good at, the initial matter is to determine what your
.... is.

17 One way to improve opportunities at the beginning of your career is to consider
doing ....

18 Your chances for gaining an interview can be reduced if your CV contains ....

19 For the interview, remember to have your .... with you if this has been
requested.

20 If you don't immediately get the position you want, think about looking online for
suggestions on ways to acquire ....

Read the text below and answer questions 21–27.

Guidance on Workplace Emergency Systems

Government regulations make it a legal requirement that every workplace has a system in place for handling fire and other emergencies. These can arise from a number of causes, but regardless a prompt, organised response is expected by persons in control of workplaces.

The underlying requirement of the *Occupational Health and Safety Act 1989* is that building owners and their tenants ensure a safe environment is provided for workers and occupants that is free from risk. This includes a duty to make sure that fire safety systems are installed and then maintained to the manufacturer's specifications, and records are kept of testing activities. As well, hazard reduction systems should be put in place such as fire exits being kept clear and fire doors kept shut.

Another important element is having an emergency plan for evacuation in the case of a fire or emergency. Initially, the most important element is that the persons appointed to compile the emergency plan must be trained to do this. The plan should be written in plain English and identify the roles and responsibilities of relevant individuals and also identify the locations of different parts of the building. It should also be displayed in a prominent position. Any plan should also cover a range of potential emergencies.

Following the adoption of the plan, an Emergency Planning Committee needs to be set up and trained and responsible individuals need to be appointed to act as Wardens. The most essential role, that of Chief Warden, involves being responsible for a number of areas, including maintaining lists of wardens, ensuring building occupants know about evacuation procedures, and carrying out inspections. In the case of emergencies, the Chief Warden identifies the nature of the emergency and the appropriate course of action and puts in place the emergency procedures, including keeping other Wardens informed. This person also liaises with the fire brigade and other emergency services.

Additionally, there will also be Floor or Area Wardens, whose duties are to operate communication equipment and carry out searches, as well as assist mobility-impaired individuals. They will also act as leaders of groups moving to assembly areas. They wear identifying coloured helmets, as does the Chief Warden.

Questions 21–27

Complete the flow-chart below.

*Choose **NO MORE THAN THREE WORDS** from the passage for each answer.*

Write your answers in boxes 21–27 on your answer sheet.

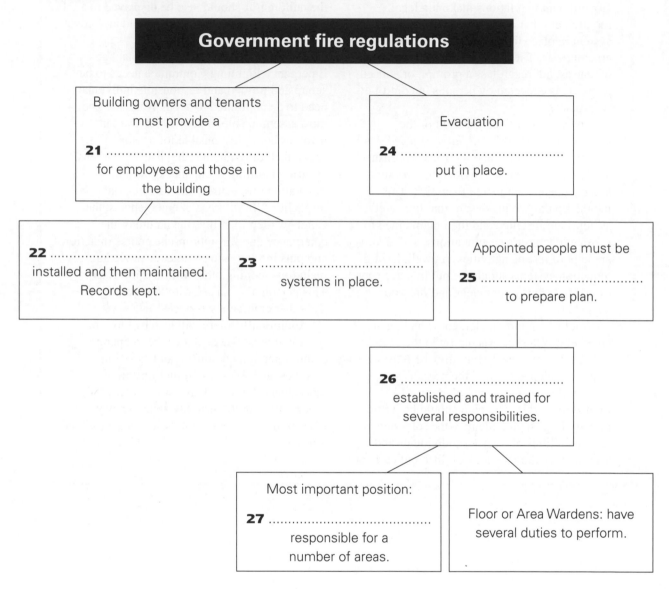

Government fire regulations

Building owners and tenants must provide a

21 .... for employees and those in the building

Evacuation

24 .... put in place.

22 .... installed and then maintained. Records kept.

23 .... systems in place.

Appointed people must be

25 .... to prepare plan.

26 .... established and trained for several responsibilities.

Most important position:

27 .... responsible for a number of areas.

Floor or Area Wardens: have several duties to perform.

Read the text below and answer questions 28–40.

The bank that changed the lives of millions

A In October 2006, a Bangladeshi economist, Muhammad Yunus, himself the product of a village upbringing and one of nine children, received the Nobel Peace Prize for his contribution to improving the lives of millions of impoverished Bangladeshis. He had developed a form of lending, since successfully copied in developing countries around the world, called microcredit. This involves lending small amounts of money to very poor people. There are now a number of banks and NGOs engaged in this form of lending, but the first was the Grameen Bank, a bank now owned by those who have been the recipients of these small amounts of money (the name 'Grameen' means 'village').

B The concept of this type of lending arose from a discussion Yunus had with a poor village woman outside her small hut after he returned to his country from the United States in the mid-1970s. She was making beautiful bamboo stools – two per day – but she had to sell these exclusively and without negotiation to the trader who had lent her the money to buy the bamboo. She had borrowed only 25 cents but she did not have this, and this debt was effectively enslaving her. At the same time he met other villagers with small enterprises and similar stories and calculated that the amount they owed in total at high interest was $27.

C He knew he could, with his income, donate this amount and free these village women from the moneylenders. However, he was aware that the problem would persist each time these women needed to borrow. Initially, he went to the banks to try to establish loans for these impoverished women but was rebuffed. The idea was completely unacceptable. Consequently, Professor Yunus decided to act himself as guarantor for their debts, clearing these and then taking over the loans. Thus began microcredit and in 1976 his revolutionary bank.

D The bank has successfully developed an operating format that has proved enormously successful and which is now emulated throughout the developing world. The bank is owned 90% by the borrowers themselves (of whom 97% are women) – with the remainder owned by the government. Tiny amounts are lent without the need to provide collateral or sign any legal documents. All loans are interest-free and can be long-term. They can also be for extremely small amounts, for example, a loan to purchase a quilt, umbrella or mosquito net requiring repayments of only 3 cents US per week.

E As well, special interest groups are catered for. One overlooked, indeed shunned group, the poorest members of all – beggars – are covered at no cost to themselves through insurance programs. These individuals, who may also suffer from physical and mental incapacity, as well as disabilities such as blindness, are now part of a special program termed the Struggling Members Program. Open to those not engaged in illegal activities, 112,000 beggars have taken up the offer to join and, of the total amount disbursed to them, 76% has been returned so far by them.

F There are also additional benefits to members, such as educational scholarships and low-interest housing loans (at an average of $US190 each). In relation to the

continued ▶

former, Grameen prioritises helping girls by assisting them maintain attendance at school in order to first complete primary school (with a total of 92,552 children being awarded scholarships for this purpose) then later tertiary education, with low-interest loans to cover tuition and other expenses having enabled 39,000 students to complete higher education up to November 2009.

G   Another developing area relates to expensive business loans, known as micro-enterprise loans, for family members wishing to expand their businesses. This gives an opportunity, for example, for the husband of a member to purchase agricultural equipment such as a power tiller or irrigation pump, or river-craft for transportation and fishing, which will help secure the future of the family. This is the most expensive of the four levels of interest rates charged on loans, being 20%. The other levels are: housing loans (8%), student loans (5%) and Struggling Member loans (interest free). One benefit of the business loan is that it does not limit the amount of the loan.

H   Muhammad Yunus's optimism in human nature has been repaid. There is a 99.3% success rate for repayment of loans. Nearly eight million poor people have taken out loans, of whom 97% have been women. Since its creation, $US8.65 billion has been lent and, at present, $US7.68 billion has been repaid. In the year to December 2009, $US1.12 billion was loaned. Apart from 1982, 1991 and 1992, the bank has always made a profit, which is disbursed to members, including new members.

I   The bank founder's belief that world peace is encouraged through the poorest of the poor having opportunities to escape the limitations and uncertainty of poverty has been validated. Today millions of people have the dignity of their own enterprise and the ability to feed and educate their children. The Nobel Peace Prize would seem to have been a justified reward for Muhammad Yunus and the people of Bangladesh who supported his radical, initially doubtful idea, one that has literally changed lives.

Questions 28–32

Do the following statements agree with the information given in the reading passage?

In boxes 28–32 on your answer sheet write

TRUE	if the statement agrees with the information
FALSE	if the statement contradicts the information
NOT GIVEN	if there is no information on this

28   Muhammad Yunus's idea extended beyond its original location.

29   His initial idea came from a meeting with a group of villagers owing money.

30   The village was very close to the capital city.

31   Before creating his bank, Yunus tried other methods of raising finance.

32   Borrowers of small amounts at the Grameen Bank have to sign legal contracts and have collateral.

*Choose the correct letter, **A**, **B**, **C** or **D**.*

Write the correct letter in boxes 33–36 on your answer sheet.

33   Beggars have special cost-free benefits related to

    A   disabilities such as blindness.

    B   the rate of interest they must repay.

    C   the amount returned to them.

    D   free insurance schemes.

34   Grameen Bank's main education priority is to provide scholarships for girls so that they can

    A   attend high school.

    B   complete primary school.

    C   finish primary school and later university.

    D   be paid tuition fees and other expenses.

35   The example of river-craft is given to illustrate that

    A   boats are necessary in the region.

    B   loans provide for the family in days to come.

    C   husbands cannot get other work.

    D   starting a new business is expensive.

36   Statistics show that the Grameen Bank has

    A   lent and been repaid millions of dollars.

    B   always made a profit over the years.

    C   lent far more than it ever got back.

    D   helped over eight million poor women.

Questions 37–40

*The text has nine paragraphs, **A–I**.*

Which paragraph contains the following information?

*Write the correct letter, **A–I**, in boxes 37–40 on your answer sheet.*

37   A description of how Yunus began his bank

38   Information about the different rates of interest on loans

39   Λ summary of Yunus's own attitude towards providing opportunities for poor people

40   An example of how someone was kept powerless by owing a very small sum of money

READING ANSWER SHEET

Pencil must be used to complete this sheet.

1		
2		
3		
4		
5		
6		
7		
8		
9		
10		
11		
12		
13		
14		
15		
16		
17		
18		
19		
20		

21		
22		
23		
24		
25		
26		
27		
28		
29		
30		
31		
32		
33		
34		
35		
36		
37		
38		
39		
40		
	Total	

This page may be photocopied by the purchaser.

Unit 2
Writing

2.1 What is in the Writing Test?

In both the General Training and Academic IELTS Writing Tests you are asked to do two tasks in one hour.

Time allowed	60 minutes It is suggested that you spend approximately 20 minutes on Task 1 and 40 minutes on Task 2.
Procedure	The Writing Test is the third section of the IELTS test. It is held in an examination room. You will be given a question booklet and an answer sheet.
Structure	Both the Academic Writing Test and the General Training Writing Test comprise two tasks.
Word length	**Task 1:** 150 words minimum **Task 2:** 250 words minimum
Task 1	**General Training** You have to write a letter describing a situation and requesting someone to do something. **Academic** You have to describe information presented in a graph, table, chart or diagram by summarising the main features, trends or comparisons.
Task 2	You have to write a discursive essay on a given topic, presenting ideas that are relevant to the issue.
Skills focus	**Task 1 (General Training):** writing a letter, using an appropriate and consistent tone **Task 1 (Academic):** summarising information presented in a visual or visuals **Task 2:** writing a longer essay that has a clear and logical structure
Scoring	You will receive a band score between 0 and 9 depending on how your response matches the task criteria. Scores can be reported in whole or half band scores, e.g. 8.0 or 7.5.

2.2 Test-taking tips

What should you do when you take the IELTS Writing Test? Here are some suggestions about how to manage the test as successfully as possible.

Manage your time

It is important to manage your time in the test, because if you don't complete both tasks, you have no chance of achieving your required band score. The test advises you to spend 20 minutes on Task 1 and 40 minutes on Task 2. You should follow this advice. As Task 2 is worth a greater percentage of your final writing mark, it is a good idea to start with Task 2.

Read the task and plan your answer

Begin by reading the tasks carefully and considering what is required. Before you begin to write, take one or two minutes to plan what you are going to write. You will get a higher band score for a well-structured answer.

Meet the minimum number of words

You will automatically get a lower mark if you fail to reach the minimum number of words for each task. You will also not be given credit for writing more than the word limit. In Task 1 you should write at least 150 words and in Task 2 you should write at least 250 words.

Check your answers

When you have finished writing, it is important to go back and check your work, so leave yourself some time to do this. You are working under pressure, so you may well make simple mistakes. Leave yourself time to edit both answers. If you have made a mistake, cross it out and correct it. You will not lose marks for poor presentation. However, do make sure that your writing can be read clearly.

2.3 Getting to know the test

The IELTS Writing Test consists of two tasks. For each task, you will be given:

▼ a general statement indicating the topic

▼ a question that may have one or more parts

▼ an instruction as to how you should answer the question.

General Training Task 1

What do I have to do?

In Task 1 of the General Training Writing Test, you are asked to write a 150-word letter. You should spend about 20 minutes on the task.

You will be given a task card, which describes a situation and includes three bullet points. Your letter should address the situation on the task card and the instructions (sub-tasks) given in the three bullet points.

It is important that you remember who you are writing the letter to, and that you use appropriate language.

Example

> ## General Training Writing Task 1
>
> You should spend 20 minutes on this task.
>
> *Last year you attended a course in a college in Australia and unfortunately you have lost your certificate.*
>
> *Write a letter to the principal of the college. In your letter:*
> - *explain who you are and the course you are studying*
> - *ask for a replacement certificate to be sent*
> - *say why you need the replacement certificate.*
>
> Write at least 150 words.
>
> You do NOT need to write any addresses.
>
> Begin your letter as follows:
>
> **Dear Sir/Madam,**

How do I approach General Training Task 1?

▼ Write 150 words.

▼ Explain the purpose of the letter.

▼ Keep your answer on topic and cover all three bullet points.

▼ Write in full sentences. (Do not use bullet points.)

▼ Relate your answer directly to the task card.

▼ Use a consistent tone.

▼ Check your writing to correct any mistakes.

Academic Task 1

What do I have to do?

In the Academic Writing Test, for Task 1 you are asked to write a description of the information in one or more visuals (charts, tables, graphs or diagrams). Your description should be more than 150 words in length and you have 20 minutes to complete the task.

Your description should give an overview of the information in the visual or visuals, summarising the main points as well as highlighting the most important details.

Example

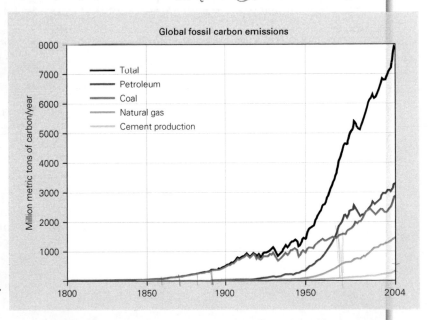

Academic Writing Task 1

You should spend about 20 minutes on this task.

highest/lowest value
(3 paragraphs)
— fluctuations

The graph shows the main sources of fossil fuel carbon emissions from 1800 to 2004.

Summarise the information by selecting and reporting the main features, and make comparisons where relevant.

Write at least 150 words.

Global fossil carbon emissions

Million metric tons of carbon/year

Total
Petroleum
Coal
Natural gas
Cement production

0000
7000
6000
5000
4000
3000
2000
1000

1800   1850   1900   1950   2004

Writing with correct grammar, spelling and vocabulary does not automatically give you a good mark in the Writing Test. In assessing your answer for Academic Task 1, the examiners will be looking for the following:

▼ Did you accurately present all the information in the visual?

▼ Did you present an overview of the main trends or differences?

How do I approach Academic Task 1?

▼ Write 150 words.

▼ Give an overview of the information, and include a brief introductory statement and a concluding statement.

▼ Summarise the main points rather than list all the information in the visual.

▼ Write in full sentences. (Do not use bullet points.)

▼ Describe the information in the visual. (Do not give your opinion or interpretation.)

▼ Check your writing to correct any mistakes.

Task 1 skill areas

Task achievement

In General Training, you are asked to respond to a situation by writing a letter. To do this successfully, you must address the three bullet points using the correct tone. In Academic Task 1, you are asked to summarise the information in the task, giving an overview of the most important factors

Coherence and cohesion (Organising ideas logically)

In both Academic and General Training Task 1, it is important to organise and link your ideas in a logical way. It is also important that your ideas relate to one another clearly. This includes using linking words to join your sentences, paraphrasing, using relative clauses and substituting nouns with pronouns. Overall, the coherence and cohesion of your response is judged by how smoothly your writing reads.

Lexical resource (Using appropriate vocabulary)

Lexical resource means the range of vocabulary you use and how effectively you use it. This involves using a wide range of words related to the task you have been given. It also means you use vocabulary accurately and appropriately.

Grammatical range and accuracy

Range refers to using different kinds of grammatical structures that are appropriate to the topic and discussion. Accuracy means using grammar and sentence structure correctly. This involves, for instance, the appropriate use of tenses and agreement, and also avoiding any errors that interfere with communication.

General Training and Academic Task 2

What do I have to do?

In Task 2 you are asked to write an essay discussing an issue. The essay should be at least 250 words in length. You have 40 minutes to complete the task.

The task card will give you a statement explaining or giving an opinion about a situation. There will then be a question about this statement. Finally you are asked to explain your answer using examples from your knowledge or experience. Your essay should have a clear structure and should clearly answer the specific question on the task card.

There is very little difference between General Training Task 2 and Academic Task 2. The only slight difference may be that Academic questions are supposed to be more abstract. However, both Academic and General Training Task 2 are marked using the same criteria and require the same skills.

Here is an example of a task card for General Training or Academic Task 2.

Example

Writing Task 2

You should spend 40 minutes on this task.
Write about the following topic:

> *Young people today spend more time than ever before playing video games. This is harmful to their physical and social development.*
>
> *Do you agree or disagree?*

Give reasons for your answer and include any relevant examples from your own knowledge and experience.

Write at least 250 words.

How do I approach Task 2?

Remember that it is a good idea to start with Task 2, as it contributes more to your overall score.

▼ Write 250 words.

▼ Make sure your writing is directly connected to the task and question.

▼ Give a clear opinion or write a clear description. When giving an opinion, it is OK if you do not agree or disagree 100% – you may partially agree or disagree.

▼ Write in paragraphs using topic sentences.

▼ Organise your answer into a logical structure and make sure each sentence contributes to your argument or response.

▼ Do not only write in simple sentences – include some complex sentences, even if this means you make a few mistakes.

▼ Use more complex vocabulary, even if you sometimes make errors in word form.

▼ Write a conclusion that is consistent with your argument.

In assessing your response to the IELTS Writing Test, the examiner will also consider your ability in the following areas.

Task 2 skill areas

Task response

As for Task 1, you must show that you have responded appropriately and thoroughly to the specific Task. This means you have answered all parts of the question, given a clear opinion relevant to the topic and explained this opinion using supporting ideas.

Coherence and cohesion (Organising ideas logically)

Coherence is organising and linking your ideas in a logical way. Cohesion means that your ideas relate to one another clearly. This includes using linking words to join your sentences, paraphrasing, using relative clauses and substituting pronouns in place of nouns. Overall, the coherence and cohesion of your response is judged by how smoothly your writing reads.

Lexical resource (using appropriate vocabulary)

Lexical resource means the range of vocabulary you use and how effectively you use it. This involves using a wide range of words related to the task you have been given. It also means using the vocabulary accurately and appropriately.

Grammatical range and accuracy

Range refers to using different kinds of grammatical structures that are appropriate to the topic and discussion. Accuracy means using grammar and sentence structure correctly. This involves, for instance, the appropriate use of tenses and agreement, and also avoiding any errors that interfere with communication.

2.4 The writing skills you need

General Training Task 1

Writing with correct grammar, spelling and vocabulary does not automatically give you a good mark in the IELTS Writing Test. In Task 1 of the General Training Writing Test you need to do the following things:

▼ Address the situation (covering all three bullet points).

▼ Consider who you are writing to and use the appropriate tone consistently.

▼ Check your writing to correct mistakes.

Responding to the task

Here is an example of a task card for General Training Task 1.

> **Example**
>
> *You have seen an advertisement for a special offer for a holiday at a beautiful tourist resort. You would like to book a holiday.*
>
> *Write a letter to the travel company. In the letter*
> - *say when you would like to arrive and leave.*
> - *describe the type of accommodation you require*
> - *ask for more information about activities available.*

In order to complete this task, you need to ask yourself the following questions:

▼ Who am I writing to?

▼ Why am I writing?

▼ What tone should I use?

In this example you are writing to a company. You do not know the name of the person to whom you are writing so your letter should start *Dear Sir or Madam*.

The reason you are writing is to find out about the special offer at the tourist resort. The bullet points provide details your letter needs to cover. It is essential that your answer addresses each of these points.

The tone of your letter should be formal or neutral (everyday language), as this is a business letter and you are writing to someone you do not know.

Purpose

The first step in writing any letter is to establish the reason you are writing: your purpose. This helps you decide whether you should use formal or informal language in your letter. Exercise 1 gives you practice at identifying purpose.

Exercise 1 Purpose

Identify the purpose of writing a letter in the following situations, and indicate whether you should use formal or informal language. The first one has been done for you as an example.

1 You saw some furniture you liked at an exhibition and you would like a catalogue.

(formal) Request for a catalogue for some furniture
....

2 You want your friend to come to your partner's surprise birthday party at a restaurant.

....

3 You recently stayed in a hotel and the service was most unsatisfactory.

....

4 You are interested in a job as a part-time sales assistant at a bookshop.

....

5 You want your friend to look after your pet dog while you go on holiday.

....

6 You are organising a high-school reunion.

....

7 You went to a restaurant and found a cockroach in your soup.

....

8 There is a gas leak in your rented flat.

....

The first line of your letter should explain your purpose in writing, without the reader having to read further. In a letter for the IELTS Writing Test, the first line should be a summary of the information in the task description (before the bullet points). As well as the purpose in writing, it may also include the time and place of the events. Exercise 2 gives you practice at writing first sentences for different situations.

Revisit the situations in Exercise 1 and this time write the first line of a letter for each situation. Make sure your first line clearly explains your purpose. The first one has been done for you as an example.

1   *I saw your furniture displayed at the Ideal Home Exhibition last week and I*

   wonder if you could send me your catalogue.

2   ....

   ....

3   ....

   ....

4   ....

   ....

5   ....

   ....

6   ....

   ....

7   ....

   ....

8   ....

   ....

Tone

Tone is the different voice you use depending on the situation and the person to whom you are writing. When you are writing to a friend, you use a different tone from the tone you use when you are writing to your bank manager. You also use a different tone when you want to complain, compared to when you want to apply for a job.

In General Training Task 1, it is important that you choose the correct tone and use it throughout your letter. In selecting tone, you need to consider:

▼ who you are writing to (Do you know the person? Are they in a position of authority?)

▼ the situation (Are you asking for something? How likely is the other person to say no?)

▼ your emotional state (What is your mood? Are you angry? happy? disappointed?).

Exercise 3 Tone

The following extracts from letters all have problems with tone. Find the problem and correct it.

1 I am very sorry to have to inform you but I want to complain about the service I received at your restaurant.

Problem: ....

Corrected version: ....

2 You must send your catalogue to the above address immediately.

Problem: ....

Corrected version: ....

3 Dear Anne
I request the pleasure of your attendance at my birthday party at my house next Saturday afternoon.

Problem: ....

Corrected version: ....

4 Unfortunately I must return to my country as my Granny has not been very well lately.

Problem: ....

Corrected version: ....

5 Dear Sir/Madam
I was excited when I saw your advertisement for an Accounts Clerk in the newspaper and I would be really happy to work for your company.

Problem: ....

Corrected version: ....

It is important when you are writing a General Training Task 1 response to keep the tone consistent throughout. This means you need to keep to one style of writing. Exercise 4 gives you some practice at considering consistency of tone.

Exercise 4 Tone

Look at the following letter and underline parts that have problems with tone. Rewrite these in a more consistent tone in the space provided. Check the answer key when you have finished for suggested solutions.

The task was:

> You have seen an advertisement for a special offer at a beautiful tourist resort. You would like to book a holiday. Write to the company and ask for some more information.
>
> Write a letter to the travel company. In the letter
> ▼ say when you would like to arrive and leave
> ▼ describe the type of accommodation you require
> ▼ ask for some more information about some activities you are interested in.

Dear Sir/Madam

I saw your advertisement for a two-week holiday in Tasmania in Cheap and Cheerful Holiday Magazine and I would like to have information on the issues below.

First, I really hope that the special offer is still valid for the school holidays from 8 to 21 July, as this is the only time that it is possible for us to get away.

Second, in your advertisement you have forgotten to say what type of accommodation you are offering. I would like to know if you have anything suitable for a party of ten people. Furthermore, would it be possible for you to inform me whether any of the cabins have wheelchair access?

Finally, we would like to go sailing, as my son loves boats and wants to be a sailor when he grows up. Is it possible to hire a boat?

I look forward to your response and hope to see you in the near future.

Yours faithfully

....

....

....

....

....

....

....

Addressing the task

Each General Training Task 1 has three parts – a situation, an instruction and three bullet points – that must be addressed in your answer.

Example

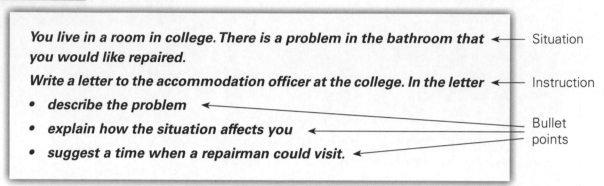

You live in a room in college. There is a problem in the bathroom that you would like repaired. ◄—— Situation

Write a letter to the accommodation officer at the college. In the letter ◄—— Instruction

- *describe the problem* ◄
- *explain how the situation affects you* ◄ Bullet points
- *suggest a time when a repairman could visit.* ◄

It is very important that you:

▼ only write about the situation described in the task

▼ cover all three bullet points

▼ use a letter format. This means you should not use bullet points or numbered points in your answer.

You should plan your answer before you write it.

Exercise 5   Addressing the task

The following plan has been drawn up for the sample task above. Using this plan, write a response to the task. When you have finished, check the answer key for a sample response.

Dear Sir or Madam

General situation

Who you are: e.g. first-year science student.

Where you live: Room 309, William Thompson Hall of Residence.

Problem

No hot water for over a week.

Water brown in colour.

How this affects me

Have to go to friend's room. Exam time.

Suggest a time

At home Monday, Wednesday and Thursday afternoons. After 3.30.

Telephone to confirm.

Polite ending

I look forward ...

Close

Using the bullet points

In General Training Task 1, it is very important that you cover all three bullet points on the task card in your answer. If you miss a bullet point you will be penalised.

It is important that your answer is at least 140 words long, otherwise it will be penalised. Therefore, it is necessary for you to not only cover the bullet points but also to expand upon them. One way of doing this is by asking yourself 'wh-' questions – who, which, what, when, what time, where, why – and maybe how.

Remember that although these 'wh-' questions are a useful way of expanding your answer, the relevance of each of them depends on the situation.

Consider this Task 1 task card.

Example

> *You want your friend to come to your partner's surprise party.*
>
> *Write a letter inviting your friend to the party. In the letter*
> * *explain about the party*
> * *describe what you are going to do at the party*
> * *say who the other guests will be.*

For the first bullet point ('explain about the party') you could give the following information:

▼ Who? Liza

▼ Why? twenty-first birthday

▼ Where? The executive suite of the Night Owls' Club in Oxford Street

▼ When? Saturday night from 8.30 pm

Exercise 6 Using the bullet points

1 Brainstorm details for the bullet point 'describe what you are going to do at the party'.

2 Brainstorm details for the bullet point 'say who the other guests will be'.

....

....

....

....

....

continued ▶

3 Put your ideas for the three bullet points into sentences.

....
....
....
....
....
....
....
....
....
....
....
....

Keeping your writing on topic

Although it is important that you expand on the points in the task, it is also important that you stick to the main focus of the topic. This means that your letter has to remain relevant to the situation at all times. Exercise 7 gives you practice at identifying information that is not important for the situation given in the task card.

Exercise 7 | Keeping your writing on topic

The task is:

> You have seen an advertisement for a job as a part-time sales assistant at a bookshop.
>
> Write a reply to the advertisement: In the letter
> ▼ describe your work/study experience
> ▼ give the hours you are available for work
> ▼ say why you are suitable for the job.

In the response letter opposite, cross out any information you consider irrelevant to the situation.

Dear Sir or Madam

I would like to apply for the position of part-time sales assistant advertised in Saturday's Daily Planet, right next to the article on talking to your plants.

I am currently studying literature at the University of Tasmania. I chose to study literature because I love books. My favourite book is Lord of the Rings by J.R.R. Tolkien and I would certainly recommend this to any of your customers.

I am available to work from Monday to Thursday night from 6.00 to 9.00 pm. I can't work later than 9.00 because my mother says the town centre is quite dangerous late at night. I can't work on Friday because I have my violin lesson.

I am well qualified for the job because I'm very friendly and I love books.

If you would like me to attend an interview you can contact me at the above address.

I look forward to hearing from you and enclose my resumé.

Yours faithfully

Organising your ideas logically

The second marking criterion for General Training Task 1 is coherence and cohesion. This means organising your ideas logically. In this area, the examiner is looking for:

▼ the way you organise your ideas

▼ the way you link ideas and sentences together.

Coherence

Every Task 1 letter needs to have three different sections. These are:

▼ the reason you are writing

▼ details of the situation (covering the three bullet points of the task)

▼ a suitable close.

It is important that you state the situation and purpose of the letter in the first paragraph, that you propose future actions in subsequent paragraphs, and that you give a polite close at the end of the letter. However, it is often convenient to change the order or combine the bullet points together in your answer.

Exercise 8 gives you practice at identifying the different sections of a letter.

You think you left your briefcase on the train yesterday morning.

Write a letter to the lost property office. In the letter

▼ describe what the briefcase looks like and what was in it

▼ explain where exactly you think you left the briefcase

▼ say what you want the lost property office to do.

The following letter is an answer to the Task 1 above. Identify the three sections of the answer and where the writer covers the bullet points.

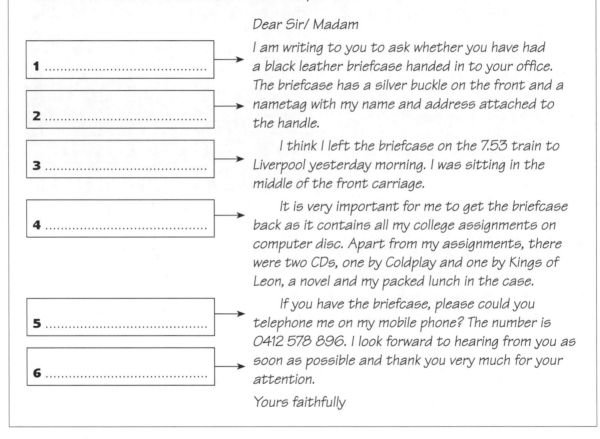

Dear Sir/ Madam

I am writing to you to ask whether you have had a black leather briefcase handed in to your office. The briefcase has a silver buckle on the front and a nametag with my name and address attached to the handle.

I think I left the briefcase on the 7.53 train to Liverpool yesterday morning. I was sitting in the middle of the front carriage.

It is very important for me to get the briefcase back as it contains all my college assignments on computer disc. Apart from my assignments, there were two CDs, one by Coldplay and one by Kings of Leon, a novel and my packed lunch in the case.

If you have the briefcase, please could you telephone me on my mobile phone? The number is 0412 578 896. I look forward to hearing from you as soon as possible and thank you very much for your attention.

Yours faithfully

1 ....

2 ....

3 ....

4 ....

5 ....

6 ....

Paragraphs

All writing needs to be organised into paragraphs. Each paragraph represents an idea. Therefore, a paragraph should have:

▼ a topic sentence that explains the main point of the paragraph

▼ further information about that main point.

As you only need to write 150 words in Task 1, your paragraphs will probably be only two sentences long. One of the sentences in each paragraph will state the topic, the other will add further information.

Topic	*I am writing to you to ask whether you have had a black leather briefcase handed in to your office.*
Further information	*The briefcase has a silver buckle on the front and a nametag with my name and address attached to the handle.*
Topic	*I think I left the briefcase on the 7.53 train to Liverpool yesterday morning.*
Further information	*I was sitting in the middle of the front carriage.*

Exercise 9 gives you practice at structuring paragraphs.

Exercise 9   Paragraphs

You have been given the following Task 1.

> You are going on holiday. Write a letter to a friend asking him or her to look after your house.
>
> In the letter
> - explain the situation
> - tell your friend what needs to be done while you are away
> - arrange to meet your friend before you go.

Select the sentences that should be put in each paragraph to make a coherent answer.

Dear Mike,

Paragraph 1

Situation: .... Request: ....

Paragraph 2

Details of request (4 sentences): ....

Paragraph 3

Arrange meeting (2 sentences): ....

Paragraph 4

Polite close: ....

Regards

John

1   I would really appreciate it if you could look after the house.

2   Would it be possible for us to meet on Wednesday so I can give you the keys?

3   I wonder if you could do me a favour while I am away.

continued ▶

4   While you are at the house, it would be good if you could water the garden and take any post out of the mailbox and place it inside.

5   As you know, I am going to England on holiday from next Monday until the 15th of July.

6   If Wednesday is OK, please telephone me as soon as possible.

7   He can get in and out of the house on his own, so all you need to do is leave some food in his bowl.

8   I look forward to seeing you in the next few days.

9   In particular, I would like you to feed the cat.

Cohesion

In order to make your writing flow, it is important to show how your ideas relate to each other. This is called cohesion, and it can involve the use of a number of devices, including:

▼ linking sentences together

▼ using referencing

▼ using relative clauses

▼ paraphrasing and using synonyms.

Linking sentences together

There are a number of ways of ordering and linking sentences together in English. Often these are shown by using linking words. The table below shows some of the more common linking words and their purpose.

Ordering/time	Cause and effect	Contrast	Adding
first	so	in contrast	and
second	therefore	but	also
finally	consequently	however	in addition
before	since	although	moreover
after	hence	nevertheless	furthermore
when	**Effect and cause**	in spite of	what is more
while	because	despite	not only … but also
then	because of	**Choice**	as well as
meanwhile	as	either … or	
during	for this reason	neither… nor	

These linking words help your writing flow more easily.

Referencing

Referencing is a method of avoiding repeating information in your writing. This is achieved by substituting key noun groups with pronouns. For example:

I am afraid I wasn't able to hand in my homework because the dog ate *it*.

In this case *it* replaces 'my homework'.

I am afraid I won't be able to attend the party because I am washing my hair. I have to do *this* on *that* night because I am very busy *that* week.

In this example, *this* refers to washing my hair, the first *that* refers to the night of the party, and the second *that* refers to the week of the party.

The word *this* is used to substitute for something that is current or near, while *that* is used for something that is more distant in time or space.

Relative clauses

Relative clauses are used to combine two sentences together that have the same subject. The subject of the second sentence is replaced by:

▼ *which* if the subject is an object or a place with no preposition before it in the original sentence

▼ *where* if it is a place

▼ *who* if it is a person.

It is important to remember that the clause must come next to the noun or noun group that it is describing, or the meaning of your sentence will be changed or incorrect.

Paraphrasing and synonyms

One useful way of making your writing read smoothly is paraphrasing. This means avoiding using the same words as the task by substituting them with other words instead. It is also important to avoid using the same words over and over. Synonyms, words that mean the same things as one another, are a useful way to achieve this. For example:

leave ⟶ depart   replace ⟶ change

Another way of paraphrasing is to use a different grammatical structure with different word forms. For example:

I am *unable to attend on this date*.

could become

I am *unavailable at this time*.

Questions 1–10

Brainstorm ways to paraphrase these words or phrases that are commonly used in General Training Task 1.

1 I would like more information about ... .

2 Would it be possible to send ... .

3 an appointment ....

4 a problem with my course ....

5 I would like to invite you to ... .

6 to rent ....

7 to be late ....

8 an assignment ....

9 holiday ....

10 I am sorry ....

Question 11

11 Look at the following General Training Task 1 and the response below. Paraphrase any words or phrases that have been overused or taken straight from the task.

> You had a minor accident at work. Write a letter to your employers.
>
> In the letter
>
> ▼ describe what happened
>
> ▼ explain the cause of the accident
>
> ▼ state what you think should be done about the situation.

Dear Mr Williams

I would like to report an accident that I had leaving work on Friday 21 October. As I was leaving work, I tripped over a raised paving stone just outside the front entrance. I fell over and tore my trousers and cut my knee. Although my cut knee was not serious, it was painful and my trousers were damaged beyond repair.

I believe that this accident was caused by problems with the paving stones just outside the front entrance. This may be because tree roots are growing under the paving stones and pushing the paving stones up. I believe that the paving stones need to be replaced if this type of accident is to be avoided in the future.

I would also like the company to pay to replace my trousers. Replacing my trousers will cost around $200. I look forward to hearing from you.

Regards

Helen

Rewrite the following section of a letter in a more coherent, shorter way, substituting pronouns for noun groups where appropriate, and combining sentences using relative clauses.

As you know, we are all going on holiday to France in September and we wondered if you would like to join us in France. We are going in September so we can celebrate my birthday on the 13th. We are having a party in a local club. In the local club, there is live music every night. The band is very good. I saw the band in London last summer and was very impressed.

We will be staying in an old farmhouse. The farmhouse has eight bedrooms so there will be room for everybody. The farmhouse is close to a beach. The beach has great waves for surfing. The beach is hidden from the road so very few people come to the beach.

....

....

....

....

....

....

....

....

....

....

....

....

....

Exercise 12 · Organising ideas logically

The following Task 1 letter has a number of problems with cohesion and coherence. All the information included is relevant. However, it should be ordered more logically and the links between sentences can be improved. Rewrite the letter, improving the ordering of the ideas and the links between sentences.

> You won't be able to hand your assignment in on time.
>
> Write to your lecturer asking for an extension. In the letter
>
> ▼ describe the situation
>
> ▼ explain why your assignment will be late
>
> ▼ say when you will be able to hand in your assignment.

Dear Mr Murray

I am sorry for any inconvenience caused but my mother has had a heart attack. I have to fly back to China as soon as possible. I do not know when I will be leaving because I am on a stand-by flight. I also do not know when I will be coming back.

My Geography assignment is due on the 14th of September so I will not be able to hand it in on that date.

Could you let me know as soon as possible whether I can have an extension? I believe that I will be away for two weeks at the most. I think that I will be able to do some work while I am in China. However, I will almost certainly need an extension on my assignment. Please could you give me permission to hand it in on the 21st of September? This would be one week later than expected.

Yours sincerely

Using appropriate vocabulary

Lexical resource is the third marking criterion for General Training Task 1. This means using a range of language related to the topic of the letter. In preparation for Task 1, you should revise vocabulary related to common letter topics, such as:

▼ issues to do with accommodation (for example, rent or lease)

▼ issues to do with employment

▼ letters about a current issue to the editor of a newspaper

▼ invitations to parties and events.

It is also useful for you to have a range of vocabulary that will help you to do the following:

▼ make requests

▼ state needs or wants

- ▼ describe likes and dislikes
- ▼ give factual information
- ▼ give opinions
- ▼ make complaints
- ▼ make suggestions or recommendations.

Word forms

Using appropriate vocabulary also means using correct word forms in your writing. One common example of incorrect word form is using an adverb instead of an adjective or an adjective instead of a verb. When you are learning vocabulary, make sure you understand the meaning fully, including how and where it can be used. For example:

I am interesting in the course.

In this case the sentence should be:

I am interested in the course.

Interested is an adverb describing the person's feelings, whereas *interesting* is an adjective describing the person himself or herself.

Exercise 13   Using appropriate vocabulary

1   Complete the table below with vocabulary items or phrases connected to the topics or purposes in the table. Some examples have been given to get you started.

Accommodation	Employment	School/lecture	Invitations/ social events
Rent Lease	Advertisement conditions	Registration	I hope you are able to attend.

Problems/ complaints	Likes/dislikes	Making Suggestions	Giving opinions
Very disappointed to find out	I'd prefer/rather	Perhaps it would be better ...	Although I accept your point of view ...

continued ▶

2 Look at the following Task 1 and complete the model letter that follows. You may need to use more than one word to fill the gaps.

> You are going on holiday and you would like to hire a car. One of your party is in a wheelchair. Write a letter to a car hire company.
>
> In the letter
> ▼ explain the reason you need the car
> ▼ describe the type of car you need
> ▼ ask what the price is and what it includes.

Dear Sir/ Madam

I found out about your **a** .... from your

b .... and I would like some more information.

My family and I are flying to **c** ....

on **d** .... and we would like to rent a car to

e .... around while we are there. We would

return the car to the **f** .... on the 29th of

December.

As there will be six people in **g** ...., we

will need a large car. We will also be **h** ....

by my brother who is in a wheelchair. Therefore, we will need a car with lots of

i .... and if possible a ramp for easy access.

Please could you let me know if you have anything **j** ....

and whether there would be an extra cost. In addition I would like to know whether your

prices include insurance.

I look forward to your reply.

Yours faithfully

3 Correct the errors in word form in this extract from a letter.

I saw your advertising in Saturday's Daily Planet and I would like applying for the position of Sales Manager. I have three years' experience to work as a salesman in Australia. I am energetic and enthusiasm in my work and I am availability to start immediately.

4 Using the plan below, respond to the following task. When you've finished, check the answer key for a sample answer.

> The local government is planning to change the bus timetable. You are not happy about the proposed changes. Write a letter to the newspaper.
>
> In the letter
> ▼ describe the changes
> ▼ explain how they will affect you
> ▼ say how you would improve the service.

Dear Sir or Madam

Paragraph 1

How do you know about the changes? What are they?

....

....

Paragraph 2

How do these changes affect you? When do these buses run? Why is the new plan inconvenient?

....

....

....

....

....

....

....

....

continued ▶

Using a range of grammar features accurately

For General Training Task 1, the final criterion is **grammatical range and accuracy**. It is not enough to write an answer that contains no mistakes. You need to demonstrate that you can write simple, compound and complex sentences accurately.

Sentences

A simple sentence contains a subject and a verb and expresses a complete idea. For example:

I would like to invite you to my party on Saturday night.

A compound sentence is made by joining two independent sentences together, using a coordinator, such as *for*, *and*, *or*, *but*, *yet* or *so*. For example:

The hotel was good *but* it was very expensive.

Complex sentences contain one or more relative clauses. For example:

I gave the assignment to the teacher when the class had finished.

Remember that all sentences must have a subject and a main verb (action). The following sentence is incomplete:

My mobile phone which was very expensive.

This is not a sentence as there is no main verb. There is no action. To make it a sentence, you could remove *which*:

My mobile phone was very expensive.

or information could be added:

My mobile phone, which was very expensive, was stolen.

It is better to make a few mistakes attempting to write complex sentences than to write perfect simple sentences throughout your letter.

Subject–verb agreement

Subjects and verbs need to agree with each other in terms of number. Problems with subject–verb agreement usually occur when the writer does not distinguish whether the subject is singular or plural. For example:

Both the bus and train finishes at 10.00 pm.

In this sentence the subject ('Both the bus and train') is plural, because you could replace it with *They*. However, the verb form used is singular. It should be:

Both the bus and train finish at 10.00 pm.

A common error of subject–verb agreement is for writers to forget the final -*s* on a verb for the singular third person (*he*, *she* or *it*). For example:

He visit his mother on Monday.

The verb needs to have an extra -*s* to agree with the singular subject.

He visits his mother on Monday.

Exercise 14   Using a range of grammar features accurately

1   Look at the examples below and decide if they are correct sentences. Rewrite those that are not correct.

   a   The bus leaving at 8.00 am.

   b   I am afraid I won't be able to attend your party.

   c   Although the room is quite close to public transport and close to the centre of the city.

   d   The day when I left my family and friends in my own country.

   e   The house where we will be staying is close to the beach.

continued ▶

f The Chinese restaurant, where I bought the meal, near to my house.

g The major assignment, which was due the day before my birthday party last week.

h My previous job, which was in an accounts office in India.

....

....

....

....

....

....

....

....

....

2 Is the subject–verb agreement correct in the following sentences? If not, rewrite the verb in the space provided to correct it.

a Everything in the house have been renovated. ....

b My flatmate and his friends is always playing loud music until late at night. ....

c The international community are very upset about the decision. ....

d The train usually departs at 11.00. However last Wednesday it were late. ....

e The noise from the building next door was very loud. ....

f There is a number of problems with my room. ....

g The job for which I applied has already been taken. ....

h The money my parents transferred to me have not yet arrived. ....

Academic Task 1

Writing with correct grammar, spelling and vocabulary does not automatically give you a good mark in the Writing Test. In Academic Task 1 you need to do the following things:

- ▼ Give a brief introductory statement.
- ▼ Give an overview that summarises the essential information in the visual(s).
- ▼ Choose the most relevant information.
- ▼ Organise the information from the visual(s).
- ▼ Describe the data presented in the visual(s) accurately.
- ▼ Write a concluding statement.
- ▼ Check your writing to correct any mistakes.

Responding to the task

In order to achieve the requirements of Academic Task 1, you need to present a clear overview of the information. To do this you should use the following structure for your response:

1 a brief statement describing what is shown in the visual(s). This statement should have a similar meaning to the task description but should not use the same words

2 an overview of the most important information presented in the visual(s). This is a summary of the most important information in the visual(s)

3 a description of any other information that you consider important in the understanding of the visual(s). In this section you choose other aspects of the visual that are important and summarise them. It is important to mention some but not all of the figures in the visual

4 a concluding statement that restates your main point again. It is not necessary for you to give an opinion about the information.

Describing one visual

In Academic Task 1 you may be asked to describe one visual. Let's look again at an example.

The graph shows the main sources of fossil fuel carbon emissions from 1800 to 2004.

Summarise the information by selecting and reporting the main features, and make comparisons where relevant.

Write at least 150 words.

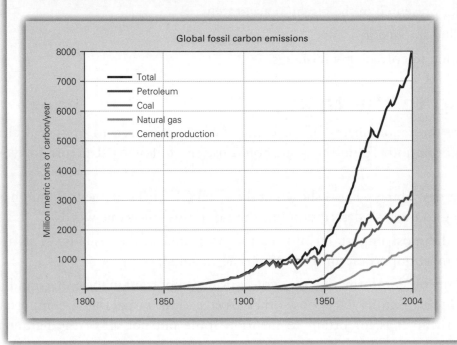

Introductory statements

You should begin by writing an introductory statement that is a restatement of the task description. You will lose marks if you simply copy the words from the task. Here is an example of a suitable restatement.

The chart *illustrates* the carbon emissions from fossil fuels between 1800 and 2004.

It is often not possible to find synonyms for the main nouns in the rubric so it is necessary to change the word order and the verb used to introduce the information instead. In the example above, the verb *shows* has been replaced with *illustrates* and the order of the noun group has been changed.

Exercise 15 | Introductory statements

Look at the Task 1 descriptions below and change them to make introductory statements.

1 The diagram shows a small town at three stages of its development, in 1900, 1950 and 2000.

....

....

2 The first graph shows the size of the cars sold in Australia from 1990 to 2008, whereas the second graph shows the price of petrol during this period.

....

....

3 The three pie charts represent the type of pets owned by 12-year-old children in Australia, the United States and the United Kingdom.

....

....

4 The diagram below shows the process by which increased carbon dioxide in the atmosphere causes global warming.

....

....

5 The chart below shows the life expectancy of men and women in five different countries around the world.

....

....

Main body

In the main body of your response you should summarise, select and report the main features presented in the visual. Look at the sample Task 1 on the previous page. From the graph we can see the following things:

▼ Coal emissions began to grow in around 1840.

▼ Coal was the only source of emissions up to about 1890.

▼ From 1925 to 2004 emissions have increased 800% from 1000 million metric tons of carbon per year to 8000 million metric tons of carbon.

▼ Coal was the equal highest source of emissions up to about 1960 when petrol emissions became higher.

▼ In 2004 petrol was responsible for almost 40% of all emissions.

▼ Emissions from natural gas and cement production also grew rapidly from 1950.

▼ Emissions from natural gas in 2004 were equivalent to the total emissions in the world in 1940.

The next step is to organise the answer. This could be done in two ways: chronologically (in order of time) or by source of emissions.

Example 1 (chronological order)

Carbon emissions first became noticeable in around 1840. From this point up to around 1930, coal was almost entirely responsible for carbon in the atmosphere. Since 1930 petrol emissions have grown rapidly. Petrol became the main source of emissions in around 1960 and in 2004 it was the source of around 40% of all carbon emissions. During this period emissions from natural gas and cement also grew rapidly. In fact natural gas emissions in 2004 equalled around 1500 metric tonnes of carbon. This was equal to the total emissions in the world in 1940.

Emissions have increased very rapidly over the past 50 years. In 1925 emissions stood at around 1000 million metric tonnes of carbon per year; by 2004 these emissions had increased to 8000 million metric tonnes, an increase of 800%.

Example 2 (source of emissions)

In 2004 petrol was responsible for 40% of all the world's carbon emissions. It began to become a significant source of emissions in 1930 before becoming the major cause of carbon in the atmosphere in around 1960. From 1840 up to 1960, coal held the greatest responsibility for carbon pollution. It is still the second-highest source of carbon emissions today. Emissions from natural gas and cement also grew rapidly in this period. In fact natural gas emissions in 2004 equalled around 1500 metric tons of carbon. This was equal to the total emissions in the world in 1940. Emissions have increased very rapidly over the past 150 years. In 1925 emissions stood at around 1000 million metric tons of carbon per year; by 2004 these emissions had increased to 8000 million metric tons, an increase of 800%.

Concluding statement

The concluding statement for a Task 1 response is a restatement of the main information you have given in your response. Therefore, the statement should be short – one or two sentences at most.

Remember it is not necessary to give your opinion or to speculate on the reasons for the information.

For the task on page 144 the concluding statement might be:

Overall, global emissions caused by the use of coal and petroleum have risen extremely quickly over the past 150 years. However, the amount of carbon in the atmosphere has become much greater in the last 50 years.

1 Look at the following visual and list the main information given.

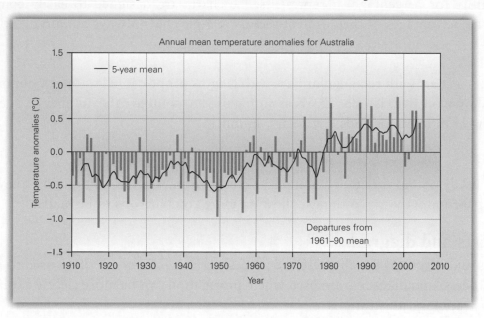

2 Use your notes to write a description of the main trends.

3 Write a concluding statement about this visual.

Types of visual

There are several different types of visual that may be used in the Writing Test – each has a slightly different purpose. However, the basic strategy for writing a Task 1 answer is the same for all of them.

Line graphs

Line graphs are used to illustrate general statistical trends. They compare two or more things.

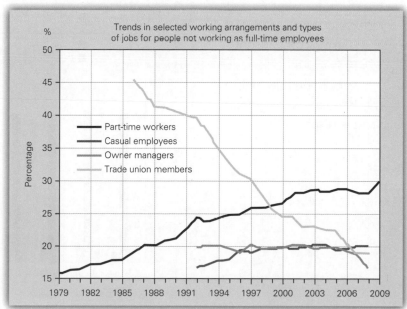

Pie charts

A pie chart is a circular graph divided into sectors. The size of each sector is proportional to the quantity (or percentage) it represents. Pie charts are designed to easily compare statistics. The percentages of the different sectors in a pie chart always add up to 100%.

Bar charts

A bar chart is a chart with rectangular bars with lengths proportional to the amounts they represent (shown on an axis). Bar charts are often used to compare the number of a certain kind of thing at different periods (e.g. years) in time.

Tables

Tables are used for more detailed statistical comparison. Unlike bar graphs, they can display data for more than two things, allowing more comparisons to be made.

Flow-charts and diagrams

Flow-charts and diagrams usually describe processes. Flow-charts are often used to show steps in a process, and diagrams are used when information can be more clearly explained with an illustration or illustrations.

So far in this section we have only looked at line graphs. Exercise 17 provides practice for a question using a bar graph.

Exercise 17 Types of visuals (bar chart)

The bar chart below shows people's satisfaction with the number of hours they work per week. Begin by making notes of the main information given, then use these to summarise the information given in the bar chart, by selecting and reporting the main features, and making comparisons where relevant.

When you have finished, check the answer key for a sample response.

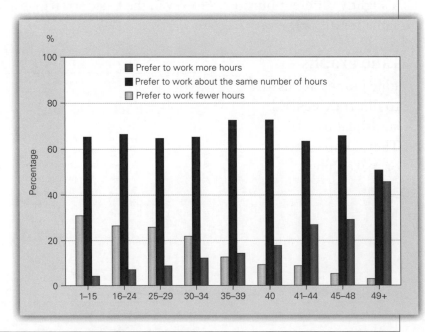

Describing and comparing more than one visual

In Academic Task 1 you may be asked to describe and compare more than one visual. In the example below you are given a table and a pie chart.

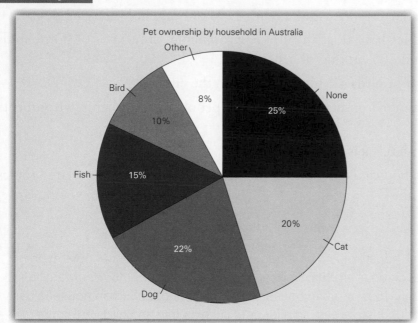

Popularity of pet by environment

	Urban (%)	Rural (%)	Suburban (%)
Dog	15	65	20
Cat	25	50	25
Fish	45	20	35
None	60	5	35
Bird	30	45	25
Other	15	60	25

Introductory statement

Although the introductory statement covers two or sometimes more than two sources of information, the purpose is the same. The introduction is a summary of the topic of the illustrations. Again, it is possible to reword the rubric to make this summary. For example:

> The pie chart shows household ownership of pets in Australia, while the table shows the environment in which these pets are kept.

Main body

The main body is a summary of the major points in the sources of information. It is also useful to combine categories to make your explanation easier. For the example on the previous page, you could combine birds and fish under the title 'small pets'. In this case the main points would be:

▼ Dogs are the most popular pet in Australia, with 22% of households having dogs.

▼ Although 65% of families have dogs in rural environments, only 15% of households have dogs in the city and 20% in the suburbs.

▼ Smaller pets such as fish or birds are more popular in the city.

▼ 60% of people in urban environments and 35% of people in suburban environments don't have pets.

▼ More households don't have pets than have pets.

When writing the main body, it is useful to combine the information into related topics to give your writing structure.

Example

Twenty-two per cent of all households own a dog, making them the most popular type of pet in Australia. However, dogs are mainly popular in rural areas, with 65% of families owning dogs, whereas only 15% of urban households and 20% of suburban households own a dog. In urban and suburban areas, smaller pets such as fish and birds are more popular.

Twenty-five per cent of all households have no pet. Although 95% of rural families have some form of pet, only 60% of people living in the city keep an animal in their home.

Concluding statement

As with other Academic Task 1 essays, the concluding statement should be a summary of the main body.

Example

The illustrations prove that although dogs are the most popular type of pet, their popularity is mainly confined to the countryside. Households in urban areas are much less likely to have a pet.

Describe and compare the following graphs. When you have finished, check the answer key for a sample response.

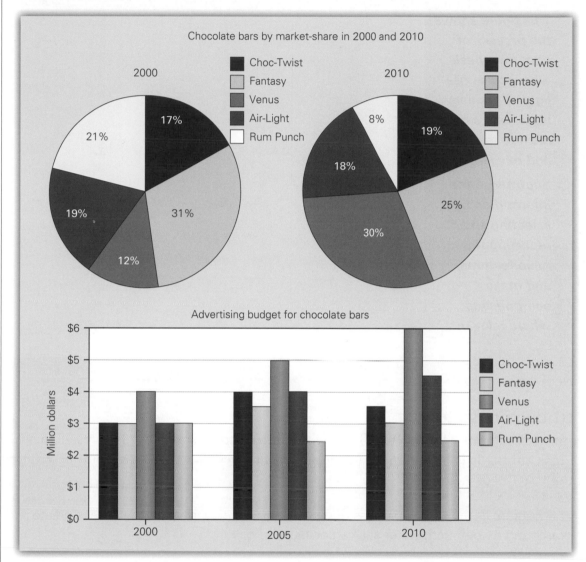

Describing a process

Some questions ask you to describe processes, shown in a diagram or flow-chart. When describing a process, it is important to:

▼ give a clear statement explaining what the diagram or flow-chart is about

▼ explain every stage shown

▼ organise the information so it is easy to follow

▼ write a concluding statement that summarises the process.

Here is an example of an Academic Task 1 task card that asks you to describe a process.

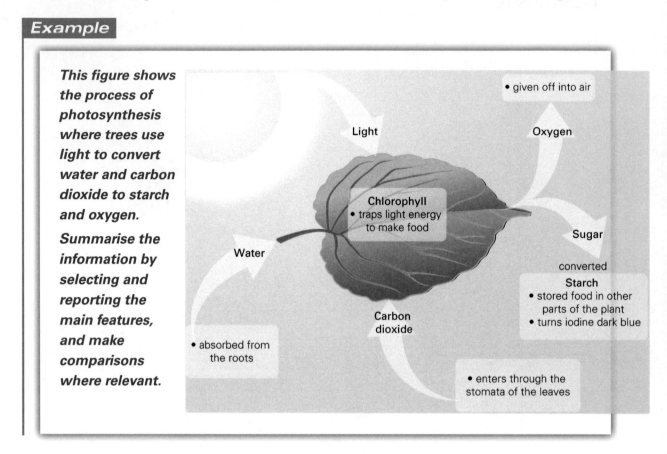

This figure shows the process of photosynthesis where trees use light to convert water and carbon dioxide to starch and oxygen.

Summarise the information by selecting and reporting the main features, and make comparisons where relevant.

Introductory statement

As for other forms of Academic Task 1, the introductory statement is a restatement of the task rubric. It is important that this statement gives the reader a general description of the visual. For example:

> The diagram describes the process of photosynthesis, in which plants and trees create starch and oxygen from water and carbon dioxide.

Main body

The main body needs to describe each stage of a process. To do this successfully it is important to paraphrase the information in the visual. This often means changing the word form to make your answer different from the illustration. For instance, you may change nouns and verbs to adjectives.

The language used to refer to a subject changes depending on whether it is new information or not. For instance, in the first sentence of the main body you may introduce the idea 'Trees and plants absorb water'. However, when this is next referred to the verb (*absorb*) becomes an adjective: *the absorbed water*.

As processes are not usually specific to a particular time (in the future or past), they are usually described in the present tense.

Example

Trees and plants absorb water through their roots and collect carbon dioxide through the stomata in their leaves. Meanwhile, sunlight is trapped by chlorophyll in the tree's leaves to form light energy, which is used to process the absorbed water and carbon dioxide to make food. When the food is created, it is in the form of sugars. These sugars are converted to starch and stored in other parts of the plant. This starch can be tested for by adding it to iodine, which will turn bright blue in its presence. Oxygen is released into the air as a by-product of this process.

Concluding statement

The concluding statement is used to summarise the main body. For example:

Trees and plants feed by using sunlight to convert carbon dioxide and water into sugars, which are processed into starch and oxygen, which is released into the atmosphere.

Exercise 19 Describing a process

The figure below shows a cross-section of an erupting volcano.

Summarise the information by selecting and reporting the main features, and make comparisons where relevant.

When you have finished, check the answer key for a sample response.

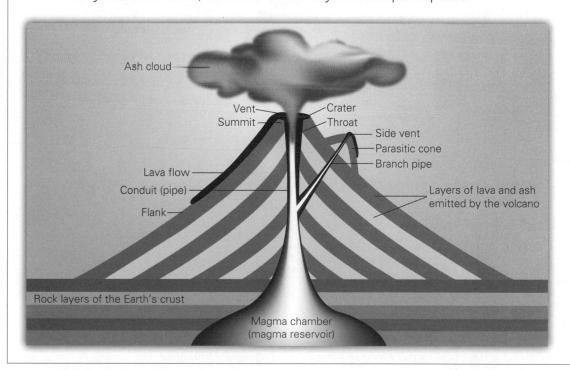

Organising your ideas logically

The second marking criterion for Academic Task 1 is **coherence and cohesion**. This means organising your ideas logically. In this area, the examiner is looking for:

▼ the way you organise your ideas

▼ the way you link ideas and sentences together.

Coherence

As we have already seen, for Academic Task 1 you should follow the structure: Introductory statement –Main body – Concluding statement. However, coherence is also about the way you find links to categorise the information within your response.

For example, if you are describing the following chart, you would organise the information by level of disadvantage, summarising the level of disadvantage for each category.

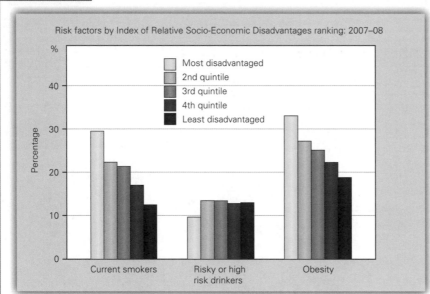

Your main points would be:

- The more disadvantaged a person is, the more likely they are to be overweight and a smoker.

- Obesity runs at nearly 20% in all levels of society.

- Obesity is 32% for the most disadvantaged percentile.

- Nearly 30% of the most disadvantaged smoke, which is more than any other group.

- Only 12% of the wealthiest percentile smoke.

- At-risk drinking is generally not dependant on the level of disadvantage. At-risk drinking stands between 11 and 13%.

- The most disadvantaged are less likely to be high-risk drinkers.

List the main points in a logical manner for the following line graph.

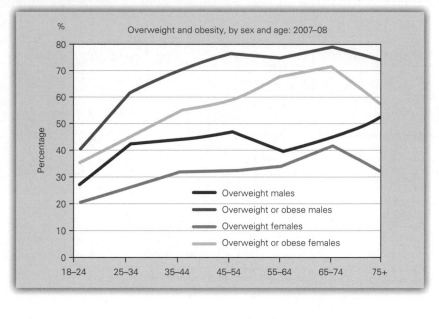

Overweight and obesity, by sex and age: 2007–08

Legend:
- Overweight males
- Overweight or obese males
- Overweight females
- Overweight or obese females

....

....

....

....

....

....

....

....

Cohesion

In order to make your writing flow in a logical way, it is important to show how your ideas relate to each other. This is called cohesion, and it can involve the use of a number of devices, including:

▼ linking sentences together

▼ using referencing

▼ using relative clauses

▼ paraphrasing and using synonyms.

Linking sentences together

There are a number of ways of ordering and linking sentences together in English. Often these are shown by using linking words. The table below shows some of the more common linking words and their purpose.

Ordering/time	Cause and effect	Contrast	Adding
first	so	in contrast	and
second	therefore	but	also
finally	consequently	however	in addition
before	since	although	moreover
after	hence	nevertheless	furthermore
when	**Effect and cause**	in spite of	what is more
while	because	despite	not only … but also
then	because of	**Choice**	as well as
meanwhile	as	either … or	
during	for this reason	neither … nor	

These linking words help your writing flow more easily.

Exercise 21   Linking sentences together

Fill in the gaps in the following Task 1 answer with appropriate linking words.

The pie charts show the size of new cars sold in Australia in 2000, 2005 and 2010,

1 .... the line graph shows the price of petrol during this period.

The number of cars sold with an engine capacity of more than four litres stood

at 25% **2** .... declining to 15% in 2005 and 10% in 2010.

3 .... sales of small cars (cars with an engine capacity under two

litres) increased from 28% in 2000 to 43% in 2010, overall sales of cars in Australia

declined by 10%.

4 .... the price of petrol increased dramatically

5 .... the period from 2000 to 2008. **6** ....

in the last part of 2009 petrol prices declined slightly **7** ....

rising again in 2010.

> *Overall,* **8** .... *did the number of cars sold decrease between*
>
> *2000 and 2010* **9** .... *the size of cars purchased became smaller.*
>
> *At the same time the price of petrol rose steadily.*

Referencing

Referencing is a method of avoiding repeating information in your writing. This is achieved by substituting key noun groups with pronouns. For example:

> Sales of new cars fell in 2009. This fall was particularly noticeable in larger models.

In this case *this* replaces the fall in sales of new cars. Here is another example:

> World population has risen dramatically over the past century. *This* rise is particularly significant in India and China. Although China has the largest population, it has made serious efforts to reduce its population.

In this example, *this* refers to the rise in world population. *It* refers to China. We substitute *this* for something that is current or near, and *that* for something that is more distant in time or space.

Relative clauses

Relative clauses are used to combine two sentences together that have the same subject. The subject of the second sentence is replaced by:

▼ *which* if the subject is an object or a place with no preposition before it in the original sentence

▼ *where* if it is a place

▼ *who* if it is a person.

It is important to remember that the clause must come next to the noun that it is describing. We will look at them in more detail on pages 196–9.

Exercise 22   Referencing and relative clauses

> Rewrite the following Task 1 response in a shorter, more coherent way, substituting pronouns for noun groups where appropriate, and combining sentences using relative clauses.
>
> *The graph shows the leisure activities of children at three different ages in three countries in 2010.*
>
> *The most popular sport for ten-year-old children in all three countries is soccer. Soccer is played by 33% of all ten-year-old children. In Britain 60% of boys play soccer and 20% of girls play soccer.*
>
> continued ▶

> *As children get older in all three countries, children play more video games. In America 78% of 12-year-old boys play video games. In America only 40% of teenage girls play video games. In America the number of children playing video games increases to 92% of 15-year-old boys.*

....

....

....

....

....

....

....

....

Paraphrasing and synonyms

One useful way of making your writing read smoothly is paraphrasing. This means avoiding using the same words over and over, by substituting them with other words instead. For example:

Sales increased greatly from 2002 to 2010.

could become

Sales grew significantly from 2002 to 2010.

Synonyms are words that mean the same thing as one another: for example, *well* and *healthy* can mean the same thing.

Exercise 23 | Paraphrasing

Brainstorm ways to paraphrase these sentences that you might find in Academic Task 1.

1 The continent with the lowest annual rainfall is Antarctica.

....

2 The servants' accommodation on the east side of the manor house was completed in the sixteenth century.

....

3 The average age of the population of Japan will increase for at least the next ten years.

....

4 Overall, the proportion of energy generated by wind power has increased substantially over the last ten years.

....

5 The proportion of monthly income spent on rent was twice as high in 2010 as in 1990.

....

6 There was a general downward trend in properties for rent in the big cities from 1990 to 2010.

....

7 The average home owner had a mortgage seven times his or her annual salary in 2010, compared to three times in 1990.

....

8 The amount of water in the dams in New South Wales was 76% of capacity in 2010, compared to 37% of capacity in 2003.

....

9 Electricity is generated by the sails of the wind turbine being turned by the wind.

....

10 The bonuses paid to bankers in the USA in 2010 were 30% higher than the bonuses paid in 2007.

....

Exercise 24 Organising your ideas logically

The following Task 1 response has a number of problems with cohesion and coherence. Find the problems and correct them.

The line graph shows the number of overseas students studying English in a college in Australia from 2000 to 2010, where the bar chart shows the students' country of origin.

The total number of English students increased dramatically at this period. In 2000, there were 400 English students at the college, when by the end of the decade there were 900, which is more than double the 2000 total.

continued ▶

> The biggest market for overseas students throughout the decade has been Asia. At the start of the decade, most of the Asian students came from Japan and Korea. Although, in the last five years that markets have been declining and more students have come from China. In 2009, 42% of all overseas students at the college came from this source.
>
> However, the number of European students has declined from 2005, there has been a steady increase in students from South American countries that are Brazil and Colombia.
>
> Overall the number of students at the college has increased, with most of the students coming from China.

Using appropriate vocabulary

Lexical resource is the third marking criterion for Academic Task 1. This means using a variety of task-specific vocabulary accurately to describe the illustration.

You will get a higher band score if you attempt to use sophisticated vocabulary and you make a few mistakes, than if you only use simple language that you know is correct.

Describing trends

When describing graphs or tables, it is important to describe the overall trend. This means describing the shape of the visual: whether the figures show a rise, a fall or remains the same. It is also important to explain the extent of this trend.

Here is some useful language for describing trends.

Upwards trend		Downwards trend		Stayed the same
Noun	**Verb**	**Noun**	**Verb**	
rise	rose	fall	fell	remained constant
increase	increased	decrease	decreased	were static
swell	swelled	decline	declined	
growth	grew	shrinking	shrunk	
upsurge	upsurged	drop	dropped	
	soared (large upwards trend)	dwindle, dwindling	dwindled	

The following language is useful for describing the *extent* or *manner* of trends.

Large movement		Small movement		Manner of movement	
Adjective	**Adverb**	**Adjective**	**Adverb**	**Adjective**	**Adverb**
significant	significantly	insignificant	insignificantly	steady	steadily
great	greatly	slight	slightly	constant	constantly
massive	massively	minor			
huge	hugely	small			
dramatic	dramatically	negligible	negligibly		
considerable	considerably	inconsiderable	inconsiderably		
rapid	rapidly	slow	slowly		
sharp	sharply				

Exercise 25   Describing trends

1   Look at the graph and use the language for describing trends to complete the description below.

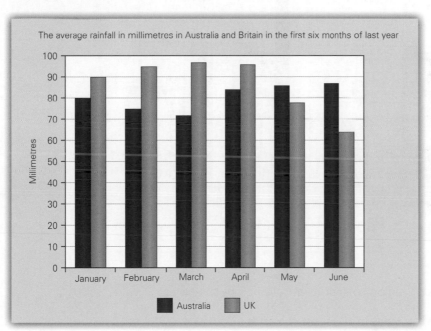

The average rainfall in millimetres in Australia and Britain in the first six months of last year

The rainfall in Britain **a** .... *from January*

before reaching a peak of around 95 mm in March. Between March and April rainfall

b .... *. From April to June there was*

continued ▶

c .... in the amount of rainfall with rainfall

levels standing just above 60 mm in June.

The level of rainfall in Australia was consistently lower than

in Britain. Rainfall stood at around 80 mm in January before

d .... to about 70 mm in March. There was

e .... in rainfall in March to around 81 mm.

After this, rainfall continued **f** .... until June.

2   Use the words in the box below to complete the description of the bar graph.

fluctuated	reached a peak	bottomed out	levelled off

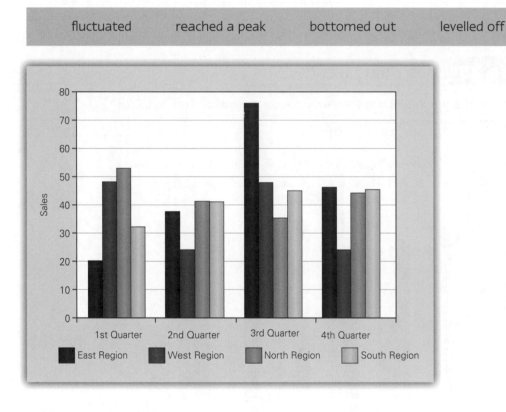

Sales in the east region rose dramatically before they **a** .... in

the third quarter. Sales in the west region **b** ....

Sales in the north region **c** .... in the

third quarter. Sales in the south region rose in the first and second quarter before they

d .... for the rest of the year.

Describing changes

When looking at a graph, it is not always possible to tell the exact number represented. It is therefore important to use language that shows this uncertainty.

Less	Not sure	More
a bit less than somewhat less than a little/slightly under	around about approximately	a bit more than somewhat/slightly more than a little / slightly over

Exercise 26 Describing changes

Use these expressions to answer the following questions. If you have no idea, guess.

1 What is the population of your country?

....

2 How many dollars to your currency?

....

3 How many kilometres is the Earth from the Sun?

....

4 How many days are there until the next public holiday?

....

5 How far is your house from the nearest shopping centre?

....

Using a range of grammar features accurately

In Academic Task 1, the final marking criterion is **grammatical range and accuracy**. It is not enough to write an answer that makes no mistakes. You need to demonstrate that you can write both simple and complex sentences accurately.

Complex sentences are ones containing one or more relative clauses.

It is better to make a few mistakes attempting to write complex sentences than to write perfect simple sentences throughout your description.

Relative clauses

As mentioned on page 157, relative clauses are used to combine two sentences together that have the same subject. A relative clause must be positioned next to the noun to which it is referring.

There are two types of relative clause: defining relative clauses and non-defining relative clauses.

Defining relative clauses

Defining relative clauses give essential information that identifies or *defines* the subject of the sentence. For example:

The average age of people *who work in the hospitality industry* is about 25.

The relative clause in this sentence is 'who work in the hospitality industry'. This clause answers the question: *what kind* of people? The clause is defining the people concerned and is essential to the meaning of the sentence.

Defining relative clauses do not need commas around them.

Non-defining relative clauses

Non-defining relative clauses give extra information that is not essential to the structure of the sentence. For example:

The water, *which has already been boiled*, is added to the mixture.

In this example the relative clause is 'which has already been boiled'. This clause is a non-defining relative clause because it is adding extra information. It could be removed and the other words would still form a whole sentence:

The water … is added to the mixture.

Commas should be placed around non-defining relative clauses to show this. Non-defining elative clauses can only begin with *which*, never *that*.

Exercise 27 Relative clauses

Use relative clauses to combine the following sentences into a passage in the space provided. Some of the sentences should not be combined.

1. The village grew from a population of 500 in 1850 to 12,000 in 2010.
2. Between 1900 and 1950 the woodland became the Newlands Estate.
3. The woodland marked the eastern border of the village.
4. In addition the Village Green was turned into townhouses.
5. The Lord's Manor House was located on the Village Green.
6. The townhouses attracted new residents to the village.
7. The final major development was the apartment blocks.
8. The apartment blocks were built on the common land to the north in the 1980s.

....

....

....

....

....

....

....

....

Sentences

Make sure that you write complete sentences. It is a common problem when using relative clauses to end up with a sentence that is incomplete. For example:

The pie chart, which shows sales by region for the last year

This is not a sentence as there is no main verb. There is no action. To make it a sentence you would have to add information:

The pie chart, which shows sales by region for the last year, indicates that the southern region sold more than the other areas.

Or you could remove *which*, but this would make only a simple sentence:

The pie chart shows sales by region for the last year.

Exercise 28 Sentences

Look at the examples below and decide if they are sentences or not. If they are not full sentences, add information of your own to write them as full sentences in the space provided.

1   The base of the fire extinguisher which is made from re-enforced steel.
2   There was a slight fall in sales of brands that contain animal product.
3   The sunlight which is stored in the photoelectric cells in the solar panels.
4   The earlier the age that children take up smoking in developing countries.
5   While the number of families living on less than $2 a day has decreased in some areas.

....

....

....

continued ▶

6 The graph show that infectious diseases, which are declining in developed countries, are spreading in developing countries.

7 It is interesting to note that the population of animals which live in the cities and large towns.

8 The rainwater collected in large containers and transported to a series of large underground vats.

....

....

....

....

....

....

Comparisons

When describing numbers it is often necessary to make comparisons between two or more different sets of figures. There are a number of ways of doing this. Two possible sentence structures you could use are shown in the tables below.

Subject	Verb	Quantifier	Adverb	Conjunction	Object
X	is	much	larger	than	Y
Y	is	considerably	smaller	than	X
A	is	a little	faster	than	B and C
B and C	are	slightly	slower	than	A

Subject	Verb	Quantifier	Conjunction	Adjective	Conjunction	Object
X	isn't	nearly	as	big	as	Y
Y	isn't	anywhere near	as	small	as	X
E	isn't	quite	as	high	as	F and G
F and G	aren't	quite	as	low	as	E

It is also possible to say that the figures are:

▼ once, twice, three (etc) times as big

▼ double/treble (etc) the size/amount.

Look at the graph and complete the sentences in the following answer, using suitable comparisons.

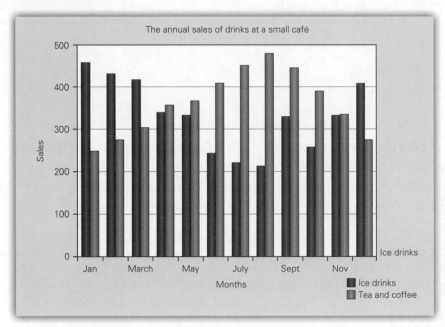

The annual sales of drinks at a small café

The graph describes the sales of iced drinks and tea and coffee

for a café throughout the year. The statistics indicate that the

type of drink people choose is seasonal. In January, sales of

1 .... However, in August the sales of

iced drinks **2** .... In April and May the sale

of iced drinks and tea and coffee **3** .... ,

standing at around the 380–390 mark.

It is interesting to note that although the sale of soft drinks bottomed

out in August, there was a sudden rise in sales before a fall of about 40 sales

in October. In spite of this rise in September, sales of iced drinks were still

4 ....

In conclusion, sales of iced drinks and tea and coffee vary at different times of

the year.

Passive construction

Passive construction is often used when describing processes, because in processes usually it is the action itself that is important and not who or what performs it. To form a passive sentence, we use the verb *to be* and a past participle.

Examples
The office *is cleaned* every night.
The new machine *was delivered* yesterday.

In these examples the objects of the verbs are given at the start of each sentence (*the office*; *the machine*). Passive construction is used when the performer of the action (the subject) is either unimportant, as in the first example, or unknown, as in the second. The most common mistake with passive construction is to use it mistakenly when the thing or person performing the action is the subject (at the start of the sentence).

Exercise 30   Passives

1   Read the following description and circle the correct (passive or active) form of the verb.

Heat **a** *is transferred / transferred* by using chemicals that **b** *are converted / convert* easily from a gaseous to a liquid state. These chemicals arrive at the compressor as a cool gas where the molecules **c** *are compressed / compresses* generating heat as more molecules **d** *are squashed / squashed* in. The resulting hot high-pressure gas **e** *is sent / sends* to the condenser where it **f** *is cooled / cools* in the air.

2   Look at the diagram opposite and correct the seven errors in active and passive construction in the model answer.

The diagram shows the procedure for enrolling, orientating and testing new students on their first day at a college.

When new students arrive at reception, they ask to fill out an arrival form and give the receptionist their passport and two photos. These are used to make their student card.

Meanwhile the Director of Studies welcomed the students to the college. The students are given an orientation speech and they are given a copy of the handbook. The students then are taken a placement test which used to help the Director of Studies to allocate them to a class.

While this happened, reception is notified the IT department of the student's arrival and each new student is issued with their own password to access college computers.

There are three main areas involve in the orientation and placement of new students.

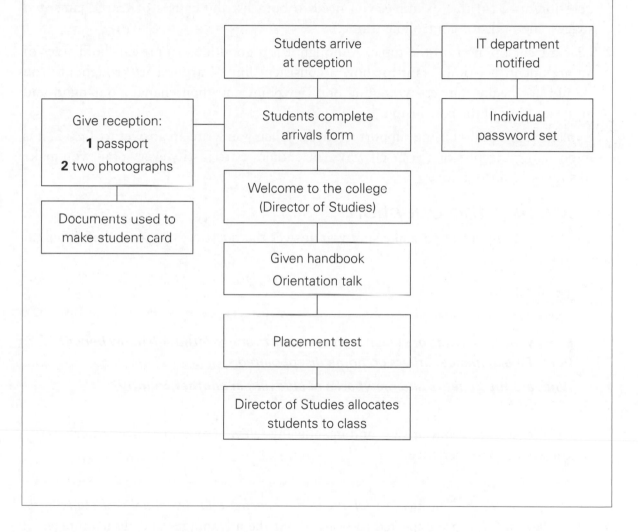

General Training and Academic Task 2

Responding to the task

In Task 2, the first of the four marking criteria is task response. The examiners are looking for you to do three things:

1 Fully respond to all parts of the question/task. Often a question/task has more than one part. (For example: 'What are the causes of these traffic jams? Suggest some methods how traffic can be controlled.') It is important that you address all sections of the question/task. (In this example, you need to both list the causes of traffic jams *and* suggest methods for controlling traffic.)

2 Give a clear opinion on the topic. Although it is a good idea to present both sides of an argument, it is important to show a consistent line of argument throughout. You should not begin your essay arguing one viewpoint and then change your mind and argue another in the conclusion.

3 Explain your opinion using supporting ideas. When you write an answer to Task 2, it is important to keep asking yourself why. You should try to justify every point you make to support your opinion.

Answering the question

In Task 2, it is important to make sure you answer the question you are asked. Look at the example below:

Example

> ***Every year, thousands of students go overseas to study. Although many benefit from the experience, others go home disappointed.***
>
> ***What are the benefits and drawbacks of studying in another country?***
>
> Give reasons for your answer and include any relevant examples from your own knowledge or experience.

In this example, the question is: *what are the benefits and drawbacks of studying in another country?* You are expected to write about the advantages and disadvantages of studying abroad.

If the question you are asked has more than one part, you should be careful to answer all sections. For example, if it was:

Do you agree that studying abroad is a valuable experience? What problems do overseas students face?

you would have to:

▼ come to a decision on whether studying abroad is a valuable experience or not

▼ outline the problems overseas students face.

Exercise 31 Answering the question

Look at the questions below and decide what you have to write about.

1 In many countries, traffic jams in city centres are a major problem. Governments around the world have tried many methods to cope with these difficulties.
What are the causes of traffic jams? Suggest some methods for controlling traffic.

....

....

2 Nowadays in Western countries, many people don't get married until they are in their thirties. In earlier times people got married much younger.
What are the advantages of waiting until you are older to get married? What do you think is the best age to get married?

....

....

3 Although being rich makes life easier, money doesn't necessarily make you happy.
Do you agree or disagree?

....

....

Brainstorming and organising your ideas

Once you have identified what you have to write about, you should think of as many relevant ideas as possible. This process is called **brainstorming**.

Do not worry if you feel your ideas are not original or clever. It is not important that the examiner agrees with you, only that you express yourself and your ideas well.

For the task on page 170 you might come up with the following arguments:

▼ Studying abroad is expensive.

▼ There are no language difficulties if you study in your own country.

▼ Living abroad gives you experience of another culture.

▼ You meet lots of people from different cultures, if you study abroad.

▼ You may experience culture shock.

▼ Sometimes a foreign qualification will help you to find a job.

▼ Studying abroad gives you a different outlook on life from meeting different people.

The next stage is to organise these ideas into a plan. One way of doing this is to divide the ideas into arguments *for* and *against*.

You can also look for other links between your ideas. For example:

Studying abroad is expensive, but sometimes a foreign qualification will help you find a job. Therefore, money spent on an overseas education could be an investment for your future.

This type of link balances the advantages and disadvantages of studying abroad and helps you to come to a conclusion.

Exercise 32   Brainstorming and organising your ideas

1   Look at the list of ideas on page 171 about studying abroad. Group the ideas into arguments *for* and *against*.

Ideas *for* studying abroad	Ideas *against* studying abroad

2   Think of other links between the ideas on the previous page. Check the answer key for suggestions.

....

....

3   Return to the questions in Exercise 31. Brainstorm as many ideas as possible and find links between your ideas. Remember to make sure the ideas you have are relevant to the question.

Planning your essay

Once you have brainstormed ideas, the next step is to divide these ideas into paragraphs. How you organise your essay will depend on the Task 2 question. You might be asked to:

▼ explain the causes or results of a situation. In this case your plan should be a series of paragraphs outlining various causes and their results

▼ discuss advantages or disadvantages. In this case it is important to discuss both advantages and disadvantages of a situation. In other words you need to think of both the positive and negative aspects of a topic

▼ Give an opinion. In this case you are asked to state what you think, so your essay should give reasons for your opinion and supporting points justifying those opinions. An alternative approach would be to discuss both the positive and negative effects of the proposal before using your evidence to justify your opinion.

Which are your main ideas? These will be the topic sentences in your paragraphs. Remember: the topic sentence tells the reader the purpose of the paragraph. It is usually the first sentence. Each paragraph should express one main idea.

Your other ideas will be used as examples and evidence to explain the ideas you have chosen to be your topic sentences. These ideas need to be made relevant to answer the question and to support your main ideas. Every sentence should add to your argument.

Think about what conclusions can be drawn from these ideas. You should use your strongest ideas to help form an opinion and to write your introduction and conclusion.

Writing your essay

The essay you write for Task 2 should have three sections: an introduction, the main body, and a conclusion.

Introduction

The first section of the essay is the introduction. It should include two things:

▼ a general introduction to the topic

▼ a thesis statement briefly expressing your views.

This means the essay must start with a paraphrase of the question. As Task 2 is only 250 words long, it is not necessary to give background information. The thesis statement should give a 'preview' of your main argument or idea.

The introduction should be no longer than 50 words.

Main body

The main body is the bulk of your essay. The main body is where you justify your opinion. It includes:

▼ your ideas

▼ evidence and examples supporting these ideas.

The main body should be three or four paragraphs in length. Each paragraph should outline one idea or discuss one topic. The reader should be able to see that your essay has a clear plan, with each paragraph adding to your argument. If you are asked to answer more than one question, at least one paragraph should be used to answer each question.

Each paragraph in the main body should have a topic sentence. This sentence explains the main point of the paragraph. The rest of the paragraph is made up of supporting evidence and examples. The topic sentence is usually the first sentence. The paragraph will often finish with either a concluding sentence or a lead in to the next paragraph.

Conclusion

The conclusion does not contain new information. It summarises the main point of the essay and repeats your opinion.

Example

> *Every year thousands of students go overseas to study. Although many benefit from the experience, others go home disappointed.*
>
> *What are the benefits and drawbacks of studying in another country?*
>
> Give reasons for your answer and include any relevant examples from your own knowledge or experience.

For the question above, the essay plan might look like this.

Introduction

Studying abroad: very popular; advantages and disadvantages
However, I believe the benefits outweigh …

Paragraph 1

Expensive but:

– a good long-term investment / better job with foreign qualification
– studying abroad teaches you new ways of doing things
– gives you a wider knowledge of your subject

Paragraph 2

Easier to study at home, no language problems but:

– mastering a foreign language is a useful career tool
– gain understanding of foreign culture

Paragraph 3

Culture shock and homesickness but:

– education doesn't only take place in the classroom
– better understanding of people and life
– more self-confidence from living outside your culture
– valuable experience of life

Conclusion

Studying abroad is better both for career and personal development.

Exercise 33 is designed to guide you step by step through the essay writing process. Remember: every sentence needs to contribute to your argument. There should be no sentences that only give background or irrelevant information to the topic.

Exercise 33 Writing your essay

You are given the following task.

> Living much longer in the future will be of great benefit to everyone.
>
> To what extent do you agree with this statement?

This task asks you to say how much you agree with the statement. This means that you should discuss the arguments about the topic and give your opinion. You may agree or disagree.

Brainstorming

There are two aspects to this task, which you should address in your essay:

▼   How could living much longer be of benefit to people?

▼   Will it be of benefit to everyone?

Using these two questions, brainstorm ideas for your answer.

Introduction

In your introduction you will restate what you are writing about (in other words, you will paraphrase the question) and give your opinion on the issue.

Write an introduction for this topic.

The main body

This paragraph is going to discuss the advantages of living much longer. Put the sentences below in the correct order to form a paragraph.

a   However, today many people can expect to live to 80.

b   Therefore, the longer people live the more interesting life will become.

c   In the past, the average life expectancy was less than 70.

d   Today, it is not uncommon for people to live to see their great-grandchildren.

e   The opportunity for generations to share experiences and learn from each other is of benefit to everyone.

The next paragraph's topic sentence is:

Many people believe they would be able to accomplish more if they lived longer.

Use your own ideas to support this topic sentence.

The fourth paragraph is about the disadvantages of living longer. The following ideas were brainstormed:

▼   quality of life

▼   living longer only of use if healthy

continued ▶

- ▼ overpopulation and limited resources
- ▼ possible aging population
- ▼ lack of opportunities for young
- ▼ benefit to everyone?

Use these ideas to write the paragraph.

Conclusion

Finally, write a conclusion using the main ideas from your essay. Your conclusion should not contain new ideas.

When you have finished, check the answer key for a suggested response to the task.

Exercise 34 Writing your essay

For further essay-writing practice, look at the essay plan on page 174 and write the essay. Check the answer key for a suggested response.

Keeping your writing on topic

In a Task 2 essay, it is essential to recognise the type (genre) of response the task requires and to plan your answer accordingly. The sample essay below does not answer the question. What problems can you identify with it?

Exercise 35 Writing your essay

Read the response to the task below and identify any problems. When you have finished, read the comments on the response in the answer key.

> As the population of the world is growing very quickly, the only long-term solution to the problem of overpopulation is for humans to settle other planets.
>
> What benefits has the world got from space exploration?
> Do you think humans will ever live on other planets?

Nowadays the topic of space exploration has become a controversial issue. In this era of globalisation the population of the world is growing and many people think that space exploration has some benefits. Other people believe that space exploration is too expensive. This essay will discuss the advantages and disadvantages of space exploration and whether human beings will live on other planets.

It is well known that humans landed on the Moon in 1969 and that governments have talked about sending further space missions to Mars and even planets further away. However, space technology is very expensive and it will cost lots of money to finance any further space travel. Furthermore, it takes a long time to travel through space and it is very dangerous. Many astronauts have been killed when their rockets blew up while travelling through space.

One solution for overpopulation would be to colonise other planets. It may be possible to find a planet that replicates the conditions of Earth. If such a planet can be found, it would be a solution to overpopulation. On the other hand, colonisation may lead to the destruction of the local people and them being turned into slaves in the same way that European countries colonised the rest of the world from the seventeenth to the nineteenth centuries.

Overall, there are many benefits to space travel and it seems inevitable that mankind will colonise other planets.

The question does not ask you to discuss the disadvantages of space travel – just the benefits. Furthermore, the question simply asks *if* humans will live on other planets; it does not ask about the consequences of humans living on other planets.

Here is a plan for a better response to the task given in Exercise 35. Using this structure, write an essay of your own on this topic. When you have finished, check the answer key for a sample response that answers the question and stays on topic.

Introduction
Benefits of space travel and living on other planets
Position

Benefit of space travel 1
Space research develops products that can be used on Earth
Improved computer technology
Heat-resistant material
Ways of living in different conditions

Benefit of space travel 2
Discoveries about the universe
Possibility of life on another planet?
Resources

Problems of establishing a colony
Distance/cost
Inhospitality of nearby planets
Life on another planet?

Possibilities of living on another planet
Maybe necessary because of overpopulation
Technology improving all the time
It would take a world effort
Maybe it will happen but not for a long time

Conclusion
Summary of benefits
Humans may live on other planets but not in near future

Cause and effect essays

So far we have been looking at essays that ask you to give an opinion or make a judgment on an issue. It is also possible that you will be asked to write an essay discussing cause and effect. This type of question asks the reason why something has happened or what would happen if a course of action was followed.

Example

> **Many people leave their homes in the countryside to live in large cities.**
>
> What factors make people want to move to the city? How realistic is it to control the numbers of people moving to the city?

In the task above you are asked to answer two questions. The first question asks you to give reasons why people wish to move to the city. The second question asks you to give your opinion on whether people can be stopped from moving to the city.

The structure for this essay could be:

Introduction
Number of reasons why people leave the countryside
Is/Isn't realistic to control the number of people living in the countryside

Cause 1
Reason why this is an important factor

Cause 2
Reason why this is an important factor

Possibility of controlling the number of people moving to the city
Why realistic or not realistic

Conclusion
Summary of main causes and possibility of controlling people's movements

Exercise 37   Cause and effect essays

Expand the plan above using your own ideas, and then use this to write an essay responding to the task. When you have finished, check the answer key for a sample response.

Organising your ideas logically

In Task 2, as in Task 1, the second criterion is **coherence and cohesion**. You must organise your ideas clearly and logically to obtain a good band score. Follow the advice below to fulfil the coherence and cohesion criteria.

Paragraphs

If you do not divide your essay into paragraphs, you will not get more than a band 5 for 'coherence and cohesion'. Your response should be divided into paragraphs logically; this means that each paragraph contains one idea and that the rest of the paragraph is used to explain that idea.

Every paragraph should contain one idea, expressed the topic sentence, which is usually the first sentence. A good topic sentence contains two parts:

▼ the subject

▼ the controlling idea.

For example:

> It is often said that large sporting competitions such as the World Cup or the Olympic Games are a substitute for war.

The subject is 'large sporting competitions such as the World Cup or the Olympic Games' and the controlling idea is that they are a 'substitute for war'.

The rest of the paragraph contains ideas and examples which explain and justify the idea expressed in the topic sentence. This can be done by giving reasons for your viewpoint and by giving examples of what you mean.

One of the signs of a good Task 2 answer is that each sentence has a clear purpose and helps to progress the argument. In other words there should be no sentences that are just used to complete the word limit.

Example

Explanation of topic sentence

Example of importance of sporting competitions

In the past, countries promoted nationalism through their armies; now nationalism is generated by sporting achievement. For this reason, countries such as Australia are prepared to spend large amounts of money to train athletes to be successful in sporting competitions. Moreover, international teams' achievements are discussed and analysed in newspapers and on the television. There are a number of advantages and disadvantages to this.

Further example

Leads into the next paragraph

Exercise 38 Paragraphs

1   What order should the following sentences go in to form a paragraph? Write the letters of the sentences to indicate the order that would be most effective.

....

A   Perhaps the main reason people don't travel around the world is that they are scared of the unknown.

B   Furthermore, as you get older it becomes more difficult to travel for long periods of time.

C   Most people would like to travel around the world but not many people actually do it.

D   Everyone worries about how they will find work or be able to make a living.

E   Therefore it is probably better to travel when you are young.

F   This is because you get extra responsibilities such as families, mortgages and jobs.

2   Identify the topic and the controlling idea in each paragraphs below.

a   Men and women have totally different attitudes to shopping. Many women enjoy browsing through shops comparing prices and quality of products. Men, on the other hand, often know exactly what they are going to buy and are only interested in getting in and out of the shops as quickly as possible.

....

b   Perhaps Australia's biggest problem today is a lack of fresh water. Increased use of water in homes and industry, coupled with years of drought, has meant that many cities have had to introduce water restrictions. This problem is likely to get worse as a rising population demands more water.

....

c   In the next hundred years, the world's oil reserves are likely to run out. It is therefore important that new sources of energy are found. One possibility would be nuclear power. However, the dangers of explosions or radiation leaks stop it from being the perfect solution. There are other sustainable energy sources such as solar, hydroelectric and wind power but these also have disadvantages.

....

3   Write suitable topic sentences for the following paragraphs. When you have finished, check the answer key for sample answers.

a   ....

First, English is important, as it is the most popular language in the world. Although Mandarin Chinese may have more speakers than English, English is the most popular second language. Therefore, if a Chinese speaker meets an Italian they will probably communicate using English. Second, English is the language most used for trade,

continued ▶

navigation, flight and many other specialist subjects, so for many jobs knowledge of English is essential.

b ....

People see their favourite celebrities as having the personal qualities and lifestyle they want for themselves. This identification takes the form of collecting memorabilia and following their hero's career in the media. In many cases fans follow their heroes because they believe under different circumstances they would be like them. This identification is usually harmless but sometimes it can lead to a more sinister trend.

c ....

First, you could get a job such as lawyer or politician, which pays a lot of money. Of course becoming rich is a lot easier if you have a special talent, such as being able to play a sport well, sing or act. Another possibility would be to start up your own business. However, this is risky, as many more businesses fail than succeed. Finally, you could always win the lottery or have a big win at the casino, but again the chances of this happening are small.

Following a logical structure

It is important that your essay has a structure that is easy for the reader to follow. This means that your argument progresses to your conclusion and that your conclusion is supported by the rest of the essay.

It is a good idea to plan your essay in advance. Exercises 19 and 20 give you practice at planning a logical paragraph structure for your essay.

Exercise 39 Following a logical structure

Below is a plan for an essay on the topic of studying history. The candidate has made notes for four paragraphs. Use these to write the final essay. When you have finished, check the answer key for a sample response.

1   There are a number of reasons why people say that the study of history has little purpose.
    The world is changing very quickly:
    – technology: Internet, robotics, more countries with nuclear weapons
    – new power centres: in the past US/Russia, now US/terrorist attacks
    – therefore past events not relevant
2   It can also be argued that by examining the past we can understand the present.
    Past events: explain alliances/attitudes of countries
    Example: the link between World War I and World War II
    No resolution to problems without understanding past

3 A further reason for studying history is that history is strongly linked to people's culture. Give your own examples.

4 In conclusion, although history may seem irrelevant, it explains the forces that made today's world.

Below, you are given sentences that belong to an essay responding to this task:

> Hunting animals is one of mankind's earliest instincts and, therefore, should not be restricted.
>
> To what extent do you agree with this opinion?

Fit the sentences in the correct order into the essay plan below.

A While many people rely on animal products for food and clothing, it is hard to justify killing animals for our enjoyment when their deaths serve no useful purpose.

B In Australia an example of this would be the Tasmanian tiger, which was hunted to extinction in the 1930s.

C Hunting for food may be an instinct but this does not extend to hunting for pleasure.

D It is in the hunter's interest to make sure that large numbers of animals survive and that their natural habitat is preserved so they can continue to enjoy their sport.

E Others believe all life is sacred and should only be sacrificed if absolutely necessary.

F However, today hunting usually involves high-velocity weapons, which kill from such a distance that the animal doesn't even know the hunter is there.

G However, in the past over-hunting has caused many animals to become extinct.

H Therefore, we have the right to decide whether animals live or die.

I Furthermore in those days, there was always a chance that the animal would escape, which made the chase more exciting.

J This may have been true when early humans hunted, as hunting was necessary for survival.

Introduction

Many people believe that they have the right to hunt animals for their pleasure.

Sentence: ....

Paragraph 1

It is often felt that human life is more valuable than animal life.

Sentence 1: ....　　Sentence 2: ....

Paragraph 2

Hunters argue that their 'sport' ensures the survival of the species.

Sentence 1: ....　　Sentence 2: ....　　Sentence 3: ....

Conclusion

Hunters often say that nothing matches the excitement of the chase and that hunting is one of humankind's first instincts.

Sentence 1: ....　　Sentence 2: ....　　Sentence 3: ....　　Sentence 4: ....

Linking your ideas

Although each paragraph should express a separate idea, your paragraphs and ideas also need to link logically to one another. This means ordering your ideas so that they flow from one to another in a way the reader can easily follow. You can do this, for instance, by ending a paragraph with a concluding sentence that leads into the topic of the next paragraph.

Just as your paragraphs need to be linked together, so do your sentences, so that your answer reads smoothly. To do this, you can use linking words of time, cause and effect, or contrast, among others.

One of the criteria for cohesion and coherence is the ability to use devices to link sentences together. Ideas can be linked together using the following sorts of linking words:

Adding information	Cause and effect	Effect and cause	Contrast	Alternatives	Ordering
Start of a sentence					
In addition Moreover Furthermore What is more	Therefore Consequently As a result	Owing to Due to As Since Because of For this reason	In contrast However Although Nevertheless In spite of Despite		First Second Finally Meanwhile During As soon as Then
Middle of a sentence					
and also not only … but also as well as	so	because	but namely for example for instance	either … or neither … nor	before after when while
End of a sentence					
too			for example for instance		

1 Fill in the gaps in the paragraph using an appropriate word or phrase from the box below.

either	also	or	first
which	finally		in addition

It is quite easy to write a paragraph in English. **a** ....
you should think of a good topic sentence, **b** ....
summarises your main idea. **c** ...., you should think of
reasons to support your topic sentence. You may **d** ....
want to give examples to support your ideas. **e** .... the
last sentence should **f** .... lead into the next paragraph
g .... act as a summary.

2 Complete the gaps in the following sentences with appropriate linking words.

a .... it is true that many cities are dangerous, the world is
probably a safer place than before.

b Biofuels are a threat to food security .... land that would
be used to grow food is used to grow crops that can be used as fuel.

c .... more land is used to grow crops for fuel, the amount
of food that can be grown is reduced.

d It is .... overeating that is causing the increase in child
obesity .... a much more sedentary lifestyle.

e The demand for fresh fish has grown significantly, ...
many food fish are becoming increasingly rare.

f .... the last ten years, the number of students studying
overseas has increased dramatically.

continued ▶

3 Choose appropriate linking words from the table to complete the Task 2 answer below.

Paragraph 1	Paragraph 2	Paragraph 3	Paragraph 4
but also	furthermore	if	while
in spite of	when	and	in conclusion
in addition	whereas	first	therefore
not only	rather	once	
because		second	
and			

> In spite of major traffic jams and pollution problems, large numbers of people continue to travel by private car to travel in the city.
>
> Why do people continue to drive in the city? How can people be encouraged to leave their car at home?

In many of the world's cities traffic is a major problem. **a** .... does traffic congestion cause great frustration among drivers **b** ....
it **c** .... increases the length of each journey.

d .... the environment in the city is seriously affected by exhaust emissions. **e** .... this situation people drive in the city
f .... it is more convenient **g** .... less time-consuming than the alternatives. People can only be encouraged to change their driving habits by making the alternatives better.

Often people drive in the city because the public transport system is underfunded and inconvenient. Most people prefer to stay in their air-conditioned cars **h** .... than travel in overcrowded buses and trains.
i ...., **j** .... people travel in their own car, they travel door to door. **k** .... when people travel by public transport they often have to change buses or trains, which adds time to their journey.

There are two ways to encourage people to stop driving in the city.
l ...., public transport needs to be improved. People will only leave their cars at home **m** .... the alternative is cheap and comfortable.
n ...., driving in the city needs to be made less convenient. This can be achieved by making parking more expensive **o** .... charging a tax

for travelling in the city. **p** .... people feel public transport is a better choice, they will use it.

q .... people will continue to use their cars **r** .... it is convenient. **s** ...., driving should be made more expensive and the money used to improve public transport.

Referencing

Referencing is when a writer substitutes a noun or a noun phrase that has already been used with a pronoun. The purpose of this is to stop the writing becoming repetitive. For example:

Genetically modified food sources are becoming more commonly used worldwide. *They* provide an opportunity to increase crop yields.

In the second sentence, 'genetically modified food sources' has been replaced by *They*.

If the subject (noun or noun phrase) is singular, it will be replaced by *he*, *she* or *it*. For example:

Manipulating plant genes may make plants more resistant to disease. However, *it* could also influence the genetic structure of people eating those plants.

In this case 'Manipulating plants genes' was replaced by *it* in the second sentence.

Exercise 41 Referencing

Make the paragraph below read more fluently by replacing the nouns and noun phrases with pronouns.

Scientists have long been worried by the ability of genetically modified plants to cross-fertilise. Scientists believe that bees and other pollen-collecting insects may transfer the modified DNA to other plants. As bees and other pollen collecting insects visit a number of different types of plant, in bees' and other pollen-collecting insects' quest to make honey, bees and other pollen-collecting insects spread genetically modified genes. The spreading of new genes means that modifying one plant may affect a wide range of life forms.

....

....

....

....

....

In the response below there are a number of coherence and cohesion mistakes. Identify and correct these mistakes.

> Every country has poor people and every country has different ways of dealing with the poor.
>
> What are some of the reasons for world poverty? What can we do to help the poor?

Although vast differences in wealth between countries, there are poor people everywhere. This essay will discuss some of the reasons for this poverty and what can be done to prevent it.

It is important to say there is no single reason for poverty. In developing countries, war and debts to wealthy nations make this inevitable that many people will struggle to survive. However, It is certainly not the case in wealthier nations for example the USA. The causes of poverty in these nations range from poor education to downsizing in major corporations. Even in developed countries, governments accept that there will always be unemployment and that life will be hard for people at the lower end of the economic scale.

Just as the causes of poverty are often unclear, there is no single solution. But, world peace would mean countries would be able to concentrate on improving their citizen's lives instead spending money on arms. Another way to raise living standards would be for wealthy nations to cancel Third World debt. Wealthy nations cancelling Third World debt would allow developing countries to use the money saved to reduce poverty.

In wealthier countries, governments need to consider how wealth is divided. It is not enough to keep creating more and more money, unless this money only goes to support people who are already rich. Governments have a responsibility to protect all citizens not just them with important positions in society.

In conclusion, there are a number of causes of poverty and when there isn't an easy way to improve living standards, stopping war and dividing wealth more equally would certainly help.

Using appropriate vocabulary

The third marking criterion for Task 2 is **lexical resource**. To get a good score in Task 2 your answer should use a variety of task-specific vocabulary accurately. You will get a higher band score if you attempt to use sophisticated vocabulary than if you only use simple language that you know is correct.

In order to get a high band score in this area, it is necessary to demonstrate an understanding of writing style. This means that your writing should avoid using slang or overly simplistic language. However, you will not get marked down for using the first person (*I*).

You should also try to avoid making errors in word formation, collocation and spelling.

You may want to keep your own word list linked to topics that may occur in the Task 2 writing.

The academic word list

One method of building up your vocabulary is to learn and practise using the academic word list. This list was compiled by Averil Coxhead at the Victoria University of Wellington, New Zealand and is made up of the 570 most frequently used words in academic English. There are websites with practice exercises for these words online. Although these words are especially used in academic English, they are also useful for the General Training module.

Exercise 43 Using appropriate vocabulary

1 Complete the sentences below using the words in the box. You may need to change the form of the word.

sector	economy	beneficial
finance	derive	variables

The **a** .... crash of 2008 badly damaged the reputation of the

b .... **c** .... It had been thought that

the banks had safeguarded their interests. However, it became apparent that they

had not taken all the **d** .... into account. Bank CEOs were paid

vast bonuses for short-term gain without **e** .... long-term

f .... to the company.

continued ▶

2 Complete the sentences below using the words in the box. You may need to change the form of the word.

data	methodical	analyse	environment
basic	context	research	

Climate change deniers claim that the **a** .... of collecting

b .... on global warming is flawed. Therefore, they believe that

climate change is **c** .... on assumptions that may or not be true.

On the other hand, many scientists claim that the **d** .... has

been taken out of **e** .... and that **f** ....

of the facts indicates a possible **g** .... disaster.

3 Complete the sentences below using the words in the box. You may need to change the form of the word.

evidence	process	assume	legal	principle

Often criminals are released because of a **a** .... error or

lack of **b** .... However, the **c** ....

system **d** .... innocence until proven guilty. This

e .... states that it is better for a guilty man to go free than an

innocent man to be jailed.

4 Complete the sentences below using the words in the box. You may need to change the form of the word.

issue	major	flexible	labour
significant	occur	income	employees

One of the **a** .... **b** ....

affecting employment today is the need for **c** .... in the

d .... market. This has **e** ....

because there has been a **f** .... shift in work patterns.

Many **g** .... now work on a casual basis and so only get an

h .... for the hours they work with no sick pay or holiday pay.

Collocations

Collocation is the name for words that usually appear together in the English language. It is useful to know some of these collocating words, as it helps to make your writing more fluent. One kind of collocation is nouns or verbs that are frequently accompanied by particular prepositions.

Exercise 44 Collocations

Complete the sentences below with a suitable word.

The distribution **1** .... (*preposition*) the world's resources

is concentrated in a few hands. One interpretation **2** ....

(*preposition*) international politics is that it is an attempt to preserve the wealth

and influence **3** .... (*preposition*) a political elite. In response

4 .... (*preposition*) this it could be argued that the standard

5 .... (*preposition*, *gerund*) has improved radically over the past

hundred years.

Exercise 45 Word groups

Find words that mean the same as the words in brackets in the box below. The words usually are found next to either the word before or the word after.

major	practice	assets	transformed	wealth
crisis	high	individual	compromises	gradual
share	compulsory	unrest	sacrificing	

When governments have tried to redistribute **1** .... (*money*), they

have often faced a constitutional **2** .... (*major problem*). This is

continued ▶

because it is hard to act in the interests of the majority without violating the rights of the

3 .... (*one person*). Although the government may start off with

4 .... (*good/worthy*) principles it has proved impossible to put them

into **5** .... (*make into reality*).

One way governments have tried to **6** .... (*divide*)

wealth is the **7** .... (*no choice*) acquisition of property.

Often this has failed because the transfer of **8** ....

(*things of value*) has caused civil **9** .... (*disturbance*). Most

governments that have **10** .... (*changed*) society have relied

on **11** .... (*slow*) change. In conclusion it is difficult for a

government to undertake **12** .... (*large*) change without

13 .... its ideals or making **14** .... (*deals*).

Word forms

Most commonly used words have a distinct root form and a changeable ending depending on their part of speech – for instance, noun, verb, adjective or adverb.

It is useful to know patterns in English word formation. For example:

▼ many nouns end in *–tion* or *-ty*

▼ many adjectives end in *-al*

▼ many adverbs end in *-aly*.

Some families of words do not have a form for a particular function. For instance, they may not have an adverb form.

1   Complete the following table of words commonly found in academic essays. Put a cross if there is no form for that word family.

Noun	Verb	Adjective	Adverb
authority		authoritarian	x
compensation			x
	to convene		
dimension	x		
	x	distinct / distinctive	
		energetic	
emphasis			
	to evaluate		x
function			
	to hypothesise		
institution			institutionally
		legislative	
	to mechanise		
		negative	
	to occur		x
potential	x		
			regionally
	to signify		
similarity	x		
			strategically
	to textualise		x
technique	x		

continued ▶

2 The words below are all commonly used in Task 2 essays and are often misspelt. Choose the correct spelling.

acess	acces	access
analise	analyze	analyse
assessment	assesment	asessment
business	buisness	busines
categary	catagory	category
consequences	consiquences	consequenses
constitusion	constitution	constution
critisism	critcism	criticism
defanate	definite	defanite
distrebution	distribusion	distribution
environment	enviroment	enviromen
explenation	explanation	ecsplanation
facilitate	faciletate	facilatate
fundimental	fundermental	fundamental
guarantee	gurantee	gaurantee
implication	implicasion	implicetion
interpritation	interpretation	interpratation
justafication	justification	justifacation
maintanance	maintenance	maintenence
modem	moden	moderm
necessary	nessecary	necesary
philosaphy	philosothy	philosophy
procedure	prosedure	precedure
proporsion	preportion	proportion
prosess	prosses	process
psycology	psychology	phsycology
recuired	reccuired	required
separate	seperate	separite
similer	simalar	similar
suficient	sufficient	suffcent
technical	tecnichal	technichal
vertion	version	vurtion

3   Correct the spelling mistakes and errors in word form in the essay below.

> Every government has a duty to provide free health care for its people.
> What are the advantages and disadvantages of governments providing free health care?

In some countries, free health care is accepted as a basic right and is provided to all citizens, regardless of income. However, in other countries people must pay for their health care. I believe that free health care should be avaliable to everyone.

The main argument against free health care is that medical treatment is expensive. Doctor's are high paid professionals and hospital care is expensive. Therefore, the people who use the health system should be the ones who pay for it. Furthermore, it is argued that medical costs need to be passed on to the consumption so that money can be made available for research.

I disagree with this point of view for two reasons. First the people who need the health sistem most are the people who are most sick. People who are sick are likely to be poor because they are unable to work or are freqently absent from work. Second, taxes are payed to the government so they will support people in times of need. If the government is unwilling to pay for essensials like healthy and education, there seems little reason to pay taxes.

Furthermore, if people are asked to pay for their own health care, like in America, the poor inevitable suffer. There have been many storys of people being turned away from hospitals because they have no insurance. Moreover, insurance companies encouraging doctors to prescribe the cheapest and not necessary the best treatment in order to increase their profits. This has led to the situation where people are not given the treatment they need because their insurance policy does not cover it. When health becomes business, quality declines and the poor suffer.

In conclusion free medicine treatment is the only way to ensure that quality health care is provided for everyone and not just the very rich.

Using a range of grammar features accurately

The final marking criterion for Task 2 is **grammatical range and accuracy**. You are required to use a wide range of grammatical structures accurately in Task 2. It is not enough simply to write an answer that has no mistakes. You need to demonstrate that you can write both simple and complex sentences accurately.

Complex sentences are ones containing one or more relative clause.

It is better to make a few mistakes attempting to write complex sentences than to write perfect simple sentences throughout your essay.

Relative clauses

There are two types of relative clause: defining relative clauses and non-defining relative clauses.

Defining relative clauses

Defining relative clauses give essential information that identifies or *defines* the subject of the sentence.

> ### Examples
>
> Delegates came from around the world. However, the delegates *who came from Pacific Island nations* were particularly concerned about the effects of global warming in their countries.
>
> The delegates *who came from Pacific Island nations* were concerned...

The relative clause 'who came from Pacific Island nations' answers the question: *which* delegates were concerned about the effects of global warming? Therefore, the clause is defining the group of people concerned and is essential to the meaning of the sentence.

> ### Example
>
> Global warming is a phenomenon which/that is caused by increased carbon emissions.

The clause 'which (or that) is caused by increased carbon emissions' is essential to the meaning of the sentence. 'Global warming is a phenomenon' is a grammatically correct sentence but it is meaningless.

Defining relative clauses do not need commas, and they can begin with either *which* or *that*.

Non-defining relative clauses

Non-defining relative clauses add extra information.

The 2010 summit on climate change, *which was held in Copenhagen*, was generally regarded as unsuccessful.

In this example, 'which was held in Copenhagen' is a non-defining relative clause because it can be removed from the sentence without changing the structure:

The 2010 summit on climate change was generally regarded as unsuccessful.

This is a meaningful sentence without the sub-clause. To show that it is not essential to the meaning of the sentence, a non-defining relative clause is surrounded by commas. It can only begin with *which*, never *that*.

The use of pronouns to join relative clauses

Who is used to join sentences when the repeated information is a person. For example:

Tony Blair, *who* was prime minister at the time, took Britain into the war in Iraq.

Where is used to join sentences when the repeated information is an event (such as the Olympic Games). It is also used when the repeated information is a place (such as the Great Wall of China) and it would otherwise be repeated with a preposition.

The World Cup finals, *where* 32 countries compete from all round the world, are probably the most popular international sporting event.
The Tower of London, *where* the Crown Jewels are kept, is a popular tourist attraction.

In the second example above, the two sentences being joined are

The Tower of London is a popular tourist attraction.

and

The Crown Jewels are kept *in* the Tower of London.

Because the preposition *in* is used in the second sentence, we use *where*.

Which is used to join sentences when the repeated information is an object or a place when there is no preposition with the noun.

The Internet, *which* was first invented in the 1960s, has become part of everyday life.
The Tower of London, *which* was first built in the eleventh century, has fulfilled many roles.

Match and combine the three parts of the clauses below to form defining relative clauses.

Subject	Object	Definition
Culture shock	an institution	prepares people for life.
The United Nations	a person	countries can discuss their problems.
An ambassador	an institution	water is used to generate electricity.
A barrister	a place	affects overseas students.
A school	a problem	represents clients in court.
A hydroelectric dam	a lawyer	represents a country abroad.

1 ....

2 ....

3 ....

4 ....

5 ....

6 ....

Use relative clauses to combine the following sentences.

7 The world climate change summit was held in Copenhagen in 2009. The world climate change summit was designed to reach an agreement to replace the Kyoto agreement. The Kyoto agreement expires in 2012.

....

....

8 Scientists have spent many years studying global warming. Scientists stated that the agreement at this conference was vital for the world's future.

....

....

9 However, economists state that action could badly damage the economy. Action might not even help control climate change.

....

....

10 The conference eventually reached an agreement. The agreement made recommendations but did not compel countries to act.

....

....

Unmarked clauses

Not all clauses are marked with pronouns such as *which* or *who*. Other clauses are recognised by the fact that they can function as a sentence on their own. In other words they have a subject and a verb.

These clauses are recognised by their function. For example:

Modern communication techniques have meant that *more information is shared around the world than ever before.*

The second (italicised) part of this sentence could be a sentence in its own right, but here it is a sub-clause. This relationship is shown by the use of *that*. In the case the sub-clause describes the effect of modern communications.

Here is another example.

Globalisation has also reinforced the isolation *felt by some ethnic groups.*

In this case the italicised clause is describing the isolation. It could be written 'which is felt by some ethnic groups', but it is not necessary to use *which is* here because the subject of the clause is not the subject of the main sentence (*globalisation*) but the object (*isolation*).

Exercise 48   Relative clauses

Decide if the following sentences from a Task 2 essay contain relative clauses, and whether the relative clauses are correct. Correct any incorrect relative clauses in the space below.

1   This isolation is felt particularly by older people, who find it more difficult to adapt to cultural changes.
2   Most people find traditions with which they grow up difficult to change.
3   However, younger people tend not to have the same respect for tradition.
4   Therefore, it is usually the young become influenced by a more global culture.
5   This can cause a generation gap makes it difficult for young and older people to understand each other.
6   Some young people also find it difficult to adapt to a culture that is far removed from their own.
7   They have lost touch with their own culture, which seems to offer them little of interest.
8   In some cases this has resulted in people becoming disconnected from their society and joining organisations are promote extremism.

....

....

....

....

continued ▶

....
....
....
....
....
....
....
....
....
....

Conditionals

Although there are three main types of conditional, it is likely that you will only need to use the first two types in your writing for Task 2. These are explained below.

First conditional

The first conditional is made up of two clauses. The first clause may begin with *if*, *unless* or *when* and it is written in the present tense. The second clause is written in the future tense, using *will*.

Examples

> *If* the price of mobile phones continues to fall, most people will not use landlines.
>
> *Unless* we stop destroying the rainforest, many animals will become extinct.
>
> *When* oil supplies run out, the world will have to look for another source of energy.

The first conditional with *if* is used when predicting the result of a future action. It shows that the author considers the proposed event (in the case above, the price of mobile phones continuing to fall) is likely to occur, and it tells what the consequences of the event will be (people not using landlines).

First conditional sentences using *unless* are a negative form of *if*. They are used to express what will happen if an action is *not* taken.

First conditional sentences using *when* show that the writer considers the situation inevitable. They tell what the writer believes will happen in the future when this event occurs.

Second conditional

The second conditional is made up of two clauses. The first clause begins with *if* and is written in the past tense. The second clause is made up of *would* and an infinitive without *to*.

The second conditional is used to show the consequences of an event that the writer believes is very unlikely to happen or impossible.

Examples

If life is found on another planet, people would have to change their view of the world.

If humans developed a second head, they would constantly argue with themselves.

Exercise 49 | Conditionals

1 Complete the following first conditional sentences, using your own ideas.

a If unemployment rises to 30%, ...

....

b Unless the government cuts spending, ...

....

c If the polar ice cap melts, ...

....

d If the world's population continues to rise, ...

....

e If drugs were made legal, ...

....

f Unless advertising of fast food is controlled, ...

....

g When the sea levels rise, ...

....

h When I pass my IELTS test, ...

....

2 Complete the following second-conditional sentences, using your own ideas.

a If the world's population reached ten billion, ...

....

b If the world ran out of natural drinking water, ...

.... continued ▶

c If man settled on another planet, ...

....

d If a new fuel was discovered, ...

....

e If people were not allowed to marry till they were thirty, ...

....

f If people only worked three days a week, ...

....

g If the government limited the amount of money people were allowed to earn, ...

....

h If everybody looked the same, ...

....

3 Complete the conditional sentences in this part of a Task 2 essay.

Record companies argue that if the public continues to download music from the Internet, actors and musicians **a** .... *(to make) any money and so there* **b** .... *(be) any new music. This argument is false because most of the music downloaded is from established artists who have already made millions from their releases. New artists rarely make money from their releases as more than 90% of the royalties go to the record company.*

Even if it **c** .... *(to be) desirable, it would seem unlikely that record companies* **d** .... *(to be able) to control the Internet. Therefore, unless companies want to become irrelevant, they* **e** .... (have) to find different ways of making money through music.*

One way music companies are making money through copyright is through preventing the borrowing of existing songs. Record companies are very quick to chase performance rights on their products. Recently a musician was sued for borrowing part of a song that was 70 years old and the original artist long dead. If companies **f** .... *(to allow) to pursue money in this way, they themselves* **g** .... *(to prevent) the creation of new music. If people can't use a series of notes without worrying about outside influences, they* **h** .... *(to probably stop) writing music.*

Editing your work

After you have finished, it is important to spend a few minutes checking your writing for both Task 1 and Task 2 for errors. The following areas are common sources of mistakes:

▼ tense

▼ punctuation

▼ word formation

▼ subject–verb agreement

Tense

Exercise 50 is designed to help you detect and correct mistakes in tense.

Exercise 50   Editing your work (tense)

The writer of this essay has made ten mistakes concerning tense. Find and correct the mistakes.

> It is the parents' responsibility and not the schools' to teach children moral values. Who is most responsible for children's moral education and what is the best way to teach right from wrong?

Both parents and schools had a major influence on a child's upbringing and so both have a role to play in the moral education of children. However, there is no easy answer as to the best method of educating children.

As parents are the first influence on children, they are the first example from which children learn. It is not only what a school teaches that is important, it is also the example that the parents set. If parents lie to their children, it is not surprising if the children also lie.

School is also a major influence on a child's life. The culture of a school will help to establish forms of behaviour. For example, if a child sees students behaving badly, they likely copied this behaviour. In other words, it is often not the school that influences the students but the child's friends.

There is no perfect way to teach right from wrong. Every child is different and responds to different methods. However, there is some ways that are more successful than others. First, it is very important to be consistent. If a child is told not to do something one day and allow to do it the next, the child will becoming confused. Second,

continued ▶

> *children will copy the behaviour of others so if a child constantly exposes to bad behaviour, it is not surprising if he/she behaves badly.*
>
> *Both school and home were important influences on a child. Children learn most from the standards that are acceptable where they grew up.*

Punctuation

Sentences

A sentence is a thought. It is a piece of information that stands alone. It has a subject and a verb. Look at this text:

> Although great advances are being made in information technology, such as the increased power of the Internet and the possibilities of instant communication with people on the other side of the world.

This is not a sentence, as the thought is not complete. The sentence starts *Although* and so should consist of two parts: a proposition and a contrasting conclusion. In this sentence, there is no conclusion. To make a sentence it would need to read something like:

> Although great advances are being made in information technology, such as the increased power of the Internet and the possibilities of instant communication with people on the other side of the world, the opportunities this provides are not open to everyone.

All sentences start with a capital letter and end with a full stop.

Commas

Commas are used to separate out information within a sentence and to make your writing read more easily. In particular, commas are used to distinguish supporting information from the main ideas of a sentence or to divide the two parts of a sentence. They are also used when linking two separate sentences joined by linking words such as *and*, *but* and *so*. For example:

> During a time of inflation, salaries increase but money buys less.

Commas are used to separate items in lists.

> Computers are used extensively in government, commerce, education, medicine, security, aviation and the domestic sphere.

Commas are also used to distinguish non-essential information in clauses.

The tsunami, which took place in 2004, caused great loss of life.

In the first two examples the commas separate the subordinate first sentence with the main clause of the sentence. In the third example, commas are used to separate the first and second item in a list of three.

Exercise 51   Editing your work (punctuation)

Add punctuation to the paragraph below to make it read more easily.

many governments believe that being 'tough on crime' and imprisoning a large number of people is an effective deterrent however there is evidence to suggest that a large percentage of people jailed have mental health issues or are addicted to drugs or alcohol in this case unless their underlying problems are addressed many offenders are likely to reoffend soon after leaving jail it may be that providing education bigger mental health budgets and more help available for addicts are better solutions to rising crime rates than locking people up

Word formation

Exercise 52 is designed to help you detect and correct mistakes in word formation.

Exercise 52   Editing your work (word formation)

Correct the errors in word formation in the paragraphs below. There are eight errors.

Since the 1950s, advertising has moved away from the direct sales of a product to the selling of a dream. Advertisements concentrate on perception lifestyle benefits rather than the product itself. For this reason car advertisements often show attractive girls or jealous neighbours to make potentially consumers reflect on how a new car might change their lives.

A further advertising technicality is to establish brand loyal. A certain brand of clothes is seen as excluding and so it establishes a niche market. Consequence, people develop brand loyalty as it helps to definitive their opinion of themselves. Often these 'exclusive' brands are little different from other products half the price.

Subject–verb agreement

Exercise 53 is designed to help you detect and correct mistakes in subject–verb agreement.

Exercise 53 Editing your work (subject-verb agreement)

Correct the errors in subject-verb agreement in the paragraphs below. There are five errors.

The danger of these types of advertising are it encourages a lifestyle that people cannot afford. If people links happiness to what they own, they will constantly buy new things. While this are good for companies' bottom lines, it has fuelled credit card debts, which many people find difficult to pay. In addition, this type of consumption encourage a society where things are thrown away after a short time. At a time when resources are becoming scarce and pollution are a major issue, it is unwise to encourage products to be discarded on the whims of fashion.

2.5 Developing an independent study program

To prepare for the IELTS Writing Test you need to devise a study program that will help you develop your writing strategies and skills independently. The first step is to identify your needs.

Identifying your needs

Think about what you need to work on in your study program and tick those items in the checklist below.

Writing checklist ✓

1 Do you need to improve your general writing? Which areas need particular attention?

Using a consistent tone ☐

Building up your vocabulary ☐

Linking your ideas ☐

Writing complex sentences ☐

Structuring your writing in paragraphs ☐

2 Which aspects of the Writing Test do you need to find out more about and practise?

The format of the test (e.g. requirements for each task) ☐

General Training Task 1 ☐

Academic Task 1 ☐

General Training and Academic Task 2 ☐

3 Which specific skills do you need to improve for the Writing Test?

Responding to the task ☐

Organising ideas logically ☐

Using appropriate vocabulary ☐

Using a wide range of grammar features correctly ☐

Editing your work ☐

When you have completed the checklist, note the section(s) where you have the most ticks, and read the relevant section below, to discover how you can develop an effective and relevant program of independent study. You can also check the Writing skills and strategies summary on page ix to make sure you've completed the relevant exercises.

Improving your general writing

Try to do some writing every day.

Reading

If you read a lot, you will become familiar with the most common styles of writing and this in turn will improve your own style of writing. Reading should also help you with your grammar, spelling and vocabulary, as it will give you examples as to how language is used.

Furthermore, reading will give you an understanding of different types (or genres) of texts. In the IELTS test you are expected to write cause and effect, discussion and argument essays. By reading newspapers and magazines you can learn about the different writing patterns that are used in each type of essay (or written piece). You can then adopt these patterns in your own writing.

Practising for specific sections of the test

If you are going to get a good band score in the Writing Test, it is important that you expand your study beyond this book. There are a number of things you can do to support the materials in this book. It may be a good idea to work together with other students from your class or friends who are also taking the IELTS test. This way you can learn from each other and help to correct each other's mistakes. If you have other people with whom to work, it will help to keep you motivated.

General Training Task 1

To practise for General Training Task 1, you can design or get a study partner to design situations where you would need to write letters. Another way to practise is to use newspapers or the Internet to find advertisements for jobs, services or courses for which you can apply. Practise writing applications for these. You can also imagine you are unhappy with the services supplied somewhere and write a letter of complaint.

General Training Task 1 checklist ✓

Task achievement

- Have you covered all three bullet points in the question? ☐

- Have you used the correct tone in your letter? For example, the language you use will be different if you are writing to a friend or writing to your manager at work. ☐

Coherence and cohesion (organising your ideas logically)

- Does your letter follow a logical order? ☐

- Have you used linking words to join your sentences? ☐

- Have you substituted nouns with pronouns and used relative clauses? ☐

Lexical resource (using appropriate vocabulary)

- Have you used a wide range of task-related vocabulary? ☐

- Have you used the vocabulary correctly? ☐

- Have you shown evidence of a good (wide range of) vocabulary? ☐

Grammatical range and accuracy

- Have you used a wide range of grammatical structures? ☐

- Have you used them correctly? ☐

Academic Task 1

To practise for Academic Task 1, you can begin by practising orally, describing a visual to a study partner and getting him or her to draw it from your description. By answering orally you can get into the habit of summarising the most significant parts of a visual at a glance. This will help you pick out the main features when you do your Task 1. You can find your own visuals to summarise from the Internet. A good site for this is the Australian Bureau of Statistics: <www.abs.gov.au>.

Academic Task 1 checklist ✓

Task achievement

- Have you accurately presented all the information in the illustration? ☐

- Have you presented an overview of the main trends or differences? ☐

Coherence and cohesion (organising your ideas logically)

- Does your description follow a logical order? ☐

- Have you used linking words to join your sentences? ☐

- Have you substituted nouns with pronouns and used relative clauses? ☐

Lexical resource (using appropriate vocabulary)

- Have you used a wide range of task-related vocabulary? ☐

- Have you used the vocabulary correctly? ☐

- Have you shown evidence of a good (wide range of) vocabulary? ☐

Grammatical range and accuracy

- Have you used a wide range of grammatical structures? ☐

- Have you used them correctly? ☐

General Training and Academic Task 2

To practise for Task 2, you can write essays about news stories you find from newspapers, television, the Internet or other media sources. In your essays you should describe the events and give your opinion about them. If possible, get your teacher or an English-speaking friend to check your work.

General Training and Academic Task 2 checklist ☑

Task response

- Have you answered all parts of the question? ☐

- Have you given an opinion? ☐

Coherence and cohesion (Organising your ideas logically)

- Have you divided your response into paragraphs? ☐

- Have you used linking words to join your sentences together? ☐

- Have you paraphrased key words? ☐

- Have you used a mix of complex, compound and simple sentences? ☐

Lexical resource (Using appropriate vocabulary)

- Have you used a wide range of task-related vocabulary? ☐

- Have you used the vocabulary correctly? ☐

- Have you shown evidence of a wide range of vocabulary? ☐

Grammatical range and accuracy

- Have you used a wide range of grammatical structures? ☐

- Have you used them correctly? ☐

Work on your areas of weakness

Decide the areas in which you particularly need help and find resources that will give you specific practice in these areas. For example you may need help with your grammar or vocabulary, or to improve your planning skills. Suitable resources may be books from libraries or bookstores, or you may be able to find resources online.

2.6 Practice IELTS Writing Tests

These practice IELTS Writing Tests have been written to simulate the real IELTS Writing Tests in style, format and length. There is one for General Training candidates and one for Academic candidates. You should simulate the conditions of the IELTS Writing Test when doing the test by yourself. Try to complete your answers in the specified time. When you finish the test, check the answer key for a sample response to each task.

Practice General Training IELTS Writing Test

Writing Task 1

You should spend 20 minutes on this task.

You are organising a graduation party for your class and you want to book a restaurant.

Write a letter to the manager of your favourite restaurant. In the letter

- *explain the reason for the party and the date and time it will be held*
- *describe some particular food you would like served*
- *say how many people will be attending and what their dietary requirements are.*

Write at least 150 words.

You do **NOT** need to write any addresses.

Begin your letter as follows:

Dear Sir/Madam,

Writing Task 2

You should spend about 40 minutes on this task.

Write about the following topic:

> *Many people have complained about the large salaries paid to top executives of major companies.*
>
> *Why do you think top executives are so well paid?*
>
> *Do you think their large salaries are justified?*

Give reasons for your answer and include any relevant examples from your own knowledge and experience.

Write at least 250 words.

Practice Academic IELTS Writing Test

Writing Task 1

You should spend about 20 minutes on this task.

> *The figures below show the percentage of prisoners returning to prison within ten years of being released.*
>
> *Summarise the information by selecting and reporting the main features, and make comparisons where relevant.*

Write at least 150 words.

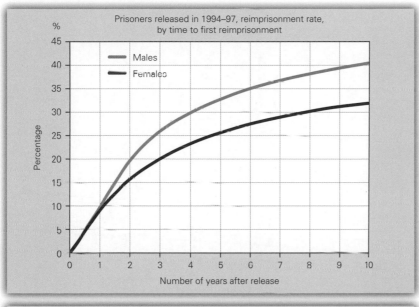

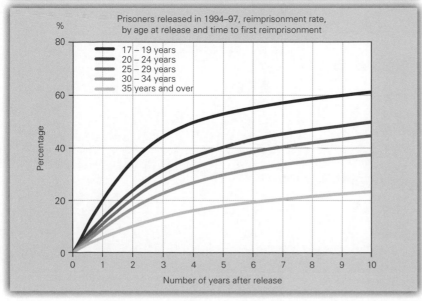

Writing Task 2

You should spend about 40 minutes on this task.

Write about the following topic:

> *Some people say children no longer need to develop handwriting skills. Others believe that handwriting is still important.*

Discuss both these views and give your opinion.

Give reasons for your answer and include any relevant examples from your own knowledge and experience.

Write at least 250 words.

Answer key

Unit 1: Reading

Exercise 1

1	B	2	A	3	D	4	A
5	C	6	B	7	C	8	D

9 A and E

Exercise 2

1 False (see first paragraph; also 'Such was the beginning of a revolution')

2 Not given

3 True (see second paragraph)

4 False ('The value of this ... object lies not in what it is, but how it is used')

5 False ('The thousands of ill-paid, ill-treated workers who once made their living ... are no more')

6 True ('Merchant marines, who had shipped out to see the world, had their shore leave ... reduced to a few hours ashore.')

7 Not given

8 True ('Sprawling industrial complexes ... gave way to smaller, more specialised plants ... in ever-lengthening supply chains.')

9 False ('... in places like Los Angeles and Hong Kong ... the cost of bringing raw materials in and sending finished goods out had dropped like a stone.')

Exercise 3

1 Yes ('One way or another, everything we do is motivated by our desire to be happy.')

2 Not given

3 No ('We're programmed to pursue it ... Whether we actually achieve it, nature doesn't much care.')

4 Not given.

5 Yes ('We are programmed to believe we'll be happier if we're ... materially secure ... All these things... would have contributed to our fitness.')

Exercise 4

1	F	2	D	3	A	4	B
5	E	6	C				

Exercise 5

7	v	8	ix	9	iii
10	viii	11	vi	12	ii

Exercise 6

1	B	2	B	3	C
4	A	5	A	6	C

Exercise 7

7	C	8	F	9	E

Exercise 8

10 its (founding) charter

11 specialised agencies

12 agree to accept

13 international conflicts

Exercise 9

14	J	15	E	16	I
17	D	18	C		

Exercise 10

1 low-technology era

2 major component

3 bridge crossing

4 modern age

5 main components

6 cantilevered

7 rivetted

8 (pairs of) hangers

9 road and railway

10 granite

11 for strength

Exercise 11

1 mitre gates

2 upper valve

3 lower valve

4 wall ports

5 control post

Exercise 12

6 economically
7 flash lock
8 guillotine gates / lifting gates
9 lock gear
10 (It) releases naturally

Exercise 13

1 **Computers** (theme) *are now a commonplace feature of daily life* (rheme) and it is hard to imagine a world without them.

For all their apparent modernity, however, **the idea behind computers** (theme) *is surprisingly ancient* (rheme).

The history of the modern computer (theme) *can be divided into distinct generations* (rheme), each distinguished by extreme changes in three areas

The changes (theme) that have taken place in less than a century *have been astonishing* (rheme).

2 a Computers are commonplace today.
   b The idea is ancient.
   c History has distinct generations.
   d Recent changes are astonishing.

Exercise 14

2 15 (news and messages)
3 5 (over 2,000 years ago)
4 10 (transistors)
5 2 (domestic sphere)
6 13 (artificial intelligence)

Exercise 15

1 mechanical
2 3 (three)
3 miniaturisation of functions (Note: Other answers are too long.)
4 computer-aided location devices

Exercise 16

1 irregular and oscillating / vibrating
2 the 1890s

3 oscillating water columns
4 westerly
5 fluctuate
6 (the) fishing (industry)
7 (low-cost) fossil fuels / nuclear generation facilities

8	A	9	F	10	G	11	E
12	D						

Exercise 17

1	B	2	C	3	A	4	A
5	D	6	A	7	E	8	B
9	F	10	D				

Exercise 18

1	B	2	C	3	A	4	C
5	A	6	B	7	C	8	A
9	B	10	C				

Exercise 19

1 Not given   2 B

Exercise 20

1 agreeable
2 sorry
3 very fast
4 devices / something used to control people
5 strong
6 frightened, excited

Exercise 21 (suggested answers)

Weather holds the key to which of the maxis will win this race. Facing stiff competition and challenging weather conditions, including a brisk 35-knot southerly, skippers will need to be on their mettle to fend off other contenders for line honours. All yachts will be under spinnaker at times, and at others will have to tack back and forth into the wind to outmanoeuvre their rivals.

We specialise in high-integrity stainless steel casting and are seeking someone with extensive experience in moulding and casting heat treatment of steel castings to oversee our production line, the general operation of the foundry and implementation of policy. We seek a motivated individual who will assist us with our organisational goals.

Exercise 22

1 Throughout their 130-year history, motor vehicles have been classified according to the type of fuel they use for locomotion. One type of alternative-fuel vehicle that originated in the earliest period of the automobile is the electric car. The original electric automobile, termed a Battery Electric Vehicle (BEV), was powered by an on-board battery pack consisting of cells storing chemical energy. In the early twentieth century, advances in another form of motor, the internal combustion engine (ICE) led to the rise of the gasoline or petrol vehicle, especially the Ford motor car. However, with concern about the environmental impact of petrol cars, a modified electric vehicle enjoyed a short revival in the 1990s, partially due to GM's EV1 electric car. Today, the principle alternative-fuel vehicle is the hybrid, which combines an internal combustion engine with a supplementary electric motor. The Toyota Prius and the Chevrolet Volt are examples of this new type of vehicle.

2 a Alternative-fuel vehicle
   b Gasoline or petrol vehicle
   c Ford (motor car)
   d GM's EV1
   e Chevrolet Volt

Exercise 23

A late surge in consumer demand has pushed up retail profits to new highs, especially in the electronics and white goods sectors. Heavily discounted bargains accounted for the highest sales of the holiday season, and the stampede to the checkout helped create a bonanza for retailers after one of the worst profit downturns in recent history. Never-to-be-repeated specials competed with discounted luxury items, which

was ultimately to the consumer's advantage. Satisfied customers responded to the bargains with enormous enthusiasm.

Exercise 24

Throughout their 130-year history, motor vehicles have been classified according to the type of fuel they use for locomotion. One type of alternative-fuel vehicle that originated in the earliest period of the automobile is the electric car. The original electric automobile, termed a Battery Electric Vehicle (BEV), was powered by an on-board battery pack consisting of cells storing chemical energy. In the early twentieth century, advances in another form of motor, the internal combustion engine (ICE) led to the rise of the gasoline or petrol vehicle, especially the Ford motor car. However, with concern about the environmental impact of petrol cars, a modified electric vehicle enjoyed a short revival in the 1990s, partially due to GM's EV1 electric car. Today, the principle alternative-fuel vehicle is the hybrid, which combines an internal combustion engine with a supplementary electric motor. The Toyota Prius and the Chevrolet Volt are examples of this new type of vehicle.

Exercise 25

1 Forgetting important things such as names, birthdays and appointments can really affect your efficiency and self-confidence. However, you can improve your memory by using a number of techniques. One of the oldest techniques is mnemonics: that is, remembering difficult information through a short rhyme. For example, music students will remember 'Every Good Boy Deserves Fruit', which is a way of remembering the notes on the lines of the treble clef: EGBDF. Another method is to associate a person's name with a pleasant, colourful image.

2 a self-confidence
   b mnemonics
   c notes
   d (colourful) image

Exercise 26

1 <u>All</u> **people** need to **consume liquids** in order to survive. <u>However</u>, the beverage of choice varies in different countries according to **cultural preferences**. <u>For example</u>, it is <u>often</u> thought that <u>all</u> **British citizens**, and <u>likewise</u> <u>all</u> **Japanese citizens**, **drink tea**, <u>either</u> black <u>or</u> green respectively. <u>However</u>, in recent times in **both** countries, <u>more</u> people, <u>especially</u> young people, are <u>also</u> drinking **coffee, colas** and **sports drinks**. <u>Even so</u>, <u>most</u> **individuals** in these countries <u>still</u> tend to drink the national **favourite beverage** <u>some of</u> the time.

2 a (all) people
  b citizens
  c young people

3 A

Exercise 27

Noun: concern (line 1); the … concern (line 9)
Verb: have been concerned (line 2); has … concerned (lines 3–4); concerns (line 4); (not) feel concerned (line 8)
Adjective: concerned (line 6); unconcerned (line 7); concerning (line 9)

Exercise 28

1 <u>Criteria</u> such as <u>elevation, steepness</u> … <u>relief</u> and <u>volume</u>, among other measures, can help determine <u>whether a particular landform is a mountain or not</u>.

2 In general, the idea that this <u>elevated geographic feature</u> stands in contrast to the <u>surrounding landscape</u> and has a certain <u>elevation</u> … helps determine the <u>classification</u>.

3 … the latter have <u>different</u> climatic <u>conditions</u> at the <u>base</u> compared with the <u>peak</u>, which means they contain <u>different forms of</u> life at different altitudes.

4 Their <u>inherent mystery</u> creates <u>a sense of wonder</u> and an <u>awareness</u> of our <u>essential smallness</u> in the universe.

5 … the <u>fear engendered</u> by <u>encountering at close quarters</u> the <u>savage, unpredictable forces of nature</u> in <u>mountainous terrain</u>, … (also a summary)

6 **Paragraph 1:** Summary 1 is best. The others are too specific.
  Paragraph 2: Summary 2 is best. It covers the time frame as well as the power. In Summary 1, 'always' is incorrect, Summary 3 is too limited and Summary 4 is not true.

7 **Paragraph 1:** Heading 4 is best. The others are either incorrect or too limited.
  Paragraph 2: Heading 3 is best. The others are too limited or are wrong.

8 No ('There is no universally accepted definition of what a mountain is.)

9 Yes ('Criteria such as elevation, steepness, relief and volume … determine whether a particular landform is a mountain or not')

10 Not given

11 inherent mystery

12 night sky

13 unpredictable forces

Exercise 29

<u>The term</u> *food security* refers to the availability and accessibility of food to a population, both households and individuals. <u>Contained within this definition</u> is the expectation that food is both physically available and priced to be accessible to local people. <u>One definition</u>, from the World Resources Institute, couches food security in negative terms: that is, a household is considered to be food secure if its occupants do not live in hunger or fear of starvation or need to acquire food in socially unacceptable ways such as scavenging, stealing or resorting to emergency supplies. <u>Other definitions</u> are more precise in that there is an expectation of more than minimum levels of food. According to the FAO, <u>households</u> should be able to have access to enough food for an active, healthy life. <u>Individuals</u> should have access to 'sufficient, safe and nutritious food to meet dietary needs and preferences'.

Exercise 30

1 However
2 whereas / while
3 Although / Even though

4   not only… but also

5   whereas / while / but

6   On the other hand / However

Exercise 31

1   the necessity to increase and expand London's Underground system

2   currently

3   if not; due to …

4   to provide a conduit for the workers … to access their place of employment in Central London

5   because

6   a   'deep level' tube system
    b   earlier

7   a   escalators
    b   earlier

8   led to; through; a consequence of this

9   Currently … are
    In the period up to 2020, … will be realised

10 a   Overall,
    b   intends to

11 C   12 A   13 B   14 C

15 1863   16 3.5 million   17 2020

18 2000   19 B, D, E and H

Exercise 32

1   mobile telephone technology

2   two types of

3   this means

4   that is

5   However

6   other telephone technologies

7   Currently

8   or

9   channels, routes

10 a code   11 C   12 A   13 B

14 A   15 B

Exercise 33

2   Other insects: ants and wasps
    Linking words: along with

3   a   honey, *besides*

b   pollination, *through*

c   almonds

d   nature

4   1C during; 2E during; 3D After; 4A ago; 5B In recent years

5   It has decimated hives

6   a   concern about honey production and supply; Linking words: *not only*

    b   concern about reliable pollination of agricultural crops and wild flowers; linking words: *but also*

7   a   monoculture diet

    b   unreliable weather

    c   other factors

    d   presence of *Varroa destructor*

8   may   9   Arguably

10 B   11 False

12 False   13 False

Exercise 34

1   **Addition and alternation:** … *and also* help save …; … *and* try to draught-proof …; … *or* wearing warmer clothes; *Also,* …

    Comparison and contrast: *Not only* will … but it can *also* …; *However,* it's important not to overheat …;

    Time (successive): *even before* a heater is switched on

    Time (simultaneous): *while* keeping costs down, *while* the heater is on

    Consequence (cause and effect): *Because* a one-degree increase …

    Consequence (purpose): *so* you can choose the right one

    Consequence (means): *by* closing doors

    Consequence (condition): *if* you're heating often

2   True   3   False

4   Not given   5   insulation

6   winter   7   cheaper

8   A

Exercise 35

1 The necessity of vitamins for bodily maintenance ... ('No dispute')

2 Fat or water soluble ('Divided according to whether ... or ...')

3 Whether taking supplementary vitamins has adverse effects when an individual's basic diet is adequate ('What there is dispute about')

4 For reasons of perceived enhanced well-being

5 35% of American males take an over-the-counter supplement

6 females with a higher socioeconomic status have a higher multivitamin intake and poor awareness of potential side effects

7 Yes ('reputable', 'respected')

8 a possible toxic effects from overdosing on a particular vitamin, and interference with prescription drugs

   b 'can include', 'or, even more serious'

9 confer with their doctor

10 agree ('which would appear to be sound advice')

11 Vitamin B supplements on migraine sufferers; use of Vitamin D in the treatment of diabetes

12 Further analysis appears to be needed

13 'this study only included those suffering Vitamin D deficiency ... uncertainty ... when the micronutrient level is adequate'

14 Further research is needed

15 No   16 Yes   17 Yes   18 No
19 Not given   20 Yes   21 B

Exercise 36

1 an elephant in the wild

2 the American prairie

3 picking up plants and animals facing extinction and moving them

4 startling

5 No

6 hugely controversial

7 '... move them to suitable locations that are outside their historic range'

8 A

9 'once confined to a handful of scientists ... are now getting a broader airing'

10 governments are discussing the issues related to a warming climate

11 an even greater rate of (temperature increases) of 40% to 70%

12 The scale of threatened extinctions

13 The scale of threatened extinctions

14 Regenerate America's prairie in parts of Texas and the Midwest

15 Fossils of elephants

16 The restoration of the US prairie

17 big grazing animals (class–subclass relationship); African elephants; the large herbivores from Africa

18 restoration of the US prairie

19 C

20 D

21 climate change

22 conservation biologist

23 rising temperatures

24 hugely controversial

25 Not given

26 No

27 Yes

Practice IELTS Reading Tests

Practice Academic IELTS Reading Test

Reading Passage 1

1 False   2 False
3 Not given   4 True
5 True
6 A   7 D   8 B   9 C
10 A   11 D   12 B   13 A

Reading Passage 2

14 v   15 iii   16 xi   17 iv
18 viii   19 i   20 vii

21 greater reporting theory
22 (simple) skin test
23 standardisation
24 false positive (result)
25 'gold standard'
26 B

Reading Passage 3

27	B	28	D	29	A	30	A
31	D	32	No	33	Yes	34	No
35	Not given			36	J	37	H
38	F	39	C	40	D		

Practice General Training IELTS Reading Test

Section 1

1	B	2	C	3	A	4	A
5	D	6	C	7	B	8	vi
9	x	10	iii	11	ix	12	viii
13	i	14	iv				

Section 2

15 career path
16 ideal job
17 volunteer work
18 typing mistakes
19 identification
20 additional skills
21 safe environment
22 fire safety systems
23 hazard reduction
24 emergency plan
25 trained
26 Emergency Planning Committee
27 Chief Warden

Section 3

28	True			29	False		
30	Not given			31	True		
32	False	33	D	34	C	35	B
36	A	37	C	38	G	39	I
40	B						

Unit 2: Writing

Exercise 1

2 (informal) Invitation to your partner's birthday party
3 (formal) Complaint about hotel service
4 (formal) Job application
5 (informal) Request to a friend to look after your pet
6 (could be either formal or informal) Invitation to a high-school reunion
7 (formal) Complaint to a restaurant, about food
8 (formal) Complaint to your landlord

Exercise 2 (sample answers)

2 As you know, it is Liza's birthday on the 22nd, so we are going to hold a party for her at the Taj Mahal restaurant in Hobart.

3 I am writing to you about the terrible service I received at your hotel during my stay from 22 to 28 June.

4 I would like to apply for the position of Shop Assistant advertised in the *Saturday Globe* on 23 September.

5 I'm writing to you to ask a favour: as you know, I am going to England on May 14 and I wondered if you could look after my dog while I'm away.

6 Next month it will be ten years since we left high school, so I would like to invite you to our ten-year reunion.

7 I wish to complain about the quality of food I received on my visit to your restaurant last Monday.

8 I wish to inform you that there is a gas leak in the kitchen of flat 1/27 Hope Street, which I rent from your agency.

Exercise 3 (Sample answers)

1   **Problem:** It is far too polite and apologetic: you are complaining.

    Corrected version: I would like to complain about the service I received at your restaurant.

2   **Problem:** It is too demanding: you are asking the other person to do something for you.

    Corrected version: Please could you send the catalogue to the above address as soon as possible?

3   **Problem:** Too formal, you are writing to a friend.

    Corrected version: Dear Anne

    I would like to invite you to my birthday party at my house next Saturday afternoon.

4   **Problem:** You are writing to college staff, so you should use formal or neutral language.

    Corrected version: Unfortunately, I must return to my country because of my grandmother's continued ill-health.

5   **Problem:** This is a job application – the tone should be formal or neutral.

    Dear Sir/Madam

    I saw your advertisement in the *Daily Globe* and I would like to apply for the position of Accounts Clerk.

Exercise 4

Dear Sir/Madam

I saw your advertisement for a two-week holiday in Tasmania in *Cheap and Cheerful Holiday Magazine* and I would like to have information on the issues below.

First, I would like to know if the special offer is still available during the school holidays from 8 to 21 July, as this is the only time that is possible for us to get away.

Second, could you send me details of the type of accommodation you are offering? I would like to know if you have anything suitable for a party of ten people. Furthermore, would it be possible for you to inform me whether any of the cabins have wheelchair access?

Finally, we would like to go sailing and wonder if it is possible to book a boat from the resort.

I look forward to your response and hope to see you in the near future.

Yours faithfully

Exercise 5 (sample answer)

Dear Sir or Madam

I am a first-year science student living in room 309 in the William Thompson Hall of Residence.

I wish to report a problem with the shower in my room. Unfortunately I have not had hot water for over a week and the water coming out of the hot tap is brown in colour. The situation has become so bad that I have to go and shower in my friend's room. I am sure you will understand that this is particularly inconvenient at examination time.

Next week I will be available on Monday, Wednesday and Thursday afternoons after 3.30 pm. Please could you telephone first to arrange an appointment and to confirm the day and time that the plumber will arrive? My number is 0414 678 921. It is best if you call after 3.00 pm as I am taking exams at the moment.

I look forward to hearing from you as soon as possible.

Yours faithfully

Exercise 6 (sample answers)

1   What? Chinese food; favourite music
    Who? DJ
    How? fancy dress; Halloween costumes

2   Who? all our friends from university; Liza's parents
    Where? surprise visit from China.

3   As you know, Saturday is Liza's 21st birthday and I would like to invite you to a surprise party for her at the Night Owls Club in Oxford Street on Saturday from 8.30 pm.

    As it is nearly Halloween, we have decided to make the party fancy dress with a horror theme. We have ordered caterers who will serve Liza's favourite Chinese food. Of course, the club's DJ will be playing all our favourite music.

All our friends from university will be at the party, as well as Liza's parents, who are coming from China especially for her birthday. Don't tell Liza, as she doesn't know anything about this.

Exercise 7

Cross out:

▼ right next to the article on talking to your plants

▼ My favourite book is *Lord of the Rings* by J.R.R Tolkien and I would certainly recommend this to any of your customers.

▼ I can't work later than 9.00 because my mother says the town centre is quite dangerous late at night. I can't work on Friday because I have my violin lesson.

Exercise 8

1 Reason you are writing
2 Details of the situation, and bullet point 1: description of the briefcase
3 Details of the situation, and bullet point 2: exactly where the briefcase was left
4 Details of the situation, and bullet point 1: description of contents of briefcase
5 Bullet point 3: what you want the lost property office to do
6 Polite close

Exercise 9

Paragraph 1
Situation: 5 Request: 3
Paragraph 2
Details of request: 1, 9, 7, 4
Paragraph 3
Arrange meeting: 2, 6
Paragraph 4
Polite close: 8

Exercise 10 (sample answers)

1 Could you send me further information about …
2 Could you please deliver …
3 a meeting / a date (depending on the circumstances)
4 a difficulty with my studies
5 I would like to ask you to come to / to attend
6 to hire
7 to be delayed
8 an essay / a project / a task / an assessment (depending on the circumstances)
9 vacation/break
10 I wish to apologise / I regret / Unfortunately
11 Dear Mr Williams
   I would like to report an accident that I had leaving work on Friday 21 October. As I was leaving <u>the office</u>, I tripped over a raised paving stone just outside the front entrance. I fell over and tore my trousers and cut my knee. Although my <u>injury</u> was not serious, it was painful and my trousers were damaged beyond repair.

   I believe that this accident was caused by problems with the <u>pavement</u> just outside the front entrance. This may be because tree roots are growing under the paving stones and pushing the paving stones up. I <u>feel</u> that the <u>path needs</u> to be replaced if this type of <u>incident</u> is to be avoided in the future.

   I would also like the company to pay <u>for the damage to my clothing</u>. Replacing my trousers will cost around $200. I look forward to hearing from you.
   Regards
   Helen

Exercise 11 (sample answer)

As you know, we are all going on holiday to France in September and we wondered if you would like to join us *there*. We are going *then* so we can celebrate my birthday on the 13th. We are having a party in a local club *where* there is live music every night. The band is very good. I saw *them* in London last summer and was very impressed.

We will be staying in an old farmhouse *that* has eight bedrooms, so there will be room for everybody. *It* is close to a beach *that* has great waves for surfing and is hidden from the road, so very few people come there.

Exercise 12 (sample answer)

Dear Mr Murray

I am sorry to have to tell you that I will be unable to hand in my Geography assignment due on the 14th of September.

Unfortunately my mother has had a heart attack and I have to fly back to China to see her as soon as possible. At the moment I am on stand-by for the next available flight, so I do not know when I will be leaving or when I will be coming back.

I believe that I will be away for two weeks at the most, and I think that I will be able to do some work while I am in China. However, I will almost certainly need an extension on my assignment. Please could you give me permission to hand it in on the 21st of September? This would be one week later than expected.

Could you let me know as soon as possible whether I can get an extension? I am sorry for any inconvenience I have caused.

Yours sincerely

Exercise 13

1 Students' own answers.
2 (sample answers)
   a car hire company
   b website
   c Cairns
   d 22 December / the 22nd of December
   e travel
   f airport
   g our group

h accompanied
i storage space
j suitable

3 I saw your **advertisement** (the letter is talking about one specific advertisement not advertising generally) in Saturday's *Daily Planet* and I would like **to apply** (after *would like* you should always use the infinitive, not -*ing*) for the position of Sales Manager.

I have three years' experience **working** (experience is followed by –*ing*, not the infinitive) as a salesman in Australia. I am energetic and **enthusiastic** (should be an adjective describing the person, not a noun) and I am **available** (*available* is an adverb describing readiness to start work, *availability* is a noun) to start immediately.

4 Dear Sir or Madam

I saw in last week's edition the article about the proposed changes to the 391 bus from East Gardens to the City.

I am sure that I am not the only one affected by this change. Reducing the number of 391 buses during the early morning rush hour will affect many people who need this link to catch a train from Central Station. Without this bus, people will be forced to abandon public transport and drive to work. This would contribute to the ever-increasing traffic jams in the city.

I suggest that the government should run this bus more frequently and schedule it to coincide with the train timetable in order to make travelling easier. Better still, the government could extend the rail link from the city to the eastern suburbs. This way they could cut down the number of drivers on the road and reduce everyone's travel time.

Exercise 14

1 **Correct:** b, e; **Incorrect:** a, c, d, f, g, h
(Sample answers)
   a The bus leaving at 8.00 am is always late.
   c Although the room is quite close to public transport and to the centre of the city, the last bus is at 9.00 pm.

d The day when I left my family and friends in my own country was very difficult for me.

f The Chinese restaurant, where I bought the meal, near to my house, is very cheap.

g The major assignment, which was due the day before my birthday party last week, was delayed for a week.

h My previous job, which was in an accounts office in India, taught me to work as part of a team.

2 a   has   b   are
   c   is   d   was
   e   (correct)   f   are
   g   (correct)   h   has

Exercise 15

1 The illustration represents three periods in the development of a small town, in the years 1900, 1950 and 2000.

2 The two graphs compare sales of Australian cars with different sizes with the petrol prices between 1990 and 2008.

3 The pie charts compare the popularity of pets owned by 12-year-old children in the United States, the United Kingdom and Australia.

4 The illustration shows the effect of increasing the amount of carbon dioxide in the atmosphere and how this causes global warming.

5 The graph compares the different life expectancies of people in five countries around the world.

Exercise 16 (sample answers)

1 The average temperature before 1961 was less than the average after 1960.

Temperatures from 1980 were consistently above average.

The five hottest years were between 1980 and 2005.

The coldest decade was the 1950s.

There is a two-degree difference between the coldest year 1919 and the hottest year 2005.

Only four years were below the average temperature between 1985 and 2000.

2 Temperatures in Australia have increased significantly since 1980. During this period there were only four years that didn't reach the average temperature between 1960 and 1990. Furthermore, the hottest eight years in the last century all occurred in the 30 years before 2005.

Temperatures were consistently 0.5 degrees below the 1960 to 1990 mean before 1957. The coldest period was between 1944 and 1957. However, the coldest single year was 1917, which was more than a degree below the mean. There is more than a two-degree difference between the hottest year 2005 and the coldest year 1917.

3 To summarise, there has been a significant increase in the average Australian temperature since 1980.

Exercise 17 (sample answer)

The bar chart shows people's attitudes to the number of hours they work in all type of jobs.

The fewer hours people work the more they would prefer to increase their number of working hours. Twenty-five per cent of employees working 15 hours a week or under wish they could work more hours. However, only 1% of people working over 49 hours a week would like to work more.

On the other hand 45% of people working over 49 hours a week would prefer to work less hours, where as only 1% of people working under 15 hours wish they could work less.

It is interesting to note that over 60% of people are satisfied working less than 15 hours a week. In addition around 55% of people working over 49 hours a week are happy to work this amount of hours. Overall more than 50% of people are satisfied with the hours they work.

To summarise, although almost 50% of people working over 49 hours a week believe they work too much, the majority of people are satisfied with the hours they work.

Exercise 18 (sample answer)

The illustrations show the market share and advertising budget for five different kinds of chocolate bar for the period from 2000 to 2010.

In 2000 Venus chocolate bar's market share stood at 12%. However, at the end of the decade, this had increased to 30%. It is interesting to note that during this period Venus was the biggest spender on advertising with a budget that increased from $4 million in 2000 to $6 million in 2010. The second-highest spender on advertising in this period was Air-Light. Despite this spending, Air-Light's market share declined 1% in this period.

The chocolate bar with the largest decline in market share was Rum Punch – its market share decreased from 21% in 2000 to 8% in 2010. During this period Rum Punch was also the least advertised brand. Fantasy also lost 5% of market share; during this time it spent no more than $3.5 million on advertising.

Overall there seems to be a correlation between the amount spent on advertising and the market share of the chocolate bar brands.

Exercise 19 (sample answer)

The image represents a volcano in cross-section during the eruption process.

The volcano is formed from a reservoir of magma stored in a magma chamber located in rock layers deep in the Earth's crust. The magma reaches the surface through a conduit pipe where it escapes the volcano through the crater. The volcano is enlarged by the layers of lava and ash that are emitted during the eruption.

During an eruption lava will flow down the flanks of the volcano and a large ash cloud will gather above the volcano. Branch pipes may split off from the main conduit and either store lava in sills under the surface of the cone or form a parasitic cone that also produces a lava flow.

The eruption of a volcano has a major effect on the geography of the surrounding area, creating a cone formed from lava and ash.

Exercise 20 (sample answer)

▼ More males than females are overweight or obese.

▼ At the age of 65, 70% of males are either overweight or obese and 40% of all males are overweight.

▼ At the age of 18, 40% of men are obese or overweight.

▼ At the age of 18, around 28% of women are overweight.

▼ At the age of 65, 35% of woman are overweight.

▼ The older a person gets, the more likely they are to become overweight up to the age of 65.

▼ The number of obese or overweight females over the age of 65 decreases by at least 10%.

▼ The number of obese males declines slightly over the age of 65 but the number of overweight males continues to increase from the age of 55.

Exercise 21

1	while	2	before
3	However	4	Meanwhile
5	during	6	However
7	before	8	not only
9	but also	10	

Exercise 22

The graph shows the leisure activities of children at three different ages in three countries in 2010.

The most popular sport for ten-year-old children in all three countries is soccer, which is played by 33% of all ten year olds. In Britain 60% of boys and 20% of girls play soccer.

As children get older in all three countries, they play more video games. In America 78% of 12-year-old boys and 40% of teenage girls play video games. For boys, this number increases to 92% for 15 year olds.

Exercise 23 (sample answers)

1 Antarctica is the continent that gets the least amount of rain per year.

2 In the sixteenth century, the east wing of the manor house was built as housing for servants.

3 There will continue to be an increase in the mean age of the Japanese population over the next decade.

4 In total, there has been a significant increase in the percentage of electricity generated by wind power over the last decade.

5 In 2010, the percentage of income per month spent on rent was double that spent in 1990.

6 The number of properties for rent in major cities decreased over the twenty years from 1990 to 2010.

7 In 1990, mortgages were three times the average salary. In 2010, this had risen to seven times the average salary.

8 In 2010, the dams in New South Wales were at 76% capacity, as opposed to 37% in 2003.

9 As the wind turbines' sails are turned by the wind, electricity is generated.

10 Bankers' bonuses in 2007 were 30% less than those paid in 2010.

Exercise 24

The line graph shows the number of overseas students studying English in a college in Australia from 2000 to 2010 while the bar chart shows the students' country of origin.

The total number of English students increased dramatically during this period. In 2000, there were 400 English students at the college, whereas by the end of the decade there were 900, which is more than double the 2000 total.

The biggest market for overseas students throughout the decade has been Asia. At the start of the decade most of the Asian students came from Japan and Korea. However, in the last five years these markets have been declining and more students have come from China. In 2009, 42% of all overseas students at the college came from this source.

Although the number of European students has declined from 2005, there has been a steady increase in students from South American countries such as Brazil and Colombia.

Overall the number of students at the college has increased, with most of the students coming from China.

Exercise 25

1 a increased consistently
  b remained almost constant
  c a dramatic fall
  d falling steadily
  e a massive rise
  f to increase slowly

2 a reached a peak
  b fluctuated
  c bottomed out
  d levelled off

Exercise 26

Students' own answers.

Exercise 27

The village grew from a population of 500 in 1850 to 12,000 in 2010. Between 1900 and 1950, the woodland that marked the eastern border of the village became the Newlands Estate. In addition, the Village Green, where the Lord's Manor House was located, was turned into townhouses, which attracted new residents to the village. The final major development was the apartment blocks, which were built on the common land to the north in the 1980s.

Exercise 28 (sample answers)

1 The base of the fire extinguisher, which is made from re-enforced steel, is encased in plastic.

2 (sentence)

3 The sunlight that is stored in the photo-electric cells in the solar panels <u>can be used for heating</u>.

4 The earlier the age that children take up smoking in developing countries, <u>the higher the rate of cancer</u>.

5 While the number of families living on less than $2 a day has decreased in some areas, <u>it has increased in others</u>.

6 (sentence)

7 It is interesting to note that the population of animals that live in the cities and large towns <u>is increasing</u>.

8 The rainwater collected in large containers and transported to a series of large underground vats <u>is cooled by refrigeration units</u>.

Exercise 29 (sample answers)

1 iced drinks were almost twice as high as sales of tea and coffee

2 were about half as high as those of tea and coffee

3 were about the same

4 considerably less than sales of tea and coffee

Exercise 30

1 **a** is transferred   **b** convert
   c are compressed   **d** are squashed
   e is sent   **f** cools

2 The diagram shows the procedure for enrolling, orientating and testing new students on their first day at a college.

When new students arrive at reception, they <u>are asked</u> to fill out an arrival form and give the receptionist their passport and two photos. These are used to make their student card.

Meanwhile the Director of Studies <u>welcomes</u> the students to the college. The students are given an orientation speech and they are given a copy of the handbook. The students then <u>take</u> a placement test, which

<u>is used</u> to help the Director of Studies to allocate them to a class.

While this <u>is happening</u>, reception <u>notifies</u> the IT department of the student's arrival and each new student is issued with their own password to access college computers.

There are three main areas <u>involved</u> in the orientation and placement of new students.

Exercise 31

1 Why are there traffic jams in the city? How can these traffic jams be controlled?

2 The advantages of marrying later. What is the best age to marry?

3 Does money make life easier? Does money make you happy?

Exercise 32

1 **Ideas** *for* **studying abroad:**
Living abroad gives you experience of another culture
You meet lots of people from different cultures, if you study abroad
Sometimes a foreign qualification will help you to find a job
Studying abroad gives you a different outlook on life from meeting different people
Ideas *against* **studying abroad:**
Studying abroad is expensive
There are no language difficulties if you study in your own country
You may experience culture shock

2 (**sample answer**) Culture shock / No language difficulties but experience / different outlook

3 Students' own answers.

Exercise 33 (sample answer)

In many ways, living longer is an attractive idea. However, it is unlikely that it would be of benefit to everyone, as it would also put strain on the world's resources.

C In the past the average life expectancy was less than 70. A However, today many people can expect to live to 80. D Today, it is not uncommon for people to live to see their great-grandchildren. **E** The opportunity for generations to share experiences and learn from each other is of benefit to everyone. **B** Therefore, the longer people live the more interesting life will become.

Many people believe they would be able to accomplish more if they lived longer. They would have extra time to concentrate on their life's work and would not have to retire at the very time that their experience becomes really valuable. If people lived longer, maybe the human race would become wiser.

However, it must be remembered that living longer will only be of advantage if the quality of life is good. Few people will want to live longer if it results in extra years of ill health. In addition, the world is not ready for more old people. Already there are problems of overpopulation and limited food supply. An aging population may place an impossible burden on the young. Longer life expectancy would be expensive, so at best it would only be of benefit to the rich.

In conclusion, living longer would probably be of benefit to the rich, but would do nothing for the majority of people.

Exercise 34

In recent times studying abroad has become very popular. Although there are many advantages to overseas study there are also some disadvantages.

One of the major problems with overseas study is that it is expensive. Tuition fees for overseas students are very high and often the cost of living is higher than in the student's own country. On the other hand, an overseas qualification may be a good long-term investment and help the person get a better job when they return home. Furthermore, study at a foreign university may give students a different perspective on their subject.

Of course studying in one's own country is easier. There are no language problems and students know what to expect from the lecturers. In contrast, overseas students may be unable

to understand lectures and find it difficult to adapt to different styles of teaching. However, overcoming these problems may provide useful skills later in life. Studying in a different environment helps students become more adaptable and gives them the confidence to deal with difficult problems.

Perhaps the main problem encountered by overseas students is culture shock. For many people it is their first time away from home and they get homesick. They miss their friends and family and find problems adapting to the language and culture. However, there is a sense of satisfaction in overcoming these problems. Overseas experience increases self-confidence and opens up people's minds to new ideas and cultures.

Overall, in spite of the difficulties of studying abroad, it is usually a positive experience.

Exercise 35 (comments)

Paragraph 1: The fact that space travel is controversial is irrelevant. The question asks about benefits of space travel, and whether humans will ever live on other planets. The candidate includes the point 'space exploration is too expensive' but the question does not ask for a discussion of disadvantages.

Paragraph 2: This paragraph begins with details of historical and future space flights. This is not relevant to the question unless it is clearly being used to explore the benefits of such missions. Once again, the writer then focuses on disadvantages rather than advantages.

Paragraph 3: In this paragraph, the writer returns to the issue of overpopulation. However, the question does not ask whether humans living on other planets is a good or bad thing – it simply asks whether it would occur. Instead of exploring the benefits of space travel, the writer has discussed the benefits of humans living on other planets, suggesting a misunderstanding of the task.

Paragraph 4: The conclusion is not supported by the essay. The writer has neither proven that there will be benefits, nor that colonisation of other planets is inevitable.

Exercise 36 (sample answer)

Space travel has long been a dream for many people. It has the potential to bring about benefits such as technological advances and discoveries about the universe. However, the idea of humans living on another planet is unlikely to happen soon.

One of the main benefits of space travel has been the applications of research. Space research has led to advances in computer technology as well as heat-resistant materials and new ways of storing food.

Space travel may also help to answer some questions such as 'are we alone in the universe?' and 'how did life start?'. In addition, space travel may reveal valuable resources that may one day be used on Earth.

Before humans are ready to occupy other planets, there are a number of obstacles that need to be overcome. The cost of developing a space program of this size would be restrictive. Furthermore, nearby planets appear to be inhospitable. Therefore, travel to a planet where humans could live would take longer than the average lifespan.

Due to the population demands of humanity, it may become necessary to inhabit other planets, at which time it is possible that more attention will be paid to space travel. Moreover, technology continues to progress and so there is the chance that there will be a technological breakthrough that will make space travel more accessible. Humans may occupy another planet but it won't be in the near future.

In conclusion, space travel has led to some technological benefits. However, there is little chance of humans living on another planet in the near future.

Exercise 37 (sample answer)

Although some people prefer to live in the countryside, there are many reasons why people move to the city. These include better work and education prospects, and more entertainment opportunities. It is probably more realistic to improve the conditions in the countryside than to stop people moving to the cities.

Many people leave the countryside, as it is easier to find well-paying work in the city. This is because companies congregate in population centres that have a well-trained workforce and the services they need. Most careers require specialist training, which is often only available in the city. As young people leave to pursue a career, country towns become populated by the elderly.

As the average age in country towns rises, the facilities are designed for older people. Therefore country life becomes boring for young people. People choose to move to the city to live a more exciting life. As people move out, shops and businesses close down. This means that people are unable to stay in the countryside because of a lack of jobs.

It is unrealistic to expect people to stay in the countryside while there are no jobs or services. Even if it was illegal for people to move to the city, they would still do so to try to improve their lives. The only way to encourage people to stay in the country is to improve the job prospects and facilities there.

The lack of employment opportunities and the consequent lack of services mean that it is inevitable that people will want to live in the city.

Exercise 38

1 C, A, D, B, F, E
2 a Shopping; different attitudes of men and women
   b Lack of fresh water in Australia; need for water restrictions will increase
   c Possible new sources of energy; nuclear or sustainable energy sources have advantages and disadvantages
3 a (sample answer) There are two main reasons why it is important to learn English.
   b (sample answer) People identify with celebrities for a number of reasons.
   c (sample answer) Although there are a number of ways to get rich, the chances of being successful are quite small.

Exercise 39

1 There are a number of reasons why people say the study of history has little purpose. First, the world is changing quickly. In recent times there have been big advances in the Internet and robotics. This means that the global situation is very different than in the past. Even the powers themselves have changed. Twenty years ago, the main threat was a war between the USA and the USSR. Now the main danger is likely to be a terrorist attack. The speed of change means history may not be relevant today.

2 On the other hand, examining the past helps us understand the present. Although situations may change, past events may explain countries' outlooks on life. For example, the end of the First World War and the Treaty of Versailles were partly responsible for the Second World War. It may be necessary to understand the past before we can solve present situations.

3 A further reason for studying history is that it is strongly linked to people's culture. Today's life is connected to life in the past in that our culture has developed from our ancestors' experiences. In Australia, many Indigenous peoples' lifestyles and artworks are inspired by their history. It is impossible to ignore history as it defines who we are.

4 In conclusion, although history may seem irrelevant, it explains the forces that made today's world. The technology and political situation may change but countries are still shaped by their history and this is impossible to change.

5 Order of sentences: (Introduction) E; (Paragraph 1) H, A; (Paragraph 2) D, G, B; (Conclusion) J, I, F, C

Exercise 40

1 a First   b which
   c In addition   d also
   e Finally   f either
   g or

2 a Although   b because
   c As   d not only … but also
   e so   f During
3 a Not only   b but
   c also   d In addition
   e In spite of   f because
   g and   h rather
   i Furthermore   j when
   k whereas   l First
   m if   n Second
   o and   p Once
   q In conclusion   r while
   s Therefore

Exercise 41

Scientists have long been worried by the ability of genetically modified plants to cross-fertilise. They believe that bees and other pollen-collecting insects may transfer the modified DNA to other plants. As <u>they</u> visit a number of different types of plant in <u>their</u> quest to make honey, <u>they</u> spread <u>these</u> genes. <u>This</u> means that modifying one plant may affect a wide range of life forms.

Exercise 42

<u>Despite</u> vast differences in wealth between countries, there are poor people everywhere. This essay will discuss some of the reasons for this poverty and what can be done to prevent it.

It is important to say there is no single reason for poverty. In developing countries war and debts to wealthy nations make <u>it</u> inevitable that many people will struggle to survive. However, <u>this</u> is certainly not the case in wealthier nations <u>such as</u> the USA. The causes of poverty in these nations range from poor education to downsizing in major corporations. Even in developed countries, governments accept that there will always be unemployment and that life will be hard for people at the lower end of the economic scale.

Just as the causes of poverty are often unclear, there is no single solution. <u>However,</u> world peace would mean countries would be able to concentrate on improving their citizens' lives instead of spending money on arms. Another way to raise living standards would be for wealthy nations to cancel Third World debt. This would allow developing countries to use the money saved to reduce poverty.

In wealthier countries, governments need to consider how wealth is divided. It is not enough to keep creating more and more money, if this money goes to support people who are already rich. Governments have a responsibility to protect all citizens not just those with important positions in society.

In conclusion, there are a number of causes of poverty and while there isn't an easy way to improve living standards, stopping war and dividing wealth more equally would certainly help.

Exercise 43

1 a economic   b financial
   c sector   d variables
   e deriving   f benefits
2 a method   b data
   c based   d research
   e context   f analysis
   g environmental
3 a procedural   b evidence
   c legal   d assumes
   e principle
4 a major   b issues
   c flexibility   d labour
   e occurred   f significant
   g individuals   h income

Exercise 44

1 of   2 of   3 of   4 to
5 of living

Exercise 45

1 wealth   2 crisis
3 individual   4 high
5 practice   6 share
7 compulsory   8 assets

9 unrest   10 transformed
11 gradual   12 major
13 sacrificing   14 compromises

Exercise 46

1

to authorise	authoritatively	
to compensate	compensatory	
consideration	considerable	considerably
consumption	to consume	consumptively
convention	conventional	conventionally
dimensional	dimensionally	
distinction	distinguish	distinctly
energy	to energise	energetically
to emphasise	emphatic	emphatically
evaluation	evaluated	
to function	functional	functionally
hypothesis	hypothetical	hypothetically
to institute	institutional	
legislation	to legislate	legislatively
mechanisation / mechanism		
mechanical	mechanically	
negative	to negate	negatively
occurrence	occurring	
potential	potentially	
region	to regionalise	regional
significance	significant	significantly
similar	similarly	
strategy	to strategise	strategic
text	textual	
technical	technically	

2 access, analyse (UK), analyze (US), assessment, business, category, consequences, constitution, criticism, definite, distribution, environment, explanation, facilitate, fundamental, guarantee, implication, interpretation, justification, maintenance, modem, necessary, philosophy, procedure, proportion, process, psychology, required, separate, similar, sufficient, technical, version

3 In some countries, free health care is accepted as a basic right and is provided to all citizens, regardless of income. However, in other countries people must pay for their health

care. I believe that free health care should be available to everyone.

The main argument against free health care is that medical treatment is expensive. Doctors are highly paid professionals and hospital care is expensive. Therefore the people who use the health system should be the ones who pay for it. Furthermore, it is argued that medical costs need to be passed on to the consumers so that money can be made available for research.

I disagree with this point of view for two reasons. First, the people who need the health system most are the people who are most sick. People who are sick are likely to be poor because they are unable to work or are frequently absent from work. Second, taxes are paid to the government so they will support people in times of need. If the government is unwilling to pay for essentials like health and education, there seems little reason to pay taxes.

Furthermore, if people are asked to pay for their own health care, like in America, the poor inevitably suffer. There have been many stories of people being turned away from hospitals because they have no insurance. Moreover, insurance companies encourage doctors to prescribe the cheapest and not necessarily the best treatment in order to increase their profits. This has led to the situation where people are not given the treatment they need because their insurance policy does not cover it. When health becomes business, quality declines and the poor suffer.

In conclusion free medical treatment is the only way to ensure that quality health care is provided for everyone and not just the very rich.

Exercise 47

1 Culture shock is a problem that affects overseas students.
2 The United Nations is an institution where countries can discuss their problems.
3 An ambassador is a person who represents a country abroad.

4 A barrister is a lawyer who represents clients in court.
5 A school is an institution that prepares people for life.
6 A hydroelectric dam is a place where water is used to generate electricity.
7 The world climate change summit, which was held in Copenhagen in 2009, was designed to reach an agreement to replace the Kyoto agreement, which expires in 2012.
8 Scientists, who have spent many years studying global warming, stated that the agreement at this conference was vital for the world's future.
9 However, economists state that action, which might not even help control climate change, could badly damage the economy.
10 The conference eventually reached an agreement, which made recommendations but did not compel countries to act.

Exercise 48

1 This isolation is felt particularly by older people, who find it more difficult to adapt to cultural changes.
2 Most people find traditions with which they grow up difficult to change.
3 However, younger people tend not to have the same respect for tradition. (no relative clause)
4 Therefore, it is usually the young who become influenced by a more global culture.
5 This can cause a generation gap makes that makes it difficult for young and older people to understand each other.
6 Some young people also find it difficult to adapt to a culture that is far removed from their own.
7 They have lost touch with their own culture, which seems to offer them little of interest.
8 In some cases this has resulted in people becoming disconnected from their society and joining organisations that promote extremism.

Exercise 49

1–2 Students' own answers.

3 a will not make
   b will not
   c were
   d would
   e will have
   f are allowed
   g will prevent
   h will probably stop

Exercise 50

Both parents and schools **have** a major influence on a child's upbringing and so both have a role to play in the moral education of children. However, there is no easy answer as to the best method of educating children.

As parents are the first influence on children, they are the first example from which children learn. It is not only what a child is told that is important, it is also the example that the parents set. If parents lie to their children, it is not surprising if the children also lie.

School is also a major influence on a child's life. The culture of a school will help to establish forms of behaviour. For example, if a child sees students behaving badly, they are likely to copy this behaviour. In other words it is often not the school that influences the child but the child's friends.

There is no perfect way to teach right from wrong. Every child is different and responds to different methods. However, there are some ways that are more successful than others. First, it is very important to be consistent. If a child is told not to do something one day and is allowed to do it the next, the child will become confused. Second, children will copy the behaviour of others so if a child is constantly exposed to bad behaviour, it is not surprising if he/she behaves badly.

Both school and home are important influences on a child. Children learn most from the standards that are acceptable where they grow up.

Exercise 51

Many governments believe that being 'tough on crime' and imprisoning a large number of people is an effective deterrent. However, there is evidence to suggest that a large percentage of people jailed have mental health issues or are addicted to drugs or alcohol. In this case, unless their underlying problems are addressed, many offenders are likely to reoffend soon after leaving jail. It may be that providing education, bigger mental health budgets and more help for addicts are better solutions to rising crime rates than locking people up.

Exercise 52

Since the 1950s, advertising has moved away from the direct selling of a product to the selling of a dream. Advertisements concentrate on perceived lifestyle benefits rather than the product itself. For this reason, car advertisements often show attractive girls or jealous neighbours to make potential consumers reflect on how a new car might change their lives.

A further advertising technique is to establish brand loyalty. A certain brand of clothes is seen as exclusive and so it establishes a niche market. Consequently, people develop brand loyalty as it helps to define their opinion of themselves. Often these 'exclusive' brands are little different from other products half the price.

Exercise 53

The danger of these types of advertising is they encourage a lifestyle that people cannot afford. If people link happiness to what they own, they will constantly buy new things. While this is good for companies' bottom lines, it has fuelled credit card debts, which many people find difficult to pay. In addition, this type of consumption encourages a society where things are thrown away after a short time. At a time when resources are becoming scarce and pollution is a major issue, it is unwise to encourage products to be discarded on the whims of fashion.

Practice IELTS Writing Tests

Practice IELTS General Training Writing Test

Task 1 (sample answer)

Dear Sir or Madam,

I would like to ask about the possibility of booking your restaurant on the 31st March for our IELTS graduation party. The party is a celebration of us getting the results we needed in an important examination. If it is possible, we would like to hold the party at 9.30 pm. Altogether, we will be a group of 19 people: 18 students and our teacher.

Last time I came to your restaurant, I particularly enjoyed the roast chicken. I have also heard that the seafood is recommended. I wonder if it would be possible to have them as set dishes? We would also like a cake to present to our teacher.

Finally, I would like to know if it is possible to prepare special vegetarian meals, as three of the guests do not eat meat.

I look forward to hearing from you as soon as possible.

Yours faithfully

Task 2 (sample answer)

The global financial crisis has highlighted the salaries paid to top executives of major international companies. At a time when many multinational companies have been struggling, it is impossible to justify the salaries their leaders are paid.

There are two reasons why top executives' salaries have increased so rapidly over the past 30 years. First, companies believe they pay enormous salaries in order to attract the best person for the job. In the past, companies have believed that the right person in the job can solve all a company's problems. These salaries are negotiated by recruitment agents who take a commission on the salary paid and therefore have an interest in making sure the top executive gets a large salary. Second, the directors appointing top executives are often from a similar background and are naturally sympathetic to their salary demands.

It is hard to justify top executives being paid 70 or 80 times more than the average salary. This is particularly true when their decisions may have often led to failure. The public is rightly upset when a top executive is paid a major bonus even though the company they run has made a loss that year and many of the employees have lost their jobs. Companies such as Qantas and Telstra paid increased salaries to top executives who were freezing employee wages and making redundancies.

Although top executives have highly responsible jobs, their work is useless without the support of the employees. Therefore, they should be paid in proportion to the salaries of the people they control.

Practice IELTS Academic Writing Test

Task 1 (sample answer)

The first line graph illustrates the rate of male and female prisoners reoffending within ten years of their release from jail. The second graph shows the percentage of people returning to prison by age.

Approximately 40% of men return to jail after ten years, compared to around 28% of females. For males and females of all ages, it is interesting to note that there is a far higher rate of return to jail for the first two years than for the next eight.

The second figure shows that the younger a person is when they are sent to jail, the more likely they are to reoffend. In fact, people aged 17 to 19 years are three times as likely to reoffend as people over 35.

Overall, men are more likely to reoffend than women, and the younger a person is when they are sent to jail the more likely they are to reoffend.

Task 2 (sample answer)

In the past, clear handwriting was essential, as it was necessary for school and university work, as well as for many job-related duties. Many people believe handwriting will no longer be useful in the future. Although computers are replacing handwriting in many areas, I still believe it is important children learn to write legibly.

People often talk about a paperless society. This means that all communication is carried out by electronic means. If this ever truly comes to pass, there will be no need to write by hand. Today, university and high school assignments have to be typed, so certainly handwriting is less important than it was before. This has made written communication simpler, as material can be reorganised and edited without being rewritten from scratch.

Although there will be less need for handwriting in the future, it is still an important skill for children to learn. Learning to write helps children learn to read, spell and punctuate. These are skills that computers can help with, but they still need input from the computer user. Furthermore, many schools and universities still require examinations to be handwritten, and this is likely to continue, as there is considerable concern about the possibility of cheating in assignments produced at home on computer.

In conclusion, although handwriting is less important than it was, it is still an important part of young peoples' education. This is because it is part of the learning process, and because there are still areas where handwritten responses are necessary.